Your Eternal Self

R. Craig Hogan, Ph.D., et alia

Greater Reality Publications
http://greaterreality.com

Contact:

Greater Reality Publications
http://greaterreality.com
800 827-3770
E-mail: info@greaterreality.com
Order copies: http://orders.greaterreality.com

ISBN 978-0-9802111-0-8

To Greta Alexander

You finally wrote your book.

Table of Contents

Preface

Humankind's understanding of our place in the universe has been stunted. We have grown intellectually at remarkable speed in the last 400 years, but advancement in understanding our spiritual nature and our place in the universe that should have paralleled our intellectual development has been thwarted. Today, humankind, especially in the West, is intellectually precocious and spiritually retarded. The result is that those areas of our lives based in technology are advanced and those that rely on understanding the meaning of life are primitive. People are engineering probes to other planets and mapping the human genome during their work days and going home to family conflicts, financial stress, and fear of death that leave their lives full of tension, fear, and unhappiness. The dissonance between our intellectual lives, flush with achievement and satisfaction, and our personal lives, filled with discontent, anxiety, and stress, is extraordinary.

But all that's changing now. In just the last three decades, some of the most brilliant minds in a broad range of disciplines have begun to use the methods of science to understand who we are in the universe, what our connection is to each other, and what happens to us when the body dies. And what we've been discovering has been beyond anything humanity could ever envision. Now we know. The facts are available for us to understand ourselves as we never could before.

Today, humankind has evolved far beyond having to accept understanding about the nature of humankind and the universe based on "faith." Søren Kierkegaard described the "leap of faith" a person must make to believe in anything beyond the physical world. Evidence, he explained, takes a person to a certain point. Beyond that, evidence is not available, leaving a chasm looming before the seeker, who must then make a "leap of faith" across the chasm of the unknown to belief. Conviction about the afterlife and the unity of all life was once assumed to require such a leap of faith—evidence for both was lacking.

That is no longer true. We need make no leaps of faith without evidence. The evidence from corroborated testimonies, carefully recorded observation, and meticulously controlled studies provides a firm roadway to the conclusion that we are eternal spiritual beings having a physical experience. We are not the temporary, disease-ridden bags of flesh that we see when we look at each other. Instead, we are eternal selves temporarily using bodies.

When humankind finally realizes that and begins to live life based on it, the family stresses we're feeling will dissolve; our children will attend schools where love and compassion are the dominant sentiments; conflicts ending in murder and wars from differences in nationality, ethnicity, and creed will extinguish; deception and dishonesty will become unknown; fear will be replaced by love as the primary emotion on Earth; personal security in life will cease to be a worry; and we will have no doubt that we are eternal beings who will never be separated from our loved ones. We will be living together as a brotherhood of man in a heaven on Earth that we create for ourselves.

Humanity just needs to hear, understand, and believe what we who study the literature now know to be true. The evidence is available.

This book is based upon evidence. Later conclusions are rooted in the evidence and facts in earlier chapters. At times, the findings derived from the carefully controlled research studies will leave you in awe and wonder. However, as audacious as the conclusions may sound, they are all based on verifiable data.

Where you see evidence, test it. Look at the credentials of the researchers; examine the methodologies; analyze the conclusions; rely on the body of evidence, not on one or two studies alone. Perform your own research by doing searches on the Web using the key words in the studies. Additional reading is available at http://youreternalself.com. Read with an open, but critical mind.

Listen to what anyone who disagrees with the research may say about it. Let their statements and evidence broaden your understanding. Apply the same standards to their statements that you apply to examining the research in this book: What are their credentials? What is the evidence they cite that refutes the evidence in the studies summarized in this book? What methodologies did they use to gain that evidence? Are their conclusions warranted based on the results of the studies they cite? Do they ignore most of the body of evidence by citing only one or two studies that confirm their biased conclusions and hiding the rest in a file cabinet?

Stay with the evidence. Reject straw man arguments that have no evidence and have no carefully designed studies behind them. Reject emotional statements that are baseless made by anyone: New-Age believers, uninformed and biased skeptics, religious fundamentalists, or people who include with their name a title identifying them as functionaries in a religious organization. Be cautious of anyone who comes to the investigation with rigid, prejudicial viewpoints, looking to proselytize you to his or her belief system or to prove yours wrong without regard for evidence.

Evaluate the credentials and credibility of the researchers. You will find that the researchers cited in this book are highly regarded physicians, scientists, psychologists, professors of humanities, investigative journalists, theologians, and a broad range of other highly educated, competent, intelligent professionals. None have motives to fabricate evidence. All have professional careers at stake in describing the clear findings of their research.

The book is meant to challenge the assumptions most of us learned as we grew up. If you follow the roadway paved with evidence keeping an open mind, you will come to the same conclusions a vast body of scientists, philosophers, theologians, scholars, and researchers have come to today, and you will join the rapidly growing ranks of those who understand that the conclusions of radical materialism based on the Enlightenment are ignorant anachronisms; the evidence will speak to you compellingly if you just read it with an open mind.

And you will certainly come to know your eternal self.

Links to the youreternalself.com Web Site

Additional readings and links with valuable information about the subjects of the chapters are on the Web site at http://youreternalself.com. This book lists the links to the youreternalself.com Web pages containing information for the chapters so you can go directly to the resources for any chapter.

The links to other Web resources are on the youreternalself.com chapter pages instead of in this book because link addresses change and Web sites sometimes disappear. I will change the links for you so they're up to date even if you're reading this book five years after it was published.

1

Where Are You?

When I stand before you, talking to you, am I talking to the skin covering your face? Humans shed and re-grow outer skin cells about every 27 days, making almost 1,000 new skins in a lifetime. Your skin is just a disposable covering and by the time I finish saying a sentence to you, some of it is gone.

Each day about 50 billion cells in the body are replaced, resulting in a new body each year. The body is just temporary. It can't be who you are. Every second, 500,000 of your body cells die and are replaced, so we'll have to keep this conversation short—much of you will be gone before we finish!

Who am I talking to when I speak to you? It's certainly not your brain. That's just a collection of fat and protein made of 85% water squeezed into the dark enclosure of your skull. Around 50,000 to 100,000 brain cells die each day, so if some of them had today's messages, no wonder you keep losing track of what your spouse tells you.

You are not your body. The body changes constantly. The body you had at age 10 when you could run like a rabbit was a different body than you have at age 90 when you shuffle like a turtle, and the molecules in it have been replaced 80 times! Last year's body is different from this year's body. The body is just flesh and bone, made of the same atoms as a bowl of warm Irish stew. That's not you.

So, when you talk to me, you'll insist you're not talking to any part of my body, or even the tofu-like mush inside my skull. You're talking to *me*. You know implicitly that you and I are above and aside from the skin and the brain.

You aren't the body. You're the mind that is greater than the body, and that means you're greater than the brain. So if your mind is greater than the brain, where are you?

Science Doesn't Know Where You Are

We'll start by correcting a common misconception. You likely have the belief that science has evidence your mind is in the three to five pounds of fat and protein compressed inside your skull. That's what you were taught in school.

But the fact is that neuroscience can't explain how people have a conscious experience, where the mind is, what memories are, or where memories are stored. That's pretty remarkable considering that the brain has been carefully mapped using CTs, MRIs, PETs, and EEGs to find out which parts of the brain are active when a person is performing activities. In spite of all the brain mapping that's been done, they can't locate the mind and they can't find memories.

Many neuroscientists are also saying that even if someone could locate mind and memories in the brain, that still wouldn't explain who has the conscious thought. In other words, yes there's a thought, but who is thinking? Who requested the thought? Yes, the brain shows activity when there's a thought, but what caused the brain to show activity? How does a human being have a conscious experience?

That's known as the "problem of consciousness" or the "hard problem," and all neuroscientists acknowledge it. They can't find a mind or memories in the brain and they don't know how the brain creates the mind. Statements by a sampling of neuroscientists illustrating this problem follow. Here and elsewhere in this book, cited writers sometimes use "consciousness" to refer to the mind. I usually use "mind" because that is the common term we all use to refer to the inner part of us that thinks, feels, and decides to act.

Stephan Patt of the Institute of Pathology at Friedrich Schiller University in Germany summarized the research on the mind and the brain:

Nevertheless all these experiments and descriptions of brain activation processes do not explain how neural activity is the cause for consciousness. Likewise, all attempts which have been undertaken to specify the neurological mechanisms of consciousness in terms of neurobiological, information processing and even social theories of consciousness have failed to prove this causal relationship.[1]

Sir John Maddox, former editor-in-chief of the renowned journal *Nature,* summed up our knowledge of consciousness in the December 1999 issue of *Scientific American*:

Nobody understands how decisions are made or how imagination is set free. What consciousness consists of, or how it should be defined, is equally puzzling. Despite the marvelous success of neuroscience in the past century, we seem as far from understanding cognitive processes as we were a century ago.[2]

Stuart Hameroff, MD, a respected researcher in neuroscience in the Department of Anesthesiology, Arizona Health Sciences Center, wrote,

Consciousness defines our existence and reality. But how does the brain generate thoughts and feelings? Most explanations portray the brain as a computer, with nerve cells ("neurons") and their synaptic connections acting as simple switches, or "bits" which interact in complex ways. In this view consciousness is said to "emerge" as a novel property of complex interactions among neurons, as hurricanes and candle flames emerge from complex interactions among gas and dust molecules. However this approach fails to explain why we have feelings and awareness, an "inner life." So we don't know how the brain produces consciousness.[3]

David Presti, Ph.D., professor of neurobiology, University of California-Berkeley, wrote,

Despite the awesome achievements of 20th-century neuroscience in increasing our knowledge about the workings of the human brain, little progress has been

made in the scientific understanding of mental
phenomena.[4]

David J. Chalmers, Ph.D., director of the Centre for Consciousness at
the Australian National University, wrote in *Scientific American,*

> Consciousness, the subjective experience of an inner self,
> could be a phenomenon forever beyond the reach of
> neuroscience. Even a detailed knowledge of the brain's
> workings and the neural correlates of consciousness may
> fail to explain how or why human beings have self-
> aware minds.[5]

Other researchers report that efforts to find the locations of
memories in the brain have proven to be unsuccessful. Karl Lashley, a
renowned psychologist and researcher in the field of learning and
memory, failed during his entire career to find the location of memories
in the brain. It prompted him to write, "Memory ought to be impossible,
yet it happens."[6]

Brian Boycott, a biologist specializing in the study of memory,
summarized the inability to find memory in any specific location in the
brain: "Memory seems to be both everywhere and nowhere in particular
in the brain."[7]

Wilder Penfield, founder of the Montreal Neurological Institute, was
able to stimulate the brain to produce segments of memories,[8] and
neurosurgeons at the Toronto Western Hospital have stimulated the
brain to recall a scene from decades before in the patient's memory.[9]
However, where the memories are stored, how the mind can intend to
recall a memory, and how memories are archived are not known.

Science simply doesn't know how the mind is produced or where it's
located, even though the brain has been carefully studied and mapped.
That has led science to begin looking elsewhere for the mind.

Many Scientists Are Suggesting Your Mind Is Not in Your Brain

Because scientists can't find the mind in the brain, many are
beginning to suggest that the mind isn't in the brain at all.

Dr. Sam Parnia, a physician from Southampton General Hospital in
England, has been studying near-death experiences among his patients.
The results were published in the February 2001 issue of the journal

Resuscitation and presented to a gathering of scientists at the California Institute of Technology in June 2001. Following is a segment of an interview he gave to the Reuters news service:

> "The brain function these [near-death] patients were found to have while unconscious is commonly believed to be incapable of sustaining lucid thought processes or allowing lasting memories to form," Parnia said— pointing to the fact that nobody fully grasps how the brain generates thoughts.
>
> "The brain itself is made up of cells, like all the body's organs, and is not really capable of producing the subjective phenomenon of thought that people have," he said.[10]

Simon Berkovich, professor of engineering and applied science in the Department of Computer Science at George Washington University wrote,

> The brain is merely a transmitter and receiver of information, but not the main place for storage or processing of information (i.e., memories).[11]

Stanislav Grof, MD, Ph.D., Freudian psychoanalyst, professor of psychiatry at Johns Hopkins University School of Medicine, and chief of psychiatric research at the Maryland Psychiatric Research Center, concluded after his lifelong study of the mind and the brain,

> My first idea was that [consciousness] has to be hard-wired in the brain. I spent quite a bit of time trying to figure out how something like that is possible. Today, I came to the conclusion that it is not coming from the brain. In that sense, it supports what Aldous Huxley believed after he had some powerful psychedelic experiences and was trying to link them to the brain. He came to the conclusion that maybe the brain acts as a kind of reducing valve that actually protects us from too much cosmic input. . . . I don't think you can locate the source of consciousness. I am quite sure it is not in the brain—not inside of the skull. . . . It actually, according to my experience, would lie beyond time and space, so it is not localizable. You actually come to the source of

consciousness when you dissolve any categories that
imply separation, individuality, time, space and so on.
You just experience it as a presence.[12]

The same conclusion was reached independently by other brain
specialists. Sir John Eccles, internationally recognized brain researcher
whose work has had a major influence on brain research, concluded

... that the mind is a separate entity from the brain, and
that mental processes cannot be reduced to
neurochemical brain processes, but on the contrary
direct them. And ... a mind may conceivably exist
without a brain.[13]

Sir Cyril Burt, educational psychologist known for his studies on the
effects of heredity on intelligence, wrote in his book, *The Gifted Child*,

The brain is not an organ that generates consciousness,
but rather an instrument evolved to transmit and limit
the processes of consciousness and of conscious
attention so as to restrict them to those aspects of the
material environment which at any moment are crucial
for the terrestrial success of the individual. In that case
such phenomena as telepathy and clairvoyance would
be merely instances in which some of the limitations
were removed.[14]

Another brain specialist, Wilder Penfield, was a ground-breaking
neuroscientist and physician. While performing surgery on patients, he
noticed that stimulating a part of the brain cortex could cause the patient
to recall a memory. However, while recalling the memory, the person's
conscious awareness was still active, aside from the memory, and no
stimulation of any part of the brain could cause any of the actions we
associate with the mind: beliefs, problem solving, decisions, or any of the
other activities that happen when a person is "thinking." The mind
activities went on even when he was stimulating the brain cortex, and
were completely unaffected by any stimulation he applied to the brain.
Penfield could stimulate small segments of memories, but he
couldn't locate the mind inside the brain. He summed up the
conclusions he formed on the basis of these experiments:

... none of the actions that we attribute to the mind has
been initiated by electrode stimulation or epileptic

discharge. If there were a mechanism in the brain that could do what the mind does, one might expect that the mechanism would betray its presence in a convincing manner by some better evidence of epileptic or electrode activation.

The mind, he wrote, "makes its impact on the brain" but isn't in the brain.[15]

Neuroscientists can't tell us how we have a conscious experience or where the mind is. Some scientists have come to the conclusion that perhaps the mind isn't in the brain at all.

That's why we know we're not speaking to the body when we speak to one another, and why we know the mind is greater than and aside from the body. The remainder of this chapter contains evidence demonstrating that the scientists coming to that conclusion are correct: your mind is not inside your brain.

The Brain Doesn't Have the Capacity to Hold the Mind or Memories

Pim van Lommel is a cardiologist and author of an article in the medical journal, *The Lancet* (December 2001). His conclusions were summarized by Tim Touber:

> Van Lommel contends that the brain does not produce consciousness or store memories. He points out that American computer science expert Simon Berkovich and Dutch brain researcher Herms Romijn, working independently of one another, came to the same conclusion: that it is impossible for the brain to store everything you think and experience in your life. This would require a processing speed of 1024 bits per second. Simply watching an hour of television would already be too much for our brains. "If you want to store that amount of information—along with the associative thoughts produced—your brain would be pretty much full," Van Lommel says. "Anatomically and functionally, it is simply impossible for the brain to have this level of speed."[16]

While small segments or individual scenes of memories can be re-experienced when the brain is stimulated,[17,18] where those memories are stored is not known, and it seems apparent that the brain doesn't have the capacity to hold them.

Not only does the brain not have the capacity to hold the memories, but many brain cells die and are replaced every second of our lives. For the memories to remain over 50 or 60 years, the brain cells would have to remain the same ones that were there when the memories were created, but that doesn't happen since they're replaced by new brain cells regularly. Dean Radin, senior scientist at the Institute of Noetic Sciences, professor at Sonoma State University, and distinguished consulting faculty member at Saybrook Graduate School and Research Center, explains this further indication that memories couldn't remain stored in the brain:

> Consider a profound mystery in biology that is not accounted for by classical assumptions: The average neuron consists of about 80 percent water and about 100,000 molecules. The brain contains about 10 billion cells, hence about 10^{15} molecules. Each nerve cell in the brain receives an average of 10,000 connections from other brain cells, and the molecules within each cell are renewed about 10,000 times in a lifetime. We lose about 1,000 cells a day, so the total brain cell population is decimated by about 10 million cells, losing in the process some 100 billion cross-linkages.[19]

Some sources today estimate that from 50,000[20] to 100,000[21] brain cells die each day. In spite of the loss of brain cells and the fact that the molecules within each brain cell are renewed about 10,000 times in a lifetime, memories from our childhood of many places we've visited can be recalled in great detail. People in old age report flashbacks of memories having remarkable clarity that they haven't recalled for decades.

Dean Radin quotes Paul A. Weiss, of Vienna's Institute of Experimental Biology, a pioneer in biology research, who also pointed out that memories remain intact in spite of the loss of brain cells and replacement of molecules in brain cells:

> And yet, despite that ceaseless change of detail in that vast population of elements, our basic patterns of

behavior, our memories, our sense of integral existence
as an individual, have retained their unitary continuity
of pattern.[22]

That fact is another indication that memories are not stored in brain cells.

Missing Large Parts of the Brain Doesn't Affect Memory.

People missing half their brain after surgery function almost perfectly normally, suggesting that the mind must be functioning outside of the brain. The procedure, called a hemispherectomy, removes half of the brain from the patient's head. The operation has been performed hundreds of times for disorders that can't be controlled using any other treatments. Remarkably, even when half of the brain has been removed, the patients retain their personalities and memories.[23] In fact, a study of children who had half their brains removed found they often were able to perform better in their school work.[24]

A number of instances have been recorded in which an adult was found to have virtually no brain, but had functioned from childhood through adulthood as a perfectly normal person; a brain wasn't necessary for normal daily functioning or storing and recalling memories. This account is from a July 19, 2007, story on Reuters:

> A man with an unusually tiny brain managed to live an entirely normal life despite his condition caused by a fluid buildup in his skull, French researchers reported on Thursday.
>
> Scans of the 44-year-old man's brain showed that a huge fluid-filled chamber called a ventricle took up most of the room in his skull, leaving little more than a thin sheet of actual brain tissue.
>
> "He was a married father of two children, and worked as a civil servant," Dr. Lionel Feuillet and colleagues at the Universite de la Mediterranee in Marseille wrote in a letter to the *Lancet* medical journal. . . . "What I find amazing to this day is how the brain can deal with something which you think should not be compatible with life," commented Dr. Max Muenke, a pediatric

brain defect specialist at the National Human Genome
Research Institute.[25]

That provides evidence for the suggestion that the mind isn't in the
brain. Mind and memory function perfectly well when half the brain is
removed or the brain doesn't develop fully.

People Can See, Hear, Smell, Taste, and Touch Without Using the Brain

> There is a community of the spirit.
> Join it, and feel the delight....
> Close both eyes
> To see with the other eye.
>
> *- Jelaluddin Rumi (Muslim Sufi mystic)*

If we are aside from and greater than the body, then you'd think we
could learn some things about the world without using the body. In
other words, if someone could prove that we can see without using our
eyes, then that would mean the eyes, retina, optic nerve, and optical
cortex in our brains aren't necessary for us to be able to see; they're just
options the mind uses in the physical realm.

But seeing without using the eyes is very common today.
Thousands of people are able to see without using their eyes through a
very common ability called "remote viewing." The remote viewer sits
quietly with his or her eyes closed and focuses on something hundreds
or thousands of miles away. The remote viewer is able to see it. Not
only that, but the person is often able to hear it, smell it, feel the texture,
sense movement, and sense emotions involved with it. In other words,
the person is doing things outside of the body while the body is sitting
quietly with its eyes closed.

The Government Found Remote Viewing Is Valid.

For several decades at the end of the twentieth century, the CIA had
a remote viewing program named Operation Stargate that attempted to
use remote viewers to spy on the Russians. The program had
remarkable results. In 1974, a remote viewer named Pat Price was to
view a mysterious, unidentified research center at Semipalatinsk, USSR,
to see what was there. He sat with his eyes closed and focused on the

area. Below is his sketch of what he saw in his mind. It had all the distinguishing marks of a gantry crane.[26]

Later, the CIA obtained satellite photos of the site. A CIA artist created the following sketch of part of the site based on photos of the actual Semipalatinsk site. It was a gantry crane:

Government Verification Study: Stanford Research Institute

The government wanted to be sure that their investment in remote viewing was going into a valid enterprise, so to find out whether people can really view things from a distance using remote viewing, the government agencies commissioned the Stanford Research Institute (SRI) to perform 154 experiments with 26,000 separate trials over 16 years. At the end of that testing period, Edwin May, Ph.D., a researcher in low energy experimental nuclear physics, headed a team of researchers that analyzed the experiments and reported to the government.

They concluded that the odds against someone merely guessing what remote viewers had described when focusing on a target at a distant location were more than a billion billion to one. His only explanation was that they genuinely were seeing without using their eyes and without regard for how many miles away the target was.[27]

Government Verification Study: SAIC

Now satisfied that remote viewing existed, the government sponsors of the remote viewing activity requested a second evaluation to find out how it works. Congress and the CIA commissioned a study by the Science Applications International Corporation (SAIC). The result of the study was that Jessica Utts, professor in the Division of Statistics at the University of California at Davis, prepared a report assessing the statistical evidence for remote viewing in the U.S. government-sponsored research. She uses the term "anomalous cognition" to refer to remote viewing. This is her conclusion:

> It is clear to this author that anomalous cognition is possible and has been demonstrated. This conclusion is not based on belief, but rather on commonly accepted scientific criteria. The phenomenon has been replicated in a number of forms across laboratories and cultures. The various experiments in which it has been observed have been different enough that if some subtle methodological problems can explain the results, then there would have to be a different explanation for each type of experiment, yet the impact would have to be similar across experiments and laboratories. If fraud were responsible, similarly, it would require an equivalent amount of fraud on the part of a large number of experimenters or an even larger number of subjects. . . .
>
> I believe that it would be wasteful of valuable resources to continue to look for proof. No one who has examined all of the data across laboratories, taken as a collective whole, has been able to suggest methodological or statistical problems to explain the ever-increasing and consistent results to date. Resources should be directed to the pertinent questions about how this ability works. I am confident that the questions are no more elusive than any other questions in science dealing with small to medium sized effects, and that if appropriate resources are targeted to appropriate questions, we can have answers within the next decade.[28]

Credible Sources Involved in Government Remote Viewing Projects Agreed It Occurred as Described.

Jim Schnabel summarized[29] statements from some government sources who had been involved in the Operation Stargate remote viewing project:

> "I never liked to get into debates with the skeptics, because if you didn't believe that remote viewing was real, you hadn't done your homework." — *Major General Edmund R Thompson, U.S. Army Assistant Chief of Staff for Intelligence, 1977-81, Deputy Director for Management and Operations, DIA, 1982-84*

> "You can't be involved in this for any length of time and not be convinced there's something here." — *Norm J., former senior CIA official who tasked remote viewers*

> "There were times when they wanted to push buttons and drop bombs on the basis of our information." — *Dr. Hal Puthoff, a former manager of the CIA remote-viewing program*

> "She went into a trance. And while she was in the trance, she gave us some latitude and longitude figures. We focused our satellite cameras on that point, and the lost plane was there." — *Former President Jimmy Carter, recalling a 1978 remote-viewing operation*

Repeated Research Studies Have Demonstrated Remote Viewing's Validity.

The Princeton Engineering Anomalies Research Laboratory (PEAR) at Princeton University began conducting its own, independent studies of remote viewing in 1978. They tested remote viewers by having a person travel to some distant location undisclosed to the remote viewer and having the remote viewer attempt to identify details about the location. The remote viewers in 334 trials were able to describe details about where the person was with odds against guessing the details of the location of 100 billion to 1.[30]

In another study, Robert Jahn, former director of the PEAR Lab, and psychologist Brenda Dunne conducted 336 rigorous trials with 48 ordinary people who were asked to do remote viewing at distances ranging from five to 6,000 miles. Almost two-thirds of the results exceeded chance levels, with odds against chance being one billion to one.[31]

Russell Targ, a physicist who pioneered development of the laser, and Harold Puthoff, another physicist who wrote the widely read *Fundamentals of Quantum Electronics*, conducted experiments on remote viewing to determine whether the phenomenon is real. In their tests, they had a person whom they called a "beacon" travel to a distant site to see whether a remote viewer could receive mental impressions about the site. The beacon and remote viewer were separated by distances of several miles so there could be no communication between them, and the beacon was instructed to go to a site randomly chosen by Targ and Puthoff without the remote viewer's knowledge. The remote viewer was to then focus on the beacon, trying to get impressions about where the beacon was and writing or sketching the scenes. This is a summary of their findings:

> Independent judges found that the descriptions of the
> sketches matched on the average 66 percent of the time
> the characteristics of the site that was actually seen by
> the beacon.[32]

These findings were far beyond chance, demonstrating that the receiver was seeing the scene where the sender was while many miles away.

Dr. Chris Roe, a parapsychologist at the University of Northampton in the UK, also verified remote viewing's validity through his studies. When the results were reviewed by Dr. Brian Josephson, a Nobel Prize-winning physicist from Cambridge University, Josephson concluded, "The experiments have been designed to rule out luck and chance. I consider the evidence for remote viewing to be pretty clear cut."[33]

I Can See Without Using My Eyes.

I'm especially able to see objects someone puts on a table or desk anywhere in the world. I can sit in my office, close my eyes, and focus on the place where the object is. In the blackness of my mind, I begin to get images of the object and impressions about it. I then write a description of the object and sketch it (although I'm not much of an artist).

In 2005, I corresponded with a computer systems analyst in New Jersey named Bill Walker about remote viewing. He asked me to do some sessions for him to show him what it is like. I sat in my office in Illinois, closed my eyes, and focused on objects he had set up in New Jersey. I e-mailed my impressions and sketches to him. Some accurately described the objects he had in his office and house, so he decided to put my remote viewing sessions on his Web site. I've reproduced them on the pages that follow to illustrate that we don't need a body to see things hundreds of miles away. You can see his Web site by going to the link at http://youreternalself.com/chapter1.htm.

This is his description from the Web site of how the sessions occurred:

> Craig Hogan and I communicated only via email. He
> lives about 700 miles away from me. All he knew about
> me was my name, email address, and that I lived in New
> Jersey. I would place an object on my table and Craig
> would email me his impressions. He said that he often
> got impressions of other objects in the room. His only
> input was an *object on Bill Walker's table*. The impressions
> included sketches and sometimes written descriptions.
> In between sessions, the only feedback I gave to him was
> the photos of matched items that I show below [on his
> Web site]. For each session, he gave anywhere from 5 to
> 20 impressions.

In the first session, Bill Walker told me he would put an object on the table in his office. When I was ready to view the object that was the "target" on his table, I sat in my office in Illinois and closed my eyes. I focused on seeing things "on Bill Walker's table." In a few seconds, I did see a green light shining down on gold brassy parts and sent my notes to him, along with my sketches of what I saw. He responded to my notes telling me that the green light was his banker's lamp with a green shade and gold bottom about six feet from the table in his office. The other sketches didn't match things in the office.

However, when he arrived home, he found that I had been sketching things on the tables in his home, not his office. The sketches, my descriptions, and the photographs he sent me after I sent him my sketches are on the pages that follow.

The First Session–An Orb

Below is the sketch of an orb I sent to him attached to an e-mail. The text I sent in the e-mail follows the sketch.

My sketch perfectly matched an orb on a table in his home. He made a photograph of the orb and put it on his Web site. The photograph is below the sketch. The object is made of metal, and he described the color in this way: "in natural light, the orbs do have both silver and gold colors."

My sketch of what I saw in my mind

Silver ribbed, amber, or gold between the ribs, a thick dimple-like thing where the ribs come together. They're curved like a cupola with arms. Gold, brassy color, round like a sugar bowl with a smooth lid, but it isn't a jar. It feels like metal.

Photograph of the actual object

A Second Session–A Plant with Round Balls on It

We did other sessions focusing on things on tables in his home, since it appeared my mind wanted to look at tables there. I knew nothing about the objects except that they were on tables in Bill Walker's home. I sat in my office in Illinois focusing on "a table in Bill Walker's home" and saw in my mind a plant with large leaves and odd little balls at the ends of the stems. I e-mailed the sketch below. In the e-mail, I wrote "like stems, organic" and "looked like two leaves, with some stems that had small circles on the end of them." Below the sketch I sent is a photograph he then sent to me of the plant on a table in his house.

My sketch of what I saw in my mind

Photograph of the actual object

A Third Session–A Peach-Colored Flower in a Pot

I closed my eyes again to look for "things on a table in Bill Walker's house" and saw another plant that had a light peach flower on it. I sketched the pot, two leaves on the sides, and a flower in the middle that I saw as "light peach." The sketch is below. I sent the description and sketch to him. He returned the photograph of a plant on a table in his house that appears at the bottom of this page. The flower is light peach.

My sketch of what I saw in my mind

light peach

green

vegetation

Photograph of the actual object

A Session for Rick Stewart in Maryland

I did another remote viewing session for Rick Stewart, a man I had never met who lived in Maryland. I viewed the object from my office in Illinois by closing my eyes and focusing on the object. This is the description I wrote in my e-mail to him and the sketch I sent:

> First drawing round thing, two feet-like things out front and round thing on top, like a toy, yellow/green color. I know there was something white somewhere on it but I forgot where by the time I sketched what I could get.

> [Another view after writing my notes and closing my eyes again] Got another round thing. This is rather like a doll, but it doesn't seem like a doll. It's more like a rolly-polly thing with a body and feet.

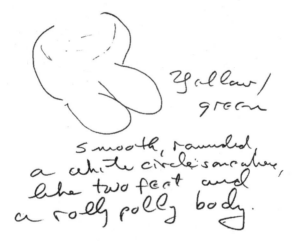

I sent it to Rick Stewart in Maryland. He returned the photograph of the target object that is at the top of the next page. Its color is yellow green and the pinwheel on the front is white.

Photograph of the actual object

I can do this at any time, with accurate descriptions like these examples around 66% of the time. It isn't just a one-time happening.

No photons came through my corneas to strike my retinas and create electrical pulses that would travel along the optic nerve to my brain. There are no sensory input devices on my body that would receive photons from 800 or 900 miles away, and without photons, an image of the object organized into a pattern with billions of pieces to match the photons would have to all travel together to where I was sitting. Something would have to encode the image (like a camera or retina), then transmit the image. There was nothing like that involved. Electromagnetic energy could not travel that far over the horizon, and studies of remote viewing with the viewers in rooms shielded by lead to block out energy (Faraday cages) show that the remote viewing is just as clear when no energy could possibly come to the viewer.[34]

The blob of fat and protein trapped inside the darkness of my skull couldn't possibly have seen a roly-poly doll or plants on tables hundreds of miles away; but I saw them. Or rather, my mind, which is outside of my brain, saw them.

The ability to remote view is very common among people. There are clubs that do remote viewing, such as the very active, proficient group in Hawaii named the Hawaii Remote Viewers Guild that does remarkable, consistently accurate remote viewing for entertainment. The links to some of these remote viewing groups, including the Hawaii group, are at http://youreternalself.com/chapter1.htm.

One estimate is that one out of a hundred people can do remote viewing successfully, meaning that among the 260 million people of all ages in the United States, 2.6 million can or will be able to do remote viewing. I am able to do it. I, and all of the many other people now doing remote viewing easily, at will, are able to close our eyes and intend to see something hundreds or thousands of miles away with nothing more to guide us than a location or a number assigned to the object or picture. Images come to our minds, but they aren't coming through our eyes.

You can try remote viewing by taking the test I have online at http://youreternalself.com/chapter1.htm.

What Remote Viewing Means for Where You Are

The data showing that remote viewing is a valid phenomenon are overwhelming. It shows without question that people can sit quietly with their eyes closed and "see" things hundreds or thousands of miles away, in places they've never been.

That means that the mind isn't in the brain. It isn't trapped inside the bony encasing of a skull. When people see using eyes, photons (light particles) come through the eye and travel along the optic nerve to the brain. In remote viewing, there is no opening in the skull for images to come in. There is no light energy coming from thousands of miles away. We can remote view objects inside dark boxes and envelopes. Studies of remote viewers in lead-lined rooms show that they still get images, so no electromagnetic signals (light, radio waves, infrared waves, microwaves) are involved. There is no energy that carries the image. The remote viewer sees instantly, regardless of distance.

What all that means is that the mind that does the seeing is outside of the brain and is linked with the object that is far away. The spirit doesn't travel to the object. There is no geographical distance where the mind is. We are one with everything in the universe, including other people's minds.

You aren't in a brain. Your mind is outside of the brain.

Evidence That We Know Information without Using the Brain

A large number of studies have demonstrated that people can know information without having contact with the source of the information. From the 1880s to the 1940s, 142 published articles described 3.6 million individual trials with 4,600 people attempting to identify the number and suit of a playing card face down in front of them. In addition, ESP tests performed on the radio added 70,000 participants to the database. The studies were performed at over two dozen universities around the world by hundreds of respected professors.[35]

The result was that participants were, on average, able to identify the cards at rates higher than chance. They knew information they could not have received unless their minds were able to obtain it without using the body. The results prompted Professor H. J. Eysenck, chairman of the Psychology Department at the University of London, to write in 1957,

> Unless there is a gigantic conspiracy involving some thirty University departments all around the world, and several hundred highly respected scientists in various fields, many of them originally hostile to the claims of the psychical researchers, the only conclusion the unbiased observer can come to must be that there does exist a small number of people who obtain knowledge existing either in other people's minds, or in the outer world, by means as yet unknown to science.[36]

A Unified Visual Image in Our Mind Can't Be Accounted for with Just Using Brain Neurons.

The fact that we can see without using the eyes indicates that no signals come to the brain, and yet the mind sees. That means the brain may not be involved in the process at all. That is predicted from other research. Studies of the brain fail to show how the light waves entering the eye can come together in the brain to form a complete image.

John Eccles, Nobel Prize winner in the study of the physiology of the nervous system, wrote *Facing Reality: philosophical adventures of a brain scientist*. In it, he explains that when we see using the eyes, the light enters the eye and turns into nerve impulses in the retina that travel along the optic nerve to the brain. However, when they arrive there, they are fragmented and sent to different areas of the brain. Science can find nothing in the brain that is able to bring the visual experience together. Eccles writes that the only explanation is that there must be a conscious mind outside of the brain that influences the brain and makes patterns using it.

The mind outside the brain apparently experiences a sight and forms the brain so it lights up with electromagnetic energy indicating that seeing is happening. The vision is a whole experience in the mind, however. We see a whole image when we look at a face or a landscape. When various parts of the brain light up as a person "sees," it appears that the mind outside of the brain is coordinating all parts of the brain so the image comes together as a whole.

Blind People Whose Brains Cannot Process Sight Images Are Able to See During Near-Death and Out-of-Body Experiences.

Blind people, including those blind from birth, can actually see during near-death experiences (NDEs) and out-of-the-body experiences (OBEs), suggesting that their minds must be independent of their bodies, which are unable to see. Kenneth Ring, Ph.D., professor emeritus of psychology at the University of Connecticut, and Sharon Cooper interviewed 31 blind and sight-impaired persons who had NDEs and OBEs, and found that 80 percent of them reported correctly "visual" experiences, some in detail. For example, they reported correctly actual colors and their surroundings. One patient who had become totally blind after having been sighted for at least 40 years "saw" the pattern and colors on a new tie during an out of body experience, even though everyone denied having ever described it to him. The results of the two-year research study were published in the book *Mindsight*.[37]

Dr. Larry Dossey, former chief of staff of Medical City Dallas Hospital, describes this case of a woman's being able to see clearly during her near-death experience:

> The surgery had gone smoothly until the late stages of
> the operation. Then something happened. As her
> physician was closing the incision, Sarah's heart stopped
> beating. . . . [When she awoke, Sarah had] a clear,
> detailed memory of the frantic conversation of the
> surgeons and nurses during her cardiac arrest; the

[operating room] layout; the scribbles on the surgery
schedule board in the hall outside; the color of the sheets
covering the operating table; the hairstyle of the head
scrub nurse; the names of the surgeons in the doctors'
lounge down the corridor who were waiting for her case
to be concluded; and even the trivial fact that her
anesthesiologist that day was wearing unmatched socks.
All this she knew even though she had been fully
anesthetized and unconscious during the surgery and
the cardiac arrest.

But what made Sarah's vision even more momentous
was the fact that, since birth, she had been blind.[38]

It appears that Sarah's mind was seeing when her body was unable
to see because she was both unconscious and blind since birth.

People Rendered Temporarily Blind Are Able to Locate Things on a Computer Screen.

Blindsight is the ability to see without normal use of the eyes. In
studies when people were made blind temporarily, they were still able to
locate things on a computer screen. The author of the study, Tony Ro, a
psychology professor at Rice University in Houston, has no explanation
for the remarkable finding, but accepts that some alternative way of
seeing is available to the brain. "These findings demonstrate that while
certain brain areas are necessary for awareness, there is extensive
processing of information that takes place unconsciously." He said these
are results "suggesting the existence of alternate visual processing routes
that function unconsciously . . ."[39]

The findings seem to fit with the others presented here
demonstrating that seeing doesn't require eyes or the use of our brain.

Blind People Perform Actions and Describe Colors that Show Vision.

David Linden, professor of neuroscience at Johns Hopkins
University, found that if the part of the brain that processes sight (the
visual cortex) is damaged, people will assert that they cannot see
anything, but when asked to pick up an object in an unknown location
within reach, many can do so on the first try. They also can judge an

emotional expression on a face, especially anger, more often than chance would predict they could. He suggests that signals from the eyes could go to a mid-brain area where they're processed even though the primary visual area is not operating. However, there is no convincing evidence of that.[40]

Lawrence Weiskrantz, emeritus professor of Psychology at Oxford University and recipient of the William James Fellow Award 1992 by the Association for Psychological Science, summarized the research showing that patients with lesions in their primary visual cortex, rendering them blind, are able to perceive colors and motion:

> Previous research has reported that blindsight patients can retain the ability to detect monochromatic light and grating stimuli, and to discriminate orientation and direction of movement in their "blind" fields. These findings have been joined by reports that these patients also are sensitive to, and are able to discriminate, wavelength in the absence of any experience of "color." This reveals that retinal pathways other than those to the striate cortex are crucially involved in vision.[41]

In all of these instances, the researchers suggest that some form of vision is left to bring signals from the eyes to the brain, although no such alternatives have been discovered. However, these findings fit with the suggestion that the eyes are not necessary to seeing.

"Echolocation" Experiments Show Blind People Can See without Physical Eyeballs.

Another phenomenon, called "echolocation," also seems to show that blind people can "see" objects in their environment even when they can't use their optical organs. In echolocation, the blind person makes sounds by tapping, clicking, or speaking, and while doing so, is able to walk or even ride a bicycle through an environment filled with obstacles. The assumption has been that the blind person hears the echoes of the sounds reflected back from objects in the environment and can interpret the sounds to identify the objects.

Ben Underwood, who lost his sight to cancer as a toddler, has two artificial eyes made of plastic. However, he walks without a cane or seeing-eye dog, plays video games, and identifies objects he passes by name: "That's a fire hydrant" or "That's a trash can."[42]

Researchers know that the brain is active when a blind person is "seeing" using echolocation:

> Scientists have discovered that in the brains of the blind,
> the visual cortex has not become useless, as they once
> believed. When blind people use another sense—touch
> or hearing, for example—to substitute for sight, the
> brain's visual cortex becomes active, even though no
> images reach it from the optic nerve. Echolocation
> creates its own images.[43]

The fact that the brain is active when the optical organs are not functioning fits with the suggestion made by some researchers that the brain may act rather like a television set that becomes active when a signal comes to it, but does not produce the signal.

Researchers have studied echolocation to try to determine how the blind can see to navigate and have concluded that it must be due to a sonar effect (hearing sounds bounce off of objects and judging their shape and distance from the sounds). However, the actions of blind people using echolocation defy the possibility that it could be due simply to a sonar effect. Ben Underwood, who has two plastic eyes, can perform feats such as hitting a moving target with a pillow at distances too far for hearing to be echoed back when the target is silent. He can identify objects too far away for him to receive echoes when he is simply making clicking sounds. He rides a bike without hitting obstacles, at speeds that preclude receiving sonar-type messages to avoid them, and he plays video games adeptly when the game is producing a cacophony of noises, and echolocation using sounds could not identify figures on a computer screen.

The fact that more than sound echoes must be involved in navigating through an environment filled with obstacles, as in the example of Ben Underwood, is another indication that the mind sees without using the brain.

People See, Hear, and Remember
When the Brain Is Not Functioning

Accounts from physicians and nurses abound about people brought back from near death who had experiences of entering a warm, loving environment where they speak with their deceased loved ones. The phenomenon was named a near-death experience (NDE) by Raymond Moody.[44] During NDEs, many people see and hear what is going on as physicians and nurses worked feverishly to revive them and they are unconscious. When they are revived, they recount statements made by those in the room, describe people and instruments, and even accurately restate conversations that went on in other rooms.

An organization of people who have had the experience, called the International Association for Near Death Studies (IANDS), now has tens of thousands of members. Dozens of books have been written, filled with cases of people who have had near-death experiences. A Gallup and Proctor poll in 1982 found that an estimated 5 percent of the adult population of the United States have had near-death experiences. Other surveys put the number at 7.5 percent.[45]

Near-death experiences, in other words, are commonplace. One of the most remarkable things about NDEs is that while brain dead, without a trace of brain function, these people see and hear what is going on in the scene where their body lies unconscious, and at times in other rooms of the same building. They then remember all of the details and recount them to the astonishment of physicians, nurses, and family members.

During the near-death experience, no sensory experiences and no memory production would be possible if the mind were located in the brain. During these times, people whose brain activity is being monitored show absolutely no life in the brain. Dr. Peter Fenwick, a neuropsychiatrist and one of the leading authorities in Britain on near-death experiences, describes the state of the brain during a near-death experience:

> The brain isn't functioning. It's not there. It's destroyed.
> It's abnormal. But, yet, it can produce these very clear
> experiences. . . . An unconscious state is when the brain
> ceases to function. For example, if you faint, you fall to
> the floor, you don't know what's happening and the
> brain isn't working. The memory systems are
> particularly sensitive to unconsciousness. So, you won't
> remember anything. But, yet, after one of these [NDE]
> experiences, you come out with clear, lucid
> memories. . . . This is a real puzzle for science. I have not
> yet seen any good scientific explanation which can
> explain that fact.[46]

Michael Sabom, MD, a cardiologist in Atlanta, Georgia, studied near-death experiences to see whether people really were seeing and hearing while their brains were completely non-functioning. He identified a sample of 32 patients who had had an out-of-body experience during cardiac arrests while their brains were unable to function so their senses couldn't be receiving stimuli. He asked the patients to describe in as much detail as they could what went on during their resuscitations. To see whether someone could simply guess the details of what was happening in the trauma scene or recall the procedure from some chance reading about it in the past, he asked 25 other patients who had cardiac arrest but no out-of-body experiences to describe the events involving their resuscitation during their cardiac arrests.

Virtually all of the patients who said they did not have an out-of-body experience (20 out of 23) made at least one major error in their account. All of the 32 patients who had near-death out-of-body experiences described the resuscitation successfully in specific facts or in the general procedure. When he checked patient descriptions against the records available about their traumas, he found that six of those who had NDEs accurately described in great detail specific facts they could not have learned while lying unconscious that were peculiar to the situation, not just general information about resuscitation:

> The recollected details in each case were quite accurate and not interchangeable with details from other near-death crisis descriptions. These specific details included things like which family members were waiting where in the hospital and their emotional reactions, the type of gurneys the patients themselves were riding, the type and description of equipment used to treat them, etc. In one thought-provoking instance, an NDE survivor made an apparent error in describing the work of a defibrillation meter—until Sabom found out that the older model the patient described was exactly the kind used back in 1973 when the patient had his cardiac arrest. Based on his research, Sabom ruled out a common explanation skeptics give for dismissing the reality of these details seen during an OBE: that the accurate portrayal of the near death crisis event is due to prior general knowledge the patient has of how a

resuscitation works, and thus his description is merely an educated guess.[47]

Another study, published in the medical publication *Journal of Resuscitation,* concluded that people with no brain function who describe a near-death experience in fact have lucid thought processes, reasoning, and memory during the period of time when their brains are not functioning. In the study, doctors at Southampton General Hospital in England interviewed 63 heart attack patients who had been evaluated to be clinically dead, but were subsequently resuscitated. To ensure that their recollections were fresh, the people were interviewed within a week of the experience. They described details and events in which they were thinking, reasoning, and consciously moving around during the period when they were unconscious, their bodies were motionless, and their brains were not functioning, according to doctors working on them.[48]

The researchers went on to collect over 3,500 similar cases of people who had been evaluated to be clinically dead, but could recall remarkable details about events during the time when they should not have been able to sense anything or remember even if they had experienced something because they were clinically dead.

Dr. Sam Parnia, one of the physicians, described a child 2½ years old whose heart had stopped beating. He was unconscious and clinically dead, but was revived. Afterward, the child's parents contacted Parnia to tell him that the boy had drawn a picture of himself portraying what it was like during the trauma, but in the picture he was outside of his unconscious body looking down at himself. In the drawing, there was a balloon-like area. When the boy was asked what that was, he said matter of factly that when you die, you see a bright light and you are connected to a cord. Six months later, he was still drawing the same scene with the same details."[49]

A study of near-death experiences in the English medical journal, *The Lancet,* concluded "that the NDE might be a changing state of consciousness (transcendence) in which identity, cognition and emotion function independently from the unconscious body . . ."[50] This is the study:

> A team of doctors in the Netherlands studied 344 patients who were resuscitated after cardiac arrest, including 62 patients (18% of those revived) who reported NDEs. They found that the NDE experiences

weren't explainable as reactions to medication; by a fear
of death on the part of the patient (a hypothesis offered
by some psychologists to explain NDEs); or by
physiological changes in the brain caused by a lack of
oxygen which can cause sensory distortions and
hallucinations. Concluded the researchers, "The NDE
pushes at the limits of medical ideas about the range of
human consciousness and the mind-brain relation."[51]

Sample Individual Near-Death Experiences Indicate the Brain Is Not Involved.

A number of verified near-death experiences on record provide
unusually convincing evidence that the brain is not involved in the near-
death experience. A small sample of these cases documented by
physicians and nurses follows.

Maria, a migrant worker brought to Harborview Medical Center's
cardiac care unit in cardiac arrest, near death, felt herself floating
upward out of the hospital. As she rose, she saw, on a third-story
window ledge of the hospital, "a man's dark blue tennis shoe, well-worn,
scuffed on the left side where the little toe would go. The shoelace was
caught under the heel." Health care workers investigated and found the
tennis shoe precisely where Maria had described it. The shoe was dark
blue, had a well-worn scuff on the left side where the little toe would go,
and the shoelace was caught under the heel.[52]

In another, similar incident, after an unconscious patient was
revived, she described floating above the hospital where she saw a red
tennis shoe on the roof of the hospital. A janitor investigated and found
a red tennis shoe, just as the patient described.[53]

Bruce Greyson, MD, professor in the Department of Psychiatric
Medicine, University of Virginia, describes a patient named Al Sullivan
who underwent an emergency quadruple bypass operation. While
unconscious, he had an NDE:

> Al Sullivan was a 55 year old truck driver who was
> undergoing triple by-pass surgery when he had a
> powerful NDE that included an encounter with his
> deceased mother and brother-in-law, who told Al to go
> back to his to tell one of his neighbors that their son with
> lymphoma will be OK. Furthermore, during the NDE, Al

accurately noticed that the surgeon operating on him
was flapping his arms in an unusual fashion, with his
hands in his armpits. When he came back to his body
after the surgery was over, the surgeon was startled that
Al could describe his own arm flapping, which was his
idiosyncratic method of keeping his hands sterile by
holding his arms at his chest and gesturing with his
elbows as he instructed staff about preparation for the
operation.[54]

In another documented case, an operating-room nurse had removed
the dentures of an unconscious heart attack victim and put them into the
special drawer on the table called a "crash cart." A week after the
incident, as the nurse was distributing medications, she came to the
heart-attack victim's room and he exclaimed excitedly, "'Oh, that nurse
knows where my dentures are. . . . Yes, you were there when I was
brought into hospital and you took my dentures out of my mouth and
put them onto that cart; it had all these bottles on it and there was this
sliding drawer underneath and there you put my teeth." At the point
when the nurse did that, the patient was in a deep coma with his eyes
closed, but he was perfectly accurate about what had happened.[55]

The nurse explained more about what the man then reported:

When I asked further, it appeared the man had seen
himself lying in bed, that he had perceived from above
how nurses and doctors had been busy with CPR. He was
also able to describe correctly and in detail the small room
in which he had been resuscitated as well as the
appearance of those present like myself. At the time that he
observed the situation he had been very much afraid that
we would stop CPR and that he would die. And it is true
that we had been very negative about the patient's
prognosis due to his very poor medical condition when
admitted. The patient tells me that he desperately and
unsuccessfully tried to make it clear to us that he was still
alive and that we should continue CPR. He is deeply
impressed by his experience and says he is no longer afraid
of death. Four weeks later he left the hospital as a healthy
man."[56]

A famous NDE suggesting people are having sensory experiences when the body's senses were blocked or not functioning was the subject of a television documentary, "The Day I Died," and reported in *Light and Death*, a book by cardiologist Dr. Michael Sabom.[57] To remove a deadly large aneurysm from beneath her brain, Pam Reynolds was put into a state of hypothermic cardiac arrest. Her body temperature was lowered to 60 degrees, her heartbeat and breathing were stopped, and the blood was drained from her head. Her brain waves flattened, showing no brain activity.

After her successful operation, she was warmed and her own blood was returned to her body. When she could communicate, she reported a startling near-death experience. She gave remarkably accurate, detailed descriptions of the surgical procedure. She reported that someone in the operating room said something about her arteries being small, and she described the Midas Rex bone saw as looking like an electric toothbrush, having interchangeable blades, and a high-pitched whirring sound.

The things she saw and heard occurred during the time when she was deeply unconscious, but before the blood was actually drained from her. During the time she described hearing and seeing details, her eyes were taped shut and her ears were plugged with devices that monitored her brain stem activity. These devices produced loud clicks measuring 95 decibels at a rate of 11.3 clicks per second, drowning out all outside noise.[58]

Pam went on to describe a remarkable NDE experience that could have happened either when she was unconscious and sensory deprived or while she was brain dead. During the near-death experience, she reported floating out of the operating room and traveling down a tunnel to a light at the end where her deceased relatives and friends were waiting. Her long-dead grandmother was there. Eventually, her deceased uncle took her back and she re-entered her body.

She said that during the experience, she saw with vision that was "brighter and more focused and clearer than normal vision." When she heard her deceased grandmother calling, the sound was clearer hearing than she had with her ears, but her auditory functions were shut down by noise and unconsciousness.

Five eminent cardiac and medical specialists (Dr. Sam Parnia, Dr. Pim van Lommel, Dr. Robert Spetzler, Dr. Peter Fenwick, and Dr. Michael Sabom) all supported the accuracy of Pam's stated experience during her clinical death, reporting that "What she saw corresponded to what actually happened."[59] She saw and heard details while both sensory deprived and unconscious, with her eyes taped shut and hearing blocked by loud clicks, or while she was brain dead.

People Commonly Describe Separating the Mind from the Body in Out-of-Body Experiences.

In out-of-body experiences (OBEs), people describe being conscious outside of their bodies and having normal sensory experiences such as traveling to locations, listening to conversations, and seeing distant people while the body is motionless. OBEs are surprisingly common. Five surveys done in the United Sates, dating back to at least 1954, show that as high as 25 percent of those polled responded that they had experienced an OBE. A 1975 survey of a randomly selected group of 1,000 students and townspeople in a small town in Virginia found that 25 percent of the students and 14 percent of the townspeople reported having an OBE.[60]

Reports of OBEs have been well-documented for hundreds of years. Fredrick Myers' book, *Human Personality and Its Survival After Death*, documents hundreds of carefully recorded and verified accounts of out-of-body experiences. [61]

In May 1980, Dr. Glen Gabbard of the Menninger Foundation, Dr. Stewart Twemlow of the Topeka V.A. Medical Center, and Dr. Fowler Jones of the University of Kansas Medical Center, presented the findings of studies of OBEs at the American Psychiatric Association's annual meeting in San Francisco. The researchers reported that those who experience OBEs describe them as being distinctly different from dreams or hallucinations. They describe feeling a real sense of separation of the mind from the body. The experiencers in the study tested normal in all psychological and physical senses. [62]

D. Scott Rogo examined over 60 studies of out-of-body experiences and found these common conclusions:

- The OBE experience was a common human experience, with roughly 10-20 percent of the adult population undergoing an OBE sometime in their lives.

- OBE experiencers weren't special types of persons (e.g. persons with pathological states of mind, or over-anxious about death, prone to fantasy, etc.).

- At least some OBE experiencers can be "detected" at distant locations during their OBE travels by the use of animal, human and sometimes physical detectors.

- At least some gifted OBE experiencers can sometimes make surprisingly correct observations at distant locations while traveling out of the body.

- At least some OBEs are certainly not dreams or hallucinations.[63]

An anecdotal example of evidence that a person's mind leaves and returns to their body during an NDE comes from the research of Dr. Melvin Morse, Associate Professor of Pediatrics at the University of Washington:

> Olga Gearhardt was a 63 year old woman who underwent a heart transplant because of a severe virus that attacked her heart tissue. Her entire family waited at the hospital during the surgery, except for her son-in-law, who stayed home. The transplant was a success, but at exactly 2:15 am, her new heart stopped beating. It took the frantic transplant team three more hours to revive her. Her family was only told in the morning that her operation was a success, without other details. When they called her son-in-law with the good news, he had his own news to tell. He had already learned about the successful surgery. At exactly 2:15 am, while he was sleeping, he awoke to see his Olga, his mother-in-law, at the foot of his bed. She told him not to worry, that she was going to be alright. She asked him to tell her daughter (his wife). He wrote down the message, and the time of day and then fell asleep. Later on at the hospital, Olga regained consciousness. Her first words were "did you get the message?" She was able to confirm that she left her body during her near-death experience and was able to travel to her son-in-law to communicate to him the message. This anecdotal evidence demonstrates that the near-death experience is a return to consciousness at the point of death, when the brain is dying. Dr. Melvin Morse thoroughly researched Olga's

testimony and every detail had objective verification
including the scribbled note by the son-in-law.[64]

Charles Tart, MD, instructor in psychiatry in the School of Medicine
of the University of Virginia and professor of psychology at the
University of California at Davis, documented an event that happened
with one of his research subjects. The subject had had previous out-of-
body experiences, so he set up a test to see whether she could have an
out-of-body experience while asleep in which she floated out of her body
and could read five numbers on a paper placed high enough in a room
that she would be unable to see the paper by physically going to the
location and trying to look at it.

He set up a bed and electroencephalograph (EEG) to measure her
brain activity while she was asleep. Electrodes were to be placed on her
head with very little slack between the electrodes and the equipment.
She could turn over in bed, but not raise her head or move from the bed.
If she had removed the electrodes to stand up, that would have been
recorded on the equipment, so she was effectively confined to the bed.

On the evening of the study, he placed a small piece of paper with
five randomly selected numbers on it, facing upward, on a shelf about
5.5 feet high on the wall of the experiment room. Someone would have
had to have been 6.5 feet off the ground to look down and read the
numbers. He hooked up the electrodes to the woman and started the
monitoring equipment, confining her to the bed because of the short
cables to the electroencephalograph. She was to sleep that evening and,
if she awoke after having had an out-of-body experience, she was to
notify Tart and tell him what she saw.

At 6:04 a.m. the next morning, she awoke and called out to Tart that
the target number was 25132. That was, in fact, the number written on
the small piece of paper. The EEG showed that the electrodes had not
been disturbed. She had demonstrated that either she had an out-of-
body experience or she clairvoyantly received the number. In either
event, it demonstrated that her mind was not confined to the fat and
protein in her skull. Her mind read the numbers from the sheet of paper
without using her eyes or her brain.[65]

Victor Zammit, formerly a lawyer of the Supreme Court of New
South Wales and of the High Court of Australia, describes a striking out-
of-body experience:

> In the United States, Karlis Osis and Boneita Perskari
> spent several years doing scientific research with an

excellent OBE subject, Alex Tanous, and were able to achieve significant results. One particular test involved Tanous traveling astrally to a different place miles away to visit a particular office to see what was on the table then report back. Tanous did not know that at this office a psychic, Christine Whiting, was waiting to see if she could see anyone coming to visit. With her clairvoyant sight she was able to see Tanous come into the office and as well she described in detail his position and the shirt with rolled-up sleeves and the corduroy pants he was wearing.[66]

The account squared with what Tanous described about his clothing and the out-of-body experience.

Psychics Know Information the Brain and Body Haven't Experienced or Sensed

Many records of psychic investigations have shown that psychics know information they are not getting from their body's senses. They describe in great detail information about people's lives, dead and alive. Psychic detectives such as Greta Alexander, who played a major role in writing this book, *Your Eternal Self*, from the other side after her death, receive specific details about cases without knowing anything about the people involved or visiting the town where the crime took place.

Consider the psychic detective case examples that follow. Statements by credible witnesses, including the police officers involved in the cases, are recorded on videotape.

An Australian series on psychic detectives entitled "Sensing Murder" aired its first episode on June 6, 2002. The psychics were under the scrutiny of the television producers and skeptics who witnessed psychics Debbie Malone and Scott Russel-Hill attempt to provide details about a case, knowing only that it was a murder, nothing else. These are the details they correctly identified:

- The victim was female.
- Her name was Sarah.
- She was in the early twenties.
- Her body was still missing.
- The victim had been dead around 13 years (It was actually 15 years).

- She was coming home from tennis.
- A car involved was a cream-colored, early 80's Holden Commodore.
- The victim was attacked getting into her little red car.
- Frankston was the area.
- Kananook was the specific place of the murder.
- She was killed with a knife.
- They identified the attacker by name.
- The incident was at night.
- The killer was with a group.
- There was a female in the group.
- One member was nicknamed "Dwarfie."
- The group leader was nicknamed "Rat-head."
- They identified the exact parking space used by the victim.
- They identified where there had been blood on the ground.
- They identified where a witness who hadn't come forward had stood.
- Scott drew up a map which was identical to the area concerned.[67]

Such sessions are commonplace. Psychic detectives are able to identify specific details about cases and lead police to victims and perpetrators. Katherine Ramsland, of CourtTV's *Crime Library*, summarizes what we know about police use of psychic detectives:

> Although skeptics galore decry the use of psychics for anything but entertainment, police departments around the country call on certain psychics when all else fails. They've been doing that for more than a century, and when forbidden to do so, they sometimes use unofficial means.[68]

A psychic detective named Phil Jordan and detectives involved in a case appeared on a television show titled *Nancy Grace* on December 30, 2005.[69] Jordan had been brought in on a case because two men had apparently drowned in a fast-moving stream in the Finger Lakes region of New York, but their bodies could not be found. He said that in his mind's eye, he saw a red flower floating down the stream where the body of the larger of the two men would be found, but it was late winter, so that didn't seem possible. He sat before a map and pinpointed pools of water where he said the larger man's body would be found.

The detectives went to the pools of water and found the larger man's body. There, they also found red flowers floating down the stream. Friends of the deceased had dropped flowers into the water upstream where the man likely fell in, as a memorial, with no knowledge of the psychic's words. The flowers had floated downstream to where the body actually was.

During the same *Nancy Grace* show, Jordan, the psychic, described what he told detectives when he was brought in on the case of a police officer killed in Akron, Ohio. He described it as a robbery gone bad, felt there were five individuals involved, said that the murdered officer knew the killer through his drug-unit police work, saw in his mind's eye a basketball hoop near the body, and felt the killer had the tip of his trigger finger missing.

Jordan hadn't seen the crime scene, but there was, in fact, a basketball court there. As a result of these statements by Phil Jordan, detectives pulled photos of suspects known to the drug unit the murdered officer had worked in, narrowing them down to 35 or 40 suspects. They asked Phil Jordan to see if men in any of the photographs seemed to be among the murderers. He picked five of the photos as being of men likely involved. The detectives interrogated all five. Three were eventually found guilty of the murder. The convicted shooter had the tip of his trigger finger missing.[70]

Psychic activity such as that reported in these documented cases happens commonly today. The psychics are using their minds to learn information they could not know if their minds had been confined to their brains.

The Mind Knows Information before the Brain Can Even Have Access to It

More evidence that the mind is outside of the brain is in the finding that the mind knows information before it's even available to the brain, then tells the brain about it so the brain registers activity, just as a television does when it receives the signal from a distant location. Descriptions of these phenomena follow.

People React to Pictures Seconds before Seeing Them.

Dr. Dean Radin, senior scientist at the Institute of Noetic Sciences, performed carefully controlled studies in which people seated before a computer monitor were shown calm pictures (pastoral scenes and neutral household objects) and emotional pictures (erotic and violent scenes). The pictures were selected at random by a computer and shown in random order. Their skin conductance levels (SCL) were measured continually during the entire test. The skin conductance test is like a lie detector that shows whether the person feels stress. As you might expect, people showed stress at seeing the emotional pictures and calm when shown the calm pictures.

But remarkably, the tests consistently showed that some people reacted to the pictures with the appropriately matched calm or stress as early as six seconds before the pictures were shown, even though the computer hadn't selected them at random yet. That suggests that the people weren't using the body to learn about the pictures.[71]

The studies were replicated by Dick Bierman, a psychologist at the University of Amsterdam and Utrecht University.[72]

What this means is that the person's mind must have already been reacting to information it received before the information even existed in the physical realm for the eyes to see. The mind told the body about it so the body could be stressed or calm, and only after the picture appeared was the brain informed.

People Can Successfully Predict Targets That Will Be Shown Before a Computer Even Selects the Target.

There has been other evidence that the mind knows things before the brain and body's senses are involved. Dr. Charles Honorton was Director of the Division of Parapsychology and Psychophysics at Maimonides Medical Center in New York. He and his colleagues looked at all the tests performed from 1935 to 1987 that were designed to determine whether someone (called a "subject") could predict which "target" was about to be shown from several possible targets. In each study, the subject was shown a selection of several targets such as colored lamps, symbols on cards, or the number on a die and asked to guess which one would be the chosen target. Then, one target was selected at random by the computer or rolling a die or some other uncontrollable, random action. The studies compared each subject's prediction with the target that was actually selected.

Honorton and his colleagues found reports of 309 experiments in 113 articles published from 1935 to 1987, done by 62 different investigators. Combined, they totaled 2 million individual trials by over 50,000 subjects. The time intervals between the guesses and the random selections of targets ranged from milliseconds to a year. The results were that the subjects were able to predict which target would be selected more often than would occur by chance guessing, with the odds against it being by chance of ten trillion trillion to one.[73]

As might be expected, when these findings were published, other researchers from around the world, from Edinburgh University to Cornell in the United States, rushed to duplicate the experiment and improve on it. They all got similar results and extended the experiments and findings:

> It was soon discovered that gamblers began reacting subconsciously shortly before they won or lost. The same effect was seen in those who are terrified of animals moments before they were shown the creatures. The odds against all of these trials being wrong is literally millions to one against.[74]

In other words, the mind outside of the body seems to know information before it is available for any of the body's senses to receive it. The mind tells the body about what is coming up and the body reacts. Only later does the brain light up with activity after the event has occurred.

People Successfully Anticipate Someone's Call or Visit.

This ability of the mind to know something before the brain could even have access to the information is common in people's everyday lives. We've all had the experience of thinking of someone and a few minutes later that person calls or knocks on the door. It could be someone we haven't seen for days or weeks.

To find out whether that really is a premonition that the person will call or knock on the door, Rupert Sheldrake, a British biologist, performed experiments in which he gave subjects a list of four people and had the subjects sit quietly beside the phone. They were then asked to select which of the four people they believed was about to call. The person among the four who would call was selected at random by rolling a die, so no one would know who was going to call.

Sheldrake studied a number of people using this setup. We would expect that the subjects would guess correctly 25 percent of the time just by chance (one out of four). However, Sheldrake had results of 45 percent correct, showing that people often did know before a person called who was going to call.[75]

That knowledge apparently was coming from a source outside of the person, another indication that the mind must not be confined to the brain.

People React to a Touch About to Happen before It Even Happens to the Body.

Benjamin Libet, Ph.D., a neurobiologist at the Medical Center of the University of California, was measuring how quickly the brain would register stimulation, such as a being touched on the arm, by using electrodes to measure when the brain responded. The surprising result was that the person involved in the test stated that he was aware (conscious) of the sensation a few thousandths of a second following the stimulation, but the person's brain didn't register the touch until after that. In other words, it seems that the person's mind knew about the stimulation to the body before the brain even started to show activity.[76]

People Prepare to Act Before the Deciding Part of the Brain Begins to Show Activity.

A similar finding resulted from other studies by Dr. Libet. He conducted experiments in 1985 that showed the motor area of the brain prepares to act a measurable length of time before a person uses the part of the brain that decides to act. He asked test subjects to decide to lift either the right finger or the whole right hand. The subjects were connected to brain-wave-measuring machines (EEGs) to see when the decision-making part of the brain was working and when the motor or muscle part of the brain was working. The times on the EEG recordings were carefully monitored. The results were that the part of the brain that governs movement was getting ready to raise the finger or hand before the decision was even made in the brain, on average by a half second but as long as 11 seconds before.[77]

The mind apparently had already made the decision before it told the brain about it.

Scientists Have Become Convinced by the Evidence that the Mind Knows Before Sensed Information is Available.

Professor Dick J. Bierman of the University of Amsterdam and Utrecht University, has been active in the field of parapsychology for over two decades, though he had been skeptical about the reality of psychic phenomena for much of that time. After receiving his Ph.D. in experimental physics, he became involved in research in artificial intelligence, specifically intelligent tutoring systems. This resulted in a focus on individual learning and later on learning during altered states of consciousness, especially learning during sleep.

His decades of research into how people know led him to change his viewpoint about psychic phenomena. This is his description of the conclusion he came to about people's ability to sense the future:

> We're satisfied that people can sense the future before it happens. . . . We'd now like to move on and see what kind of person is particularly good at it.[78]

Professor Brian Josephson, a Nobel Prize winning physicist from Cambridge University, similarly concluded,

> So far the evidence seems compelling. What seems to be happening is that information is coming from the future.[79]

A meta-analysis of all precognition experiments conducted at Stanford Research Institute from 1973 to 1988 was conducted by Edwin May, Ph.D., a researcher in low-energy, experimental nuclear physics, and his colleagues. The analysis was based on 154 experiments with more than 26,000 separate trials conducted over 16 years. They concluded that the studies showed that people were able to predict the future, with the statistical results of this analysis showing odds against chance that were more than a billion billion to one.[80]

Sensory experience confines a person to knowing about what is happening currently, in the immediate environment of the body. These studies and the conclusions by the researchers who have reviewed them indicate that the mind must be obtaining information from some source outside of the body and brain that it knows and remembers. That suggests that the mind is not in the brain.

People Draw Creativity from Some Source Outside of the Brain

The remarkable abilities some people display defy the notion that a merely mechanical brain could suddenly produce remarkable creations. Machines perform as they were built to perform, but the mind can perform feats far beyond a brain machine's capabilities. Some examples follow.

Child Prodigies Have Abilities that Come from Somewhere Other than the Brain.

Jay Greenberg: Music prodigy

Jay Greenberg is 12 years old, but already has written five full-length symphonies and is now enrolled in the Juilliard School of Music.[81] Greenberg says that music just fills his head and he has to write it down to get it out. He doesn't know where it comes from, but it comes fully written, playing like an orchestra within his head: "It's as if the unconscious mind is giving orders at the speed of light," he reports. "You know, I mean, so I just hear it as if it were a smooth performance of a work that is already written, when it isn't." [82]

But he's not alone. He was preceded by Mozart (who played whole pieces of music at four and wrote his first composition at five), Mendelssohn (who wrote his first piece at age 11), and Camille Saint-Sans (who at age 10 could play any of Mozart's piano concertos from memory).

Where are Greenberg's creations coming from? "It's as if he's looking at a picture of the score, and he's just taking it from the picture, basically," says Sam Zyman, a composer and Greenberg's teacher at Juilliard. In fact, at around age two, Greenberg started drawing instruments. Before he knew what a cello was, he had drawn a picture of one and had written the name. His mother, who has no musical background, reported, "He managed to draw a cello and ask for a cello, and wrote the word cello. And I was surprised, because neither of us has anything to do with string instruments. And I didn't expect him to know what it [a cello] was." At age three, he was drawing the notes for the cello performance.[83] He had not been taught how to draw notes or create a cello performance, yet they came to him.

In 2007, his mother reported that ". . . he told us he often hears more than one new composition at a time. Multiple channels is what it's been termed." Says Jay, ". . . my brain is able to control two or three different musics at the same time — along with the channel of everyday life." He doesn't revise his compositions. They usually come out right the first time. [84]

Akiane: Art and poetry prodigy

Akiane is an accomplished artist and poet who began drawing at age four. She is considered the only known child "binary" genius, meaning she is a prodigy in both realist painting and poetry.[85] Akiane has had solo art exhibitions at ages 9, 10, 11, and 12. She had a life-changing spiritual transformation at age four, bringing her entire family, including her atheist mother, to God. Like Jay Greenberg, she explains that her poems often arrive fully conceived.[86]

Olivia Bennett: Art prodigy

Olivia Bennett began painting at age five. Now 17, her work is well known and has been compared to that of the art master Georgia O'Keeffe.[87]

Materialists assert that these prodigies result from mysteries of the brain, but they can't explain how. It's clear that unusual abilities of these magnitudes couldn't come from three to five pounds of fat and protein squashed inside a skull. If the phenomenon were simply a product of the same machine brain 6 billion people on the planet share in common, we would expect a sizable percentage of the machines to be equally talented. But machines don't suddenly take on remarkable properties, and few people are prodigies.

For a list of child prodigies in various fields, go to http://youreternalself.com/chapter1.htm.

Creativity Comes from Outside the Brain.

> The words or the language, as they are written or
> spoken, do not seem to play any role in my mechanism
> of thought. . . . Conventional words or other signs have
> to be sought for laboriously only in a secondary
> stage. . . .when words intervene at all, they are, in my
> case, purely auditive. – *Albert Einstein*[88]

Graham Wallas created a sequence that creativity seems to go through that is widely accepted today:[89]

- **Preparation** – Knowledge of the facts, insights, and general knowledge base about the subject that is the focus of the creative endeavor.

- **Incubation** – Great ideas seem to require some time from the moment the person begins exploring a problem to the time a creative idea comes.

- **Illumination** – This is a flash of insight about a new approach or new idea. Wallas described it as a mysterious phase in which the creative insight seems to appear almost magically from nowhere.

- **Verification** – The idea is tested to be sure it works.

The "illumination" step is the most revealing. Creative people describe the insight or answer just "coming to them." If the insights were coming from the brain as a machine, we would not have this sudden insight. New ideas would come at the end of a logical process, like putting figures into the cells of a spreadsheet and having the correct results appear. The mechanical process would be to think through the knowledge, and at the end of the thought process the answer would be apparent. That isn't what creative people describe happening. The insights seem to come fully formed from a source the person can't identify.

Creative people such as musicians, writers, and theoretical mathematicians and physicists commonly describe these mysterious, sudden insights. Larry Dossey, chief of staff, Medical City Dallas Hospital and director of the Biofeedback Department of the Dallas Diagnostic Association, describes such a burst of creativity that came to a renowned concert artist, Rosalyn Tureck. At the age of 17, Tureck was playing a Bach fugue when she says she had this remarkable experience:

> Suddenly she lost all awareness of her own existence. On coming to, she saw Bach's music in a totally new way, with a new structure that required the development of a novel piano technique. She worked it out over the next two days, applying it to four lines of the fugue, which she played at her next session. Her teacher felt her interpretation was marvelous but could not be sustained or applied to Bach's entire oeuvre. "All

I knew," Tureck said, "was that I had gone through a
small door into an immense living, green universe, and
the impossibility for me lay in returning through that
door to the world I had known."[90]

Later, she became the first woman invited to conduct the New York
Philharmonic Orchestra.

Mozart described his musical composition in much the same way the
child prodigies describe theirs, as coming whole into the mind:

All this fires my soul, and, provided I am not disturbed,
my subject enlarges itself, becomes methodized and
defined, and the whole, though it be long, stands almost
complete and finished in my mind, so that I can survey
it, like a fine picture or a beautiful statue, at a glance.
Nor do I hear in my imagination the parts *successively*,
but I hear them, as it were, all at once. What a delight
this is I cannot tell! All this invention, this producing,
takes place in a pleasing, lively dream.[91]

Physicist Michael Faraday, renowned for his work with
electromagnetism, said that his thinking was almost entirely visual. He
originated his theories without the help of a single mathematical
formula.[92]

Max Knoll, Professor of Electrical Engineering at Princeton
University and inventor of the electron microscope, described this
inspiration with a suggestion that it comes from some greater source:

The fact that an idea suddenly emerges full-blown call[s]
for the existence of . . . a special intuitive function. The
content of this idea is best described in . . . timeless,
nonspatial . . . terms. . . . Always unmistakable are the
suddenness and activity of the intuitive event, and its
tendency to occur in a state of relaxation, and after a
protracted "period of meditation." . . . This . . . cannot be
attributed . . . to higher thinking functions.[93]

Savants Have Abilities Outside
the Capabilities of Their Brains.

Savants normally are autistic in most areas of their mental
development, meaning they are withdrawn, don't react normally to their

environments, don't communicate well, and have mental deficits. However, savants have abilities called "splinter skills," meaning they are focused in a highly specialized area such as recalling facts, numbers, license plates, maps, and extensive lists of statistics after being exposed to them only once.

Kim Peek, whose life inspired the movie *Rain Man* with Dustin Hoffman and Tom Cruise, had macrocephaly resulting from damage to the cerebellum. He was missing parts of his brain, so he didn't learn to walk until age four and still walks in a sidelong manner. He cannot button up his shirt and has difficulty with other motor activities. His IQ scores are well below average.

However, in spite of his deficiencies, he can recall books in their entirety, from memory. He has photographic recall of about 98% of what he reads one time. His ability to read came suddenly at age three:

> At age three Kim asked his parents what the word
> "confidential" meant. He was kiddingly told to look it up
> in the dictionary and he did just that. He somehow knew
> how to use the alphabetical order to locate the word and
> then proceeded to read, phonetically, the word's
> definition (Since that time Kim has read, and can recall,
> some 7600 books).[94]

The most reasonable explanation for the savant's unexplainable ability is that memory and the mind aren't in the brain. A person not focused on the physical realm has access to a great variety of other abilities and memories. The savant's knowledge seems to come from the same place from which a psychic receives knowledge. It is outside of the immediate physical environment.

A materialist might suggest that the brain simply has greater capabilities in a highly focused area when the other parts of the brain that should have developed are allocated to that focused area. However, there is no research to indicate that other parts of the brain somehow become converted to the focused skills; in fact, damage to the brains of savants means parts of the brain simply don't work.

The abilities can develop suddenly, showing that this ability doesn't develop gradually as unused parts of the brain are dedicated to the unusual abilities. When they are acquired suddenly, the effect is known as the "acquired savant syndrome."[95] That was the case with savant Orlando L. Serrell.[96] Orlando was simply an ordinary boy until, at age 10, he was struck by a baseball on the left side of his head. He fell to the ground, but didn't report it to his parents or receive medical attention, although he suffered from a headache for a long time. However, he found that he then was able to perform calendrical calculations of incredible complexity. That means if you ask Orlando what day of the week January 4, 2015, will fall on, he will be able to tell you, "Saturday," instantly, without a pause to calculate and with perfect accuracy. The boy's brain didn't develop over time so that more brain was focused on calendrical calculations. The change happened immediately after the accident.

At six years of age, an autistic child named Matt Savage suddenly began playing *London Bridge Is Falling Down* perfectly on the piano without trial and error to learn it, "from nothing to playing perfectly," his mother said.[97] Today he is an accomplished jazz pianist. Before that day when he spontaneously started playing the piano, he did not like to be exposed to any noise.

The Evidence the Mind Knows without the Brain Having Access to the Information Is Overwhelming

Edward F. Kelly is currently Research Professor in the Department of Psychiatric Medicine at the University of Virginia. He is author of *Computer Recognition of English Word Senses, Altered States of Consciousness and Psi: An Historical Survey and Research Prospectus,* and *Irreducible Mind: Toward a Psychology for the 21st Century.* He asserts that the reality of psychic knowledge (knowing outside of the brain) has been experimentally established beyond any reasonable doubt, and any viable theory of human personality will have to accommodate this fact.[98]

Dreams Don't Play Back Memories in the Brain

If life memories were stored in the brain, we would expect that when the person relaxes the focus of wakeful awareness by sleeping, the brain would access those memories and play them back in dreams because it would require little effort. Without wakeful control, the memories would simply spill out into dreams. If memories were stored in the brain like a movie on a DVD, when the brain was searching for some source of images during the dream state, it would pull out some of its stored movies—they're already there, so it would take little energy to just play them back. At the very least, the brain would play back some of the memories during sleep in exactly the same way they occurred when the memories were experienced.

Instead, when you relax into a half-sleep or are in a full-dream sleep, you witness scenes of people you don't know doing things you don't anticipate, saying things you didn't remember anyone saying in your lifetime. Your mind is off in the same place your memories, creativity, thoughts, and the mind are, where entirely new creations evolve in ways different from what your eyes, ears, nose, tongue, and skin actually experienced as sensual input. If the brain were a machine, you could no more do that than you could get a dry martini out of an old Coke machine. Let a toaster run by itself for decades and it will never produce a cup of coffee. The capability for novelty and creativity just isn't in a machine.

Instead, the person's mind sails off into flights of fancy. It creates entirely new dramas with some of the same characters in the person's life, but some entirely new characters the dreamer has never met and will probably never meet in life. In other words, the mind, in sleep, goes to the same place where memories are stored, outside of the brain. But since it has a universe of resources to draw from, it sets about creating an entirely novel life for itself, like another Earth realm, using the person's life experiences only as the basis for the dreams.

At times, dreams have important messages or contain vivid images of and conversations with deceased loved ones. That couldn't come out of the brain.

How Does the Mind Interact with the Brain?

The research seems clear that when we have a memory, it isn't that the brain creates the memory. The brain does take on the same state it was in when the memory was first created. It has sights, sounds, smells, tastes, and sensations of touch, and it plays them in a sequence as though the memory were being lived again. The mind then feels all the same emotions because it believes it's in the original, remembered state, even though the memory might have been created at some remote time.

Those who speak about this re-creation of memory in the brain use the term, "whole-brain memories."[99] They can't find out where memories are stored in the brain, but they know that a memory uses many parts—the sight, sound, smell, taste, touch, emotional, psychomotor, and psychokinetic areas of the brain—so they assume the memories must be stored in many parts of the brain in some mysterious, not-understood way. However, there is no evidence to assume that memories are stored in the brain, and the requirements on the brain to accomplish that would be impossible to realize. We just know that when the mind wants to recall something, it wills the memory into existence and the brain takes on the same states it had when the memory was formed so the person sees the image, hears the sounds, feels the textures, smells the odors, and feels the emotions, but the source of these experiences is unknown.

The only viable explanation for what is happening is that the mind, outside of the brain, brings whole memories to the brain and reorganizes the brain to duplicate what the mind was experiencing when the memories were formed. The brain, in other words, is like a television. The signal coming into it aligns its components to create images of the Simpsons on the screen, just as a memory is recreated in the mind. But the television doesn't create the image of Bart Simpson; Bart's image and zany actions aren't stored in the television. The television is just the instrument that allows Bart to be experienced again as he was when his image was first created, outside of the television set.

When the television set is damaged, perhaps by having a short circuit burn out a part, the television will not function properly. We could turn on Larry King but we might not be able to hear sound, or the picture may be distorted or fuzzy. However, that doesn't mean Larry King has been struck dumb or has become fuzzy. The signal, just like a person's mind, is perfectly fine when the television or the brain is damaged; they just don't function well enough to receive and process the signals correctly.

Some recent research supporting the view that the mind outside of the brain forms the brain to have experiences is presented in Chapter 10.

Then Where Are You?

Neuroscientists can't locate your mind or your memories in the brain, so many are now suggesting that the mind is not in the brain. The data seem to support that because the brain doesn't have the capacity to hold all the memories, and missing large parts of the brain doesn't affect memory or thinking. At the same time, many people, including me and units of the United States Government, can see objects and scenes thousands of miles away without using our eyes. Blind people see clearly in near-death experiences and have the remarkable ability to locate objects and even ride bicycles without using physical eyes. People having near-death experiences when the brain is completely nonfunctioning as shown on brain-monitoring equipment see, hear, and know more clearly than when they are fully awake, and what they experience is stored in memory while the brain shows no functioning. Out-of-body experiences demonstrate that people lying in bed at one location can see scenes far away without using their closed eyes. People's minds react to pictures before a computer has even chosen them, showing the brain couldn't be involved, and we commonly know someone is going to call or visit with no sensory organs sending information to the brain to tell us that. Musical scores and creative ideas pop into people's minds in ways a brain machine couldn't manage. Savants have remarkable abilities beyond the brain's capacities. And in dreams we sail off into flights of fancy rather than playing back memories stored in the brain.

The data all clearly indicate that the mind simply is not in the brain. You're outside of the body in an entirely different realm. That will have profound implications for your relationships with other people because your mind is one with their minds. It will prove to you the truths about the afterlife because if you're not limited in the body, you don't die when the body dies.

The body is useful for having experiences, but it's just like a television. You turn it on so you can experience the Simpsons or Larry King. But just as the signal comes from outside the television, your mind is outside the brain and the body, and like the first television you had decades ago that you don't have any use for or affection for today, you will find that you don't need or care about the body when it stops functioning. That's what we'll explore in the next chapters.

For more about the mind and the brain, log onto http://youreternalself.com/chapter1.htm.

2

What Are You?

> The mind – the thing that is "you" – your "soul" if you
> will – carries on after conventional science says it should
> have drifted into nothingness. — *Dr. Sam Parnia,*
> *Southampton General Hospital, London, England, and the*
> *University of Southampton*

You know that you are your mind that goes through the day using the brain and the body as it creates realities. The physical world is the scenery for the plays you create. But you are not the scenery. You know that your mind isn't in the brain. No neuroscientist can locate it there; the brain couldn't hold all of your life memories; stimulating the brain doesn't result in a single mind function; and people have sensory experiences without using the brain at all. You aren't in the brain. You're mind is outside of the brain.

That leads to a remarkable conclusion. When the body stops functioning, your mind must still be there. Your mind simply continues as it was when it was using the body, just as when you take off your overcoat and leave it in the closet, you walk into the living room and hug your loved ones without a thought for where your coat is. We know that's true from all the evidence we've accumulated over the last two centuries. The mind, that continues after the body dies, is your real self.

If your self is a mind apart from the brain and the body, then what are you? You are an eternal being having a physical experience. This chapter explains that fact.

As a note for Christians taught that it is sinful to speak to people who have crossed over to the next plane of life or that people go into a long sleep after death, those things are absolutely not true. For more, link to http://youreternalself.com/chapter2.htm.

Why Do Some Have Difficulty Realizing We're Eternal Beings?

If we had been reared to understand that we're not the body, today we would just assume that is true. Many people don't believe that today because they were taught, by model and example since childhood, that we are just the body. Our culture has a desperate fear of death, as though death were somehow a bad thing—the end of existence. Large amounts of money are expended during the last few weeks of life trying to keep the body alive just a little longer, even though, at times, the mind is already gone. People prefer living in a vegetative state or conscious but in pain for a few extra days, hooked up to monstrous, expensive machines, instead of dying peacefully, with loved ones a few weeks earlier at home. When people want to remember a loved one who has died, they go to the cemetery and stare at the ground, as though the person was the body buried there. It's no wonder that children walking beside their sobbing elders across the cemetery lawn learn to fear death and feel the body is all there is to life.

The problem arose because humankind matured intellectually over the past two millennia, but spiritually remained backward. Belief in the tribal gods held sway at the beginning of the first millennium BCE. Then, during the Axial Age (c. 800 BCE – 200 BCE) and through the time of Yeshua (Jesus) in the first century CE, humankind was repeatedly given insights into the greater self we each are that is not confined to a body. Our ancestors should have used the knowledge to mature away from the harsh, militaristic, partisan tribal gods toward a spirituality of peace, love, brotherhood, and confidence in our eternal natures. That's what the spiritual teachers were describing.

These words we're just coming to understand today were spoken by Yeshua ben Yosef[1] (the Aramaic name that Jesus and his family used) in the first-century CE:

> I will not leave you as orphans; I will come to you. Before long, the world will not see me anymore, but you will see me. Because I live, you also will live. On that day you will realize that I am in my Father, and you are in me, and I am in you. – *Yeshua ben Yosef*

In the first century CE, Yeshua knew that he would not die when he stopped using the body and knew that he would continue to be with his followers and even appear to them. That is a perfect description of what we today know to be true about death, the afterlife, and our oneness with each other and the Higher Power. But the people who came to assume control of spiritual affairs reinterpreted all of Yeshua's teachings to fit their assumptions and perspectives, eventually developing an organized religion that preferred the more primitive religious beliefs: exclusivity, intolerance, tribal hierarchy, power, judgment, death as separation until a distant heaven for the obedient and eternal punishment for the disobedient, and wealth for the functionaries.

Gradually, a huge organization with opulent cathedrals and an autocratic, wealthy ruling class evolved; religion gave no freedom of thought to the people and would not encourage them to learn about the mind of God that was continually communicating with them. Yeshua's understanding of the afterlife, the Higher Power, and the need for love, peace, brotherhood, and servanthood was overshadowed by the powerful, wealthy religious organization that eventually developed after his death. The religious functionaries told the people that their beliefs were naïve and untrustworthy, that the inner voice they heard was demons and delusion, and that only the religious leaders understood the Divine truths. Over the centuries, humankind came to believe those falsehoods. Many people still believe them today.

In the end, the beliefs that only religions can know the truth of the universe, and that the Higher Power will speak unique truths only to ministers or priests, are agnostic or atheistic; they reveal an implicit belief that the Higher Power either doesn't exist or disdains to communicate to people directly.

The result is that over the two millennia since the Axial Age and Yeshua, humankind has been in a spiritual dark ages. Religion punished anyone who spoke about spiritual subjects not sanctioned by the religion. During that time, our species became intellectually mature, but remained spiritually retarded. For most people today, the term "spirituality" means going to church and swearing allegiance to a set of doctrines. But neither has anything to do with spirituality. This misconception illustrates the depth of our ignorance about spiritual realities.

And so, when bright people in the seventeenth century began to learn about the material realm through a rapidly evolving science, humankind declared its independence from religion. The intellectuals of the time felt they no longer needed to have a religious interpretation of life and the mind because they believed both were accidents in time, governed by natural laws, not a god's laws. God became superfluous.

But abandoning religion left humankind with no spiritual foundation. Today, most people don't know what spirituality is or how to learn about spirituality and their own spiritual selves. Many have shunned religion, God, and spirituality altogether, while others, especially in the United States, have adapted their beliefs to the current secular trends that require no real thought about an inner spiritual life, just membership in and attendance at some church. For their beliefs about life and the universe, they have turned to materialistic science because it has a ring of authoritative truth and its assertions can be proven on demand, unlike the statements about the inner self made by the great spiritual teachers.

Materialistic science became the twenty-first century religion and scientists became its priests. Humankind has exchanged the God of legalistic religions, which kept people ignorant about personal spirituality and the inner self, for materialistic science, which promoted the premise that discussions of the inner self and personal spirituality are naïve, primitive, and ultimately meaningless. While at funerals they talk about a distant heaven, the real fear for most is that the mind is in the brain and the death of the brain is the end of existence for the mind.

So the odd belief that humankind evolved from rocks is a very recent belief that developed because humankind was not able to grow spiritually for two millennia and had little on which to base its beliefs as confidence in religions fell away. Today, we are rediscovering the truths about the universe, life, God, and humankind that have always been there, but were shrouded by religion. We're learning from each other what we always knew to be true by listening to each other's accounts of our natural, everyday encounters with the afterlife. We just haven't been sharing our convictions with confidence because of a society formed by the centuries-old religious beliefs and the current scientific disdain for such conversations.

Today, we're gaining a perspective on the odd mythology about man being a soft rock; people are learning that it's just profound ignorance produced from the lack of spiritual growth by humankind and a demonizing of the inner voice that speaks the truths about life. The result of this rediscovery of the self will be a revolution in science. As Peter Russell wrote in *From Science to God: A Physicist's Journey into the Mystery of Consciousness*, "Our inability to account for consciousness is the trigger that will, in time, push Western science into what the American philosopher Thomas Kuhn called a 'paradigm shift.'"[2]

Do Scientists Believe There Is an Afterlife?

There might have been more skeptics about the afterlife among scientists in the nineteenth and early twentieth centuries when science had not turned to learning about the mind and the survival of consciousness, but today the landscape has changed. Scientists are the ones making the discoveries about whom we are physically, psychologically, and spiritually. Now, a steadily increasing number of scientists and other educated professionals are becoming convinced of the reality of the afterlife from the emerging scientific data; the number of skeptics is shrinking.

Here's why new discoveries are at first opposed by a herd of hard-nosed skeptics. At the emergence of every new worldview or paradigm shift in humankind's intellectual history, a group of highly intelligent, well-educated men and women has stubbornly refused to look at or be convinced by the data. They are as consistently a presence in humankind's progress as are the pioneers who persevere and eventually have their new understanding adopted. If humanity listened to the herd of skeptics present during most of our intellectual advancements, we'd still be living in caves using stone tools. Thankfully, the discoverers always eventually emerge victorious, although sometimes not until after their deaths and at other times with deep wounds from the gauntlets they had to run to have their discoveries understood and accepted.

Often, these skeptics speak from simple ignorance. In January 1905, more than a year after the Wright brothers had flown at Kitty Hawk, *Scientific American* ridiculed the notion of manned flight using machinery. At the time, the Wrights were called "The Lying Brothers." The author wrote,

> If such sensational and tremendously important
> experiments are being conducted in a not very remote
> part of the country, on a subject in which almost
> everybody feels the most profound interest, is it possible
> to believe that the enterprising American reporter, who,
> it is well known, comes down the chimney when the
> door is locked in his face—even if he has to scale a
> fifteen-storey skyscraper to do so—would not have
> ascertained all about them and published them
> broadcast long ago?[3]

The writer didn't have the facts, but that didn't deter him from writing
that the statements by the Wright Brothers and others were lies.

Sometimes their resistance is from fear. The trouble Galileo had in
convincing people that the Sun, not the Earth, is at the center of the solar
system came from the professors who feared his ideas would undermine
the Aristotelian principles they were teaching. He was nicknamed "The
Wrangler" and had to leave his medical studies because the professors
made life so miserable for him. I believe many of today's neuroscientists
who still dismiss the data about the mind being outside of the brain do
so because of fear. What would happen to their disciplines, their
prestige in the field, and their book in progress if the data were proven
to be true?

But most often, the herd of stubborn skeptics resists any new
conceptions coming from outside their ranks from pure elitist arrogance.
They believe their understanding of reality and the universe must be
correct because they're the learned scientists, and others don't have the
credentials to suggest or understand scientific truths. In 1772, the
prestigious French Academy of Science studied cases of stones falling
out of the sky presented by many ordinary people. After a lengthy
examination of undeniable reports and the remarkable stones
themselves, they asserted, against all the data, that stones falling from
the sky were delusions because all scientists agreed there are no stones in
the sky. It wasn't until 1803 that they conceded there are such things as
meteorites.

Virtually all important discoveries were maligned by a herd of
skeptics when they were first advanced:

- Penicillin wasn't accepted by the medical establishment for ten
  years after it was discovered.

- Pasteur's suggestion that germs cause disease was called "a ridiculous fiction."

- When Ignaz Semmelweis urged physicians to wash their hands before surgery to deter infections, he was so ridiculed for his suggestion that he ended up in a mental hospital and his ideas weren't accepted until after he died.

- One British geologist wrote of Darwin's evolution theories, "I laughed till my sides were sore," and a British ornithologist wrote, that he had "utter contempt" for Darwin's theory.

- Wegener, who developed the theory of continental drift, was so ridiculed that he died an outcast from the scientific community in 1930, 20 years before he was proven correct.

- Bell's telephone was turned down by the U.S. Post Office and British Post Office as ridiculous.

- Peyton Rous' suggestion that some cancer is caused by viruses was proven clearly in research, but wasn't accepted for nearly 50 years.

- Roentgen's x-rays were described as an "elaborate hoax."

- Edison's light bulb was called "a completely idiotic idea."

- The military tank was called "idiotic and useless."

- John Baird, inventor of the television camera, was called a swindler.

- Chandrasekhar, who won a Nobel Prize for discovering black holes, was so viciously attacked by the scientific community when he suggested they exist that he couldn't continue his career in science in his native England.

- Doppler's discovery of the Doppler Effect wasn't accepted for two decades because it conflicted with the prevailing notions of science.

- Faraday, the pioneer in electricity, was called a charlatan by his fellow scientists.

- The discoverer of an influential, revolutionary form of geometry (non-Euclidean geometry) kept it secret for 30 years out of fear of ridicule and his work wasn't published until after his death.

- The discovers of a microscope with atom-scale resolution eventually received a Nobel Prize, but initially were greeted with hostility, shouts, and laughter in scientific meetings when they described it.

- The idea of sending rockets into space was called essentially impracticable.

- "Space travel is bunk," the Astronomer Royal of Britain wrote before the first successful manned launches into space.

- Ken Olson, president, chairman, and founder of Digital Equipment Corporation wrote in 1977, "There is no reason anyone would want a computer in their home."

- IBM turned down the newly invented photocopier asserting that the market for it was likely no more than 5,000 businesses.

- Julius Mayer, who conceived the Law of Conservation of Energy, couldn't get an article about it published by any physics journal.

- The work of George Ohm, the pioneer in electricity who developed the now familiar Ohm's Law, was called "a tissue of naked fantasy" and wasn't accepted for 10 years after he advanced it.

The list could continue through all revolutionary ideas advanced in the history of humankind. The skeptics are present at every one of these advancements, and remain simply uninformed, misinformed, arrogant, and closed-minded until they are passed by and the new ideas are adopted.

Max Planck, the German theoretical physicist who originated quantum theory, wrote,

> A new scientific truth does not triumph by convincing its opponents and making them see the light, but rather because its opponents eventually die, and a new generation grows up that is familiar with it.[4]

New discoveries that matter to humankind will never come from the herd of skeptics. They are prisoners of their paradigms.

When you examine the evidence for the afterlife, listen to either ordinary people who experience things they have no reason to fabricate and who speak with genuine excitement and candor, or to the educated intellectuals who acknowledge themselves to be open minded and willing to let truth be found wherever it lies, even if that is outside of their present understanding. If you are willing to listen to these genuine, open-minded people and not the ever-present herd of uninformed skeptics, you will become convinced of the reality of the afterlife. The evidence is incontrovertible. If, instead, you shrink back from the light of newly emerging truth, you will be destined to live huddled in darkness with the skeptics.

Below is a sampling of the vast amount of information that intellectual advancements and science have provided that proves to everyone who reads the literature that we are eternal selves having a physical period of our existence. If someone doesn't believe the afterlife is as real as this life, they simply don't know or won't believe the literature.

People Are Coming to Realize that the Afterlife Is As Real As This Life

The widespread accessibility to information today has resulted in a sharing of knowledge unprecedented in humankind. As people compare their experiences with the afterlife, they are discovering that what they individually always felt to be true is shared by most other people. Emboldened, they're willing to state their beliefs. These aren't hallucinations or superstitions; they're the discovery of truths apparent to most people that have been described throughout the history of civilization. The afterlife is as real as this life.

In 1970, 77 percent of Americans polled said they knew the reality of the afterlife. In a 2000 poll, however, 82 percent of Americans said they knew the reality of the afterlife. Among Jews, 19 percent said they knew the afterlife is real in the 1970s. By 1998, 56 percent said they were convinced of it in.[5] Humankind is outgrowing the superstitions of both religion and science that exist about the afterlife by becoming more knowledgeable about it.

Millions of Everyday People Are Having After-Death Communications

Experiencing the presence of loved ones who have died is very common. In a study reported in the *American Journal of Psychiatry*, two-thirds of those surveyed in the U.S. reported having sensed the presence of the person who passed on.[6] Their experiences can hardly be called unusual.

In 1987, the Gallup Poll organization published the results of a survey designed to find out how many people had after-death communication experience of any kind in Britain. The survey showed that 48 percent of those asked felt they were personally aware of this kind of experience in their lives.[7]

A broad range of studies of after-death communication have shown that after-death communication is very common.[8]

> Rees found that 50% of widowers reported visions of departed spouses that occurred while they were in a wakened state.[9] [Jan Holden reported a percentage of 70% to 80% of widows and widowers.[10]]

> Haraldsson, in a national survey in Iceland, reported that 31% of respondents reported visual encounters with the dead.[11]

> Kalish studied adults in Los Angeles and found that 55% of blacks, 54% of Mexican-Americans, 38% of Anglo-Americans, and 29% of Japanese-Americans reported such encounters.[12]

> These experiences have also been reported in traditional Hopi Indians.[13]

> The fact that these experiences are so common has led one investigator to advocate abandoning the word "hallucination" to describe them.[14]

In 1988, Bill and Judy Guggenheim began The ADC Project, in which they interviewed 3,300 people who had experienced after-death communications. The accounts were emotional, heartwarming, and at times startling. They described them in their book, *Hello from Heaven*[15] that includes 353 of the actual stories they heard. Reading the clear, heartfelt stories by ordinary people who insist they communicated with their deceased loved ones cannot help but convince all but the most hardened skeptics that our loved ones are alive and well after death, just in a different form and a different place that is close by.

The number of people who have had such experiences with deceased loved ones is increasing, in part because of the openness to the phenomena today. Communication with deceased loved ones is a common, everyday occurrence. To deny it is to suggest that most people in the world today are insane, delusional, or lying. A common phenomenon like this is as real as seeing total eclipses of the sun. We wouldn't deny the reality of total eclipses of the sun even if we had never seen one because so many millions of people have experienced them. The same is true of after-death communication. It's simply a common fact.

People don't talk about their after-death communication experiences because of the odd notion in our culture that if we talk about such experiences, we're delusional. But if you bring up the subject of near-death experiences or after-death communication in a group and let people know it's OK to talk about them, the stories will start to roll out.

The same is true for psychotherapists and physicians, who care for people at times of crisis. They often hear accounts of psychic activity and the afterlife, and many have themselves had such experiences. They don't feel comfortable talking about the experiences because of the criticism they fear they would receive from colleagues. But when they're given the opportunity to speak about them in a safe group, the stories abound.

Dr. Elizabeth Lloyd Mayer, psychoanalyst, researcher, clinician, author of groundbreaking papers on female development, the nature of science, and intuition, and professor of psychology at U.C. Berkeley and U.C. Medical Center, studied and spoke about clairvoyance. She wrote about the common reaction from physicians and psychotherapists when she spoke about her own psychic experiences:

> As word of my new interest [in psychic experiences] spread, my medical and psychoanalytic colleagues began to inundate me with accounts of their own anomalous experiences, personal as well as clinical. . . . the stories they shared with me were often ones they'd never revealed to another professional associate. Their accounts—by e-mail, snail mail, at conferences, in seminars, in hall corridors, or at dinner—made as little sense to me as they did to the colleagues telling me about them. The stories were all about knowing things in bizarrely inexplicable ways. . . . I was particularly fascinated by how eagerly my colleagues shared even the most weirdly personal stories with me. Their eagerness puzzled me, until I realized how badly people

wanted to reintegrate corners of experience they'd
walled off from their public lives for fear of being
misbelieved.[16]

The same reluctance to speak, but great desire to share their
experiences, is true for healthcare professionals who have seen evidence
of the afterlife in their own lives and their patients' lives.

Examples of these common contacts with those continuing to live in
the afterlife follow.

People Having After-Death Communications Learn Things They Couldn't Know Otherwise

It is common for someone having an after-death communication
(ADC) to receive messages about things the person could not have
known if the messages didn't come from the deceased.

This account of an after-death communication came from a patient of
Dr. Allan Botkin, formerly a psychotherapist with a large Chicago area
VA hospital, with whom I co-authored the book, *Induced After-Death
Communication: A New Therapy for Grief and Trauma.*[17] It illustrates the
striking reality of the communication for the experiencer, and the fact
that those experiencing after-death communication often learn things
they could not have known.

> Jerry had come to see me for psychotherapy about an
> unrelated matter, but after developing some trust in me,
> felt he could tell me his spontaneous ADC story
> "without being labeled a nutcase." Jerry was living in the
> Midwest and his ex-wife was living on the East Coast
> with their three children. One night, he experienced the
> clear image of his ex-wife while he was asleep. "She
> looked beautiful, peaceful and happy," he said, "and she
> wanted to tell me about something of great concern to
> her." Jerry said she told him that he needed to start
> playing a more important role in rearing their children
> and even offered very specific suggestions about each
> child. Jerry said his experience was much clearer than a
> dream.
>
> Jerry awoke right after his experience, baffled by its
> remarkable clarity. He could remember the entire

experience, and for him it felt like a real conversation with his ex-wife. After lying awake a while trying to make sense of his experience, he managed to get back to sleep.

The next morning as he was making coffee, the phone rang. It was his ex-wife's sister. Tearfully, she told Jerry that his ex-wife had been killed in a car accident during the night.

Suddenly, the meaning of his experience became clear. Since then, Jerry's ex-wife has appeared to him five times in spontaneous ADCs, each time offering further advice about their children. "Every time," he said, "she did all the talking." And after each experience, Jerry followed her advice closely. In all instances, the advice turned out to be very helpful.

As he told me [Dr. Botkin] the story, Jerry laughed at one point and said "She hasn't changed much. She was always hyper-verbal and bossy." When I asked him if he thought that his wife had really visited him after she died, he said defiantly, "I am sure of it. I am as sure of it as I am that I'm looking at you right now. Nobody can ever tell me that it wasn't real, not you or anyone else. I don't care what other people think about this because they really don't know. I didn't believe in this stuff before it happened, but now I have no doubt whatsoever."[18]

In another case, a woman's life was saved by the appearance of an apparition, and she learned about the identity of the apparition later:

In some cases people appear apparently with the express purpose of saving loved ones from danger. This happened to Elaine Worrell who lived with her husband Hal on the top floor of an apartment building in Oskaloosa, Iowa. One day she saw a young man in her hallway who led her downstairs into the apartment of a young widow whom she barely knew. She found the young woman collapsed on a bed after having slashed her wrists. After she recovered, the young woman showed her a photograph of her late husband; Elaine

recognized it immediately as the young man who had
led her downstairs and into the apartment.[19]

Pre-death and Deathbed Visions Are Common

Everything we know about the afterlife tells us that the Higher
Power has set up life so the transition into the next plane of eternal life is
as easy as possible; the universe is filled with love and compassion. Pre-
death visions are an example of that preparation for a gentle transition.

Pre-death visions are visions of deceased loved ones patients
commonly have in the weeks before they die. *Deathbed visions* are the
visions dying patients have in the days or hours immediately preceding
death. Both help the person prepare for the transition. They are God's
counselors, bringing reassurance to those about to cross over.

Dr. James L. Hallenbeck, director of palliative care services with the
Veterans Administration Palo Alto Health Care System, estimates that
these pre-death visions or deathbed visions of deceased loved ones occur
for at least 25 percent of deaths.[20]

Stephen Wagner estimates the number of people who experience
deathbed visions as even more because only about 10 percent of dying
people are conscious shortly before their deaths. Looking just at those
who are conscious, between 50 and 60 percent experience deathbed
visions.[21]

Children are truth-tellers because of their youthful naiveté, so when
they experience such visions, they describe them matter-of-factly. In
Closer to the Light, Dr. Melvin Morse describes children's deathbed
visions, explaining that they are astonishing scientific proof of the
validity of the near-death experience.[22]

Dr. Diane Komp, a Yale pediatric oncologist, described a 7-year-old
girl who sat up in bed just before her death from leukemia and said, "The
angels, they are so beautiful, can't you hear them singing Mommy?" A
boy dying of leukemia said that God spoke to him and that he asked
God to live another year so he could explain his death to his 3-year-old
brother. Amazingly, against medical odds, the boy lived one more
year.[23]

Elisabeth Kübler-Ross described a healthy 4-year-old girl who had a
vivid dream she described to her mother. She said she saw a beautiful
golden heaven and that it was "really, really, real," with gold angels,
diamonds, and jewels. It was a fun place. There, she met Jesus. She told

her mother not to worry because Jesus would take care of her. She then went out to play and sadly was murdered only hours later.[24]

In 1959, Karlis Osis, Ph.D., psychology professor at the University of Freiburg, and Erlendur Haraldsson, Ph.D., psychology professor at the University of Munich, studied deathbed visions in the U.S. and India by interviewing doctors and nurses who had been present when people died. They mailed out questionnaires to 5,000 physicians and 5,000 nurses, providing information on over 35,000 observations of dying patients. Over 1,300 dying patients saw apparitions and almost 900 reported visions of an afterlife.

The researchers found the following consistencies:

1. Some dying people reported seeing angels and other religious figures, but most reported seeing familiar, deceased people.

2. Very often, the friends and relatives in these visions communicate that they have come to help take them away.

3. The dying person is reassured by the experience, expresses great happiness with the vision, and is quite willing to go with the deceased greeters.

4. Often, the dying person's mood and health change when they have such a vision. During these visions, a once depressed or pain-riddled person is elated and relieved of pain.

5. During the vision, the dying person is acutely aware of their real surroundings and conditions, not immersed in a fantasy.

6. The experience and reactions afterward are the same for all experiencers, whether they believe in an afterlife or not.[25]

Osis and Haraldsson reported their findings in a book titled *At the Hour of Death*, concluding, in typical researcher-scientific language,

> In our judgment, the similarities between the core phenomena found in the death-bed visions of both countries are clear enough to be considered supportive of the post-mortem survival hypothesis.[26]

In other words, the deathbed visions are another support for the conclusion that people live on after the body dies.

Carla Wills-Brandon, MA, LMFT, a licensed marriage and family therapist, is the author of nine books exploring addiction, self-esteem, sexual trauma, death, the afterlife, and spirituality. She describes her husband's experience of a deathbed vision before the death of his father, whom they called "Da." Her husband told her the story the morning after he sat up all night with his father in the hospital. He said to her,

> "Tonight while snoozing in the chair in his room, I had a wonderful dream about Da. In this dream he said to me he was going soon, but that he would always watch over us. Upon awakening, I looked over at Da as he slept and noticed he was very at ease. Suddenly, I saw something rise from his body. It was absolutely beautiful. A whirl of pastel color, vibrant in not only appearance but also movement, was leaving his chest area. It was so comforting." The following week, Da gently passed away in my husband's arms.[27]

Wills-Brandon, in her book, *One Last Hug Before I Go: The Mystery And Meaning Of Deathbed Visions*,[28] describes other experiences told to her by caregivers who had been at the bedside of someone passing. She explains that countless hospice workers have seen a wisp of "something" leave the body at the moment of death and that the patients commonly describe visions of deceased relatives, angels, or celestial beings of light.

The caregivers themselves often describe receiving visits during dream time from deceased relatives or even the dying person. Wills-Brandon describes one caregiver's account. She had just returned home exhausted from caring for her dying mother at the nursing home:

> My mother had been very ill for some time. . . . After dinner with my husband and children, I went to bed. During the middle of the night, I awoke from a very deep sleep. I had dreamed my mother had come to visit me. In this dream, she was with my father who had passed 5 years ago. Both of them looked happy and healthy. My mother blew me a kiss. Then she and my father turned around and walked off, over a hill. When I awoke, tears filled my eyes, but I also felt a sense of peace. My parents had looked so joyful. I looked at the clock and noted it was 3 a.m., then lay back down and went to sleep. The next morning my brother called to tell me my mother had left us. When I asked him about the time of her death, he replied she had passed at 3 a.m.[29]

Dr. Peter Fenwick, neuroscientist and fellow of the Royal College of Psychiatrists, describes the account of a woman who witnessed the spiritual image of her husband's death:

> Suddenly there was the most brilliant light shining from my husband's chest, and as this light lifted upward, there was the most beautiful music and singing voices. My own chest seemed filled with infinite joy, and my heart felt as if it was lifting to join this light and music. Suddenly, there was a hand on my shoulder, and a nurse said, "Sorry, love. He's just gone." I lost sight of the light and the music and felt so bereft at being left behind.[30]

The deathbed visions are quite common and aren't explained by any medical or psychological influence. Apparently, those on the next plane of life are helping the dying person make the transition into the afterlife.

We Know Deathbed Visions Are Not Medical or Psychological Hallucinations.

The word "hallucination" is often used by people who are unable to bring themselves to accept the reality of the afterlife. They use the word to dismiss the millions of reports of people communicating with their deceased loved ones. However, the communications don't have any of the characteristics of drug-induced or psychological hallucinations.

In the 1959 article cited earlier, Karlis Osis, Ph.D., and Erlendur Haraldsson, Ph.D., found over 1,300 dying patients who saw apparitions, with almost 900 reporting visions of an afterlife. The researchers examined the patients and data carefully to rule out hallucination and other factors. They concluded the following:

> The typical deathbed vision experience was of a shorter duration, more coherent and more related to the situation of dying and an afterlife than the rambling experiences of a sick brain. . . .

> Most of the visions did not exemplify the normal characteristics of ordinary hallucinations. The patient was rational, logical and well oriented in all respects except his insistence that he was seeing something real. . . .

> Delirium was not the basis for the deathbed apparitions; the apparitions seemed to have an external source and

were not mere projections of wishful thoughts or unfulfilled desires. . . .

Two-thirds of the apparitions seen by the dying were of deceased people; only one-third were of living persons. The opposite is typical of hallucinations by persons in normal health.

Of the apparitions seen, 83 percent were of relatives: mothers, fathers, spouses, siblings and offspring. This contrasted sharply with hallucinations of the mentally ill who most often conjure up strangers or bizarre characters.

The majority of patients who saw apparitions described the mission of the apparition(s) as aiding them in making the transition to the Other World. . . .

The predominant reaction of patients who see apparitions coming to take them away is that of serenity and peace.[31]

Osis then carried out two more studies in the next two decades. The conclusions of the researchers were that the visions were not due to medical or psychological problems:

Medical Factors

- There was no acceptable evidence that drugs were generating the afterlife visions. Those patients who received drugs (e.g. morphine and Demerol) did not have a greater frequency of afterlife visions than other patients.

- There was no acceptable evidence that brain disturbances were generating the afterlife visions. Brain disturbances caused by disease, injury or uremic poisoning decreased the afterlife vision phenomenon or did not affect it at all.

- The presence of a medical history suggestive of hallucinogenic factors did not increase the frequency of afterlife visions.

- Osis and Haraldsson had a separate search of medical literature done for them to find any hallucinations in dying patients. No support was found for this thesis.

Psychological factors:

- Such factors as stress, patient expectations of dying or recovering, or a desire to see someone they loved did not affect how often people had death-bed visions. No evidence was found from the data to suggest that psychological factors encouraging hallucinations also encouraged afterlife visions. Patients didn't automatically see in their visions people they specifically wanted to see; and people who didn't expect to die also saw death-bed visions. These results, noted Osis, lent support to the hypothesis that the people seen in the visions were not just wishful projections of the patient.

Cultural factors:

- Patients often saw something that was "unexpected, untaught and a complete surprise to them."

- Afterlife visions often did not conform to religious beliefs about the afterlife. Among Christian American patients, there were many reports of visions of heaven; visions of hell and devils were almost totally absent. Christian ideas of "judgment," "salvation," and "redemption" were not mirrored in their visions. In India, basic Hindu afterlife beliefs like reincarnation and dissolution in Brahma were never mentioned in their visions.

- Eleven core phenomena suggestive of an afterlife were found to be common to both Indian and American death-bed visions. Similarities outweighed the differences by a large margin, indicating a universal human experience rather than a culturally-produced experience.[32]

The deathbed visions were not due to any medical or psychological influences. They could be explained only as visions of deceased loved ones helping the dying person through the transition process.

James L. Hallenbeck, assistant professor of medicine at Stanford University and director of palliative care services with the V.A. Palo Alto Health Care System, describes the one disease he knows of that mimics pre-death visions, but explains that they are quite different:

> The one disease process I know of that can mimic these predeath visions is Parkinson's disease, especially when associated with Lewy bodies dementia. These patients also have visual hallucinations, usually of people. The distinction is that usually the people in visions are unknown to the patient. Initially, the Parkinson patient may be aware that these people are not real; they may be only shadow figures. When turned to, they disappear. As the disease progresses, the patient usually becomes more paranoid and very disturbed by more persistent and troublesome visitations.[33]

Deathbed visions are consistently of people the person knows, are clear and rational, contain reasonable, uplifting messages, and are always calm and never disturbing.

Jennifer Hammargren, a chaplain for VistaCare Hospice Services in Salt Lake City, Utah, explains that when dying people see visions of their deceased loved ones, they bear no resemblance to hallucinations:

> Some patients [reacting to drugs] describe bugs crawling on the walls and seeing things that aren't pleasant, which Hammargren often finds is a reaction to the drugs her patients are being given. But those experiences are vastly different in description and "feel" from the ones that happen with loved ones, she said.[34]

Carla Wills-Brandon explains why deathbed visions could not be hallucinations in her book, *One Last Hug before I Go: the Mystery and Meaning of Death Bed Visions*. Some skeptics suggest that they are hallucinations created by the dying brain, but Wills-Brandon explains that this is not a plausible argument because in some situations the dying did not know that the relatives who were visiting in the visions were already dead. A dying brain would not be able to limit visions to people who are dead when the dying person felt these relatives were still alive.

She also explains that medications would not give rise to such visions because people on medications are not coherent and the deathbed visions are quite coherent even if they are on medications.[35]

The fact that deathbed visions are not due to drugs, fever, or the illness is explained also in a publication by the staff of the University of Virginia Health System, Division of Perceptual Studies:

> Furthermore, the little research that has been done suggests that such visions may not be related to the hallucinations that drugs, fever, and certain illnesses can produce, and that drugs and fever may even inhibit rather than generate them.[36]

Visions Are Sometimes of Loved Ones the Person Couldn't Know Had Died

The deathbed visions are always of people who had passed away at the time of the vision. A compelling reason the deathbed visions could not be hallucinations or imagination is that some people have a vision of someone they could not know had actually died.

In 1926, Sir William Barrett, a professor of physics at the Royal College of Science in Dublin, studied as many accounts as he could find of deathbed visions and published the summation of his findings in *Death Bed Visions*. Barrett found accounts of deathbed visions of people the dying person didn't even know had passed away:

> On the night of January 12, 1924, Lady Barrett rushed home from the hospital to tell her husband about a remarkable deathbed vision seen by one of her patients, Dora, who delivered a child safely but died after the delivery. As Dora lay dying, she suddenly looked across the room and broke into a radiant smile. When Lady Barrett asked what she saw, Dora replied, "Lovely brightness—wonderful beings." Dora was fully and intensely absorbed in the vision. Then she announced to Barrett that she saw her father who was indicating to her how glad he was that she was coming to join him. When the nurses brought Dora her newborn baby for her to see, Dora wondered aloud whether she should stay for the child's sake, but then announced that she couldn't

turn her back on the beautiful world she was seeing in
her vision. She wanted to go there.

It must have been an extremely real and attractive vision
for a mother to willingly give up her own baby, and her
life as well, to embrace it. But such complete and total
belief in the reality of her death-bed visions by the dying
is not uncommon. What makes the case so strong is
what happened next. Dora turned to Lady Barrett with
a puzzled expression. "He has Vida with him," she said.

. . . Vida was Dora's sister, who had died three weeks
before. Because her family was afraid it would upset
Dora's fragile health, Dora had not been told that Vida
had died. Thus Dora's surprise at seeing her sister with
her deceased father.[37]

As a result of his extensive study of deathbed visions, Barrett found
two compelling reasons to believe the visions are real visitations from
deceased relatives:

1. It was very common for the dying people who saw these visions
    to identify friends and relatives whom they thought were still
    living, but in each case, it was later discovered that these people
    actually were dead. Communications in 1926 were quite slow,
    and it often took weeks or even months to learn that a friend or
    loved one had died.

2. Barrett found that children quite often expressed surprise that
    the "angels" they saw in their dying moments did not have
    wings. If the deathbed vision were just a hallucination, a child
    would see angels because angels are depicted with large, white
    wings.[38]

Michael Tymn summarizes a report from Dr. Minot J. Savage, a
Unitarian clergyman and author, that was published in Savage's book,
Life Beyond Death (1899). Two young girls, Jennie and Bessie, ages 8 and
9, were close friends, and both contracted the usually fatal disease
diphtheria at the same time. Jennie died, but Bessie's family did not tell
her because she was very ill and they felt there was no need to upset her.
Realizing she was about to die, on the day of her death Bessie began to
tell brothers and sisters which of her belongings she wanted them to

have. She included some items she wanted to go to Jennie, showing that she didn't realize Jennie had died.

Savage described what happened later in the day as Bessie approached death:

> . . . she began seeing deceased grandparents and others gathered around her bed. And then she turned to her father, with face and voice both expressing the greatest surprise, and exclaimed, "Why, Papa, why didn't you tell me that Jennie had gone? Why didn't you tell me of it?"

Bessie still had no way of knowing Jennie had died unless she genuinely saw her in her deathbed visions.[39]

People in the Room with a Dying Person Sometimes All See the Same Vision

Victor Zammit, B.A., Grad. Dip.Ed., M.A., LL.B., Ph.D., a retired lawyer of the Supreme Court of New South Wales and the High Court of Australia, cites[40] records from the Society of Psychical Research in which apparitions of dead relatives have appeared at the bedside of dying patients and have been seen by more than one person there:

> There are many cases on record with the Society of Psychical Research where the apparitional visitor has been seen by others at the bedside of the dying person, sometimes by several persons simultaneously:
>
> - In one well-documented case a deathbed apparition was seen by the dying woman, Harriet Pearson, and three relatives who were caring for her.[41]
>
> - In another case of a young boy dying, two witnesses independently saw his recently deceased mother at the child's bedside.[42]

These accounts of people in the room with someone about to pass away seeing the same vision also provide further proof that the visions could not be hallucinations. Hallucinations are individual. However, deathbed visions have occurred that are seen by others around the dying person.

Deathbed visions seem to be genuine contacts from deceased loved ones preparing the person for death. Those on the next plane of life are continually in contact with loved ones on the Earthly plane and help them with this transition into the next plane of their eternal life. No one dies alone.

Distant People Appear to Loved Ones at the Moments of Their Deaths

Accounts of people appearing at the moments of their deaths to people hundreds or thousands of miles away are very common. The founders of the Society for Psychical Research began their studies by collecting and studying cases of telepathy, apparitions, and other psychic phenomena. They were most impressed by the visions people saw of the deceased at the moment of death, even though the dying person was hundreds or thousands of miles from them. This is one of their reports from an experiencer:

> I sat one evening reading, when on looking up from my book, I distinctly saw a school-friend of mine, to whom I was very much attached, standing near the door. I was about to exclaim at the strangeness of her visit when, to my horror, there were no signs of anyone in the room but my mother. I related what I had seen to her, knowing she could not have seen, as she was sitting with her back towards the door, nor did she hear anything unusual, and was greatly amused at my scare, suggesting I had read too much or been dreaming.

> A day or so after this strange event, I had news to say my friend was no more. The strange part was that I did not even know she was ill, much less in danger so could not have felt anxious at the time on her account, but may have been thinking of her; that I cannot testify. Her illness was short, and death very unexpected. Her mother told me she spoke of me not long before she died. . . . She died the same evening and about the same time that I saw her vision, which was the end of October, 1874.[43]

They reported another case described by a puzzled teacher:

About fourteen years ago, about 3 o'clock one summer's afternoon, I was passing in front of Trinity Church, Upper King Street, Leicester, when I saw on the opposite side of the street a very old playmate, whom, having left the town to learn some business, I had for some time lost sight of. I thought it odd he took no notice of me; and while following him with my eyes, deliberating whether I should accost him or not, I coned after him by name, and was somewhat surprised at not being able to follow him any further or to say into which house he had gone, for I felt persuaded he had gone into one. The next week I was informed of his somewhat sudden death at Burton-on-Trent, at about the time I felt certain he was passing in front of me. What struck me most at the time was that he should take no notice of me, and that he should go along so noiselessly and should disappear so suddenly, but that it was [my playmate] I had seen, I never for one moment doubted. I have always looked upon this as a hallucination, but why it should have occurred at that particular time, and to me, I could never make out.[44]

In some cases the deceased person was even seen by more than one person after their death, as in the following example:

Some years since, when living at Woolstone Lodge, Woolstone, Berks, of which parish and church, etc., etc., my husband was clerk in Holy Orders, I left the fireside family party one evening after tea, to see if our German *bonne* could manage a little wild Cornish girl to prepare her school-room for the morning. As I reached the top of the stairs a lady passed me who had some time left us. She was in black silk with a muslin "cloud" over her head and shoulders, but her silk rustled. I could just have a glance only of her face. She glided fast and noiselessly (but for the silk) past me, and was lost down two steps at the end of a long passage that led only into my private boudoir, and had no other exit. I had barely exclaimed "Oh, Caroline," when I felt she was something

unnatural, and rushed down to the drawing-room again,
and sinking on my knees by my husband's side, fainted,
and it was with difficulty I was restored to myself again.
The next morning, I saw they rather joked me at first;
but it afterwards came out that the little nursery girl,
while cleaning her grate, had been so frightened by the
same appearance, "a lady sitting near her in black, with
white all over her head and shoulders, and her hands
crossed on her bosom," that *nothing* would induce her to
go into the room again; and they had been afraid to tell
me over night of this confirmation of the appearance,
thinking it would shake my nerves still more than it had
done.

As chance would have it, many of our neighbours called
on us the next morning—Mr. Tufnell, of Uffington, near
Faringdon, Archdeacon Berens, Mr. Atkins, and others.
All seemed most interested, and Mr. Tufnell would not
be content without noting down particulars in his own
pocket-book, and making me promise to write for
inquiries that very night, for my cousin, Mrs. Henry
Gibbs. She had been staying with us some time
previously for a few days, and I had a letter half written
to her in the paper case.

I wrote immediately to my uncle (the Rev. C. Crawley,
of Hartpury near Gloucester) and aunt, and recounted
all that had happened. By return of post, "Caroline is
very ill at Belmont" (their family place then), "and not
expected to live"; and die she did on the *very day* or
evening she paid me that visit.[45]

One account, told to me by Mike Thomson, an acquaintance of mine,
was of the unexpected appearance of his ex-wife's Uncle Neely. Mike
had been divorced from his ex-wife for seven years and hadn't seen her
family since the divorce. One day, driving alone down a highway, he
felt that someone was sitting next to him. He looked at the passenger's
seat and there sat his ex-wife's Uncle Neely, whom he hadn't seen since
the divorce. Mike was shaken because he had been driving alone. His
ex-wife's uncle said to him, "Mike, the Mass is over. Thanks be to God."
That was an old joke Mike had with Uncle Neely. Mike converted to

Catholicism for his wife, but hated going to mass. When the family attended Mass together, Uncle Neely would smile at Mike as they walked out after Mass and say, "Well Mike, the Mass is over. Thanks be to God," with the double meaning, "Thank God, the Mass is over!"

Mike glanced forward, and when he looked back to the passenger seat, Uncle Neely was gone. When he arrived home, Mike was upset and worried; he thought he might be losing his mind, so he didn't tell anyone about the strange event. About an hour later, his son came into the room and said, "Dad, Mom called. She said she had some bad news. Uncle Neely died today." As Mike found out later, Uncle Neely had died at the moment he appeared in Mike's car.

Victor Zammit describes five other such apparitions:[46]

> . . . Second Lieutenant Leslie Poynter . . . was killed in action. At 9 p.m. on the evening of his death he appeared to his sister in England, walked into her bedroom, bent over and kissed her and then, smiling happily, faded from view. It was not until two weeks later that the family received a telegram informing them of his death earlier in the day on the same date.[47]

> . . . Mrs. Pacquet's . . . brother Edmund appeared to her six hours after he had drowned at sea and acted out how he had been caught around the legs by a rope and dragged overboard.[48]

> . . . Mrs. Gladys Watson . . . was awakened from a deep sleep by someone calling her name. On waking she saw her paternal grandfather who told her "Don't be frightened. It's only me. I've just died." When she woke her husband, he refused to believe it and telephoned the family home only to learn that the grandfather had died unexpectedly a few minutes before.[49]

> . . . Lord Brougham, an English peer . . . was traveling in Sweden. He suddenly saw an apparition of a university friend he had not seen or thought about for years. Later he received a letter confirming that the friend had died in India at the exact time of the apparition. While at university the two had often speculated on the question of survival and had drawn up an agreement written in

their blood that whichever of the two died first would
appear to the other.[50]

. . . Mrs. Arthur Bellamy of Bristol . . . made a similar
agreement with a school friend whom she had not seen
for years. A night after the friend's death a lady was seen
by Mr. Bellamy sitting on the bed beside his sleeping
wife. He later identified her from a photograph as the
same friend.[51]

Dr. Minot J. Savage, the Unitarian clergyman cited earlier, describes
an incident in which a young boy received a visit from someone who
had just passed away, as reported by Michael Tymn:

Savage . . . relates the case of a small boy who had
befriended a judge of some prominence living in the
neighborhood. After the boy was put to bed one night,
his parents heard him crying. They rushed to him and
asked him what was wrong. "Judge says he's dead! He
has been here and told me that he is dead!" the boy
sobbed. The next morning the parents found out that
the judge had died at about that time the night before.[52]

Physicians Working with the Dying Come to Know the Reality of the Afterlife

Physicians work with dying patients regularly. We would expect
them to know something about death and the afterlife from their
experiences. In fact, a 2005 survey of physicians found that 76 percent
believe in God and 59 percent believe in some sort of afterlife.[53] Those
beliefs are in the face of strong sanctions within the scientific and
medical communities at large against speaking of belief in God or the
afterlife, a result of the materialistic ignorance from the seventeenth
through nineteenth centuries that is now falling away.

Interestingly, among members of the National Academy of Sciences
in the physical sciences, most of whom work with only matter and
energy (not people, life, and death), 79 percent do not believe in God.[54]
That discrepancy between the beliefs of professionals who work with
people, life, and death, and those who work with matter and energy only
suggests that a reason for skepticism among some in the herd of skeptics
is simply from not being exposed to the realities of life and death.

Some striking examples of physicians whose experiences and research have confirmed the reality of the afterlife follow.

Dr. Janis Amatuzio – Dr. Janis Amatuzio, a practitioner in forensic medicine for nearly 25 years, has come to be known as the "compassionate coroner." In her work, she has heard extraordinary stories from grieving family members, patients near death, police officers, clergy, and colleagues – stories of the spiritual and otherworldly experiences concerning the transition between life and death. She wrote, "I have come to realize that for some experiences there is no explanation, just a deep knowing that I have encountered the Divine."[55]

Dr. Elisabeth Kübler-Ross – Dr. Kübler-Ross, an internationally renowned physician, author, speaker, and expert on death and dying, was listed as one of the 100 most important thinkers of the century by *Time* magazine in 1999. She received 20 honorary degrees for her achievements and was included in the International Biographical Centre's list of the foremost women of the twentieth century. This is her conclusion after decades of study of death and dying:

> Many people are beginning to be aware that the physical body is only the house or the temple, or as we call it the cocoon, which we inhabit for a certain number of months or years until we make the transition called death. Then, at the time of death, we shed this cocoon and are once again as free as a butterfly to use the symbolic language that we use when talking to dying children and their siblings.[56]

Sir Arthur Conan Doyle – Conan Doyle was a physician turned writer, knighted for his service as a historian during the Boer War. He is best remembered as the creator of Sherlock Holmes stories. Conan Doyle was highly skeptical of mediums and the afterlife when he began investigating psychic phenomena in 1886. After he studied the evidence for the afterlife, he became a strong believer.

Dr. Enrico Morselli – An Italian neurologist and Director of the Clinic of Nervous and Mental Disease at the University of Genoa. He began as a bitter skeptic, but after investigation of the afterlife, changed his belief.

Dr. Gustave Geley – Professor of medicine at the University of Lyons. Dr. Geley studied evidence for the afterlife and became so convinced that he gave up his practice as a teacher and physician in 1919 to become director of the Institute Metaphyschique International in Paris to investigate mediumship.

Dr. T. Glen Hamilton – A graduate of Manitoba Medical College, Hamilton, instructor in clinical surgery at Winnipeg General Hospital. He became interested in psychic phenomena in 1918 and conducted extensive studies on Canadian mediums. These were his conclusions:

> . . . we hold the survival theory to be valid in accounting for every fact known in regard to the trance personalities. It accounts for their stated opinions that they were indeed deceased (discarnate) individuals. It admits of the possibility that they, as discarnate persons, shared some manner of inter-communication, which enabled them to plan, to co-operate, and to commit themselves to organized activities in the séance room, activities which extended over a period of many years.[57]

He had mediums come to his laboratory where, under strictly controlled conditions, he set up a battery of fourteen electronically controlled flash cameras to photograph any apparitions the mediums could summon. He invited four other physicians, two lawyers, an electrical engineer, and a civil engineer to observe and corroborate anything that happened. He summarized the results in this sentence: "Time after time, I saw dead persons materialize."[58]

Dr. Barbara R. Rommer – A founding member of the Holy Cross Medical Group in Fort Lauderdale. Dr. Rommer practiced medicine from 1974 until her death in 2004. She was also a researcher of near-death experiences, authoring two books on the subject, including *Blessings in Disguise*, published in 2000. Based on her research, she concluded,

> I believe that the only part of us that dies is our physical body, once referred to as our "husk" by a Catholic priest who related his own near-death experience to me. The body is physical matter but is not our true essence. Our true essence, our soul, our spirit, our life force, and our very being, that part of us which has a personality, most probably does not die. I must admit that I have received what I consider to be confirmation of this from my

husband, Salvatore (Sonny) Pepitone, who entered his
spirit form on June 25, 1997.[59]

Dr. Robert Bridges – A physician who became poet laureate of
England. Dr. Bridges wrote,

> Man is a spiritual being: the proper work of his mind is
> to interpret the world according to his highest nature, to
> conquer the material aspects of the world so as to bring
> them into subjugation to the spirit.[60]

Dr. Michael Schroter-Kunhardt – A German psychiatrist who
conducted a comprehensive review of the scientific literature about the
survival of consciousness. Dr. Schroter-Kunhardt concluded that the
paranormal capacities of the dying person suggest the existence of a
time-and-space transcending immortal soul.[61]

Skeptical Researchers Studying Mediums Become Convinced of the Afterlife

People today who still are not able to accept the abundant data that
proves the afterlife is as real as this life have not read the evidence or
participated in medium activities. They assume that the mind is
confined to the brain, so evidence of the mind outside of the body
couldn't be valid, and that justifies their not reading it. Because they
haven't read the evidence, they assert that there is no evidence, and since
they are not themselves aware of any evidence to the contrary, they are
assured that the mind must be confined to the brain and that reinforces
their belief that any evidence of the mind outside of the brain must be
invalid. That circular reasoning leaves them in an ignorance of their own
making.

Instead of looking to the uninformed and close minded for any
understanding of life, the universe, and the eternal self, we need to take
seriously the conclusions of researchers who have studied the afterlife
and mediums in depth, especially those who began their studies as
skeptics determined to review the evidence objectively, to participate in
rigorously controlled medium sessions themselves, and to expose any
fraud they found.

The eminent scholars who have participated in medium activities
and have studied the literature have come to the undeniable conclusion
that the afterlife is as real as this life. A small sampling of them follows.

Victor James Zammit, B.A., Grad. Dip.Ed., M.A., LL.B., Ph.D., has devoted his life to critical examination of the evidence available for the afterlife, accepting only evidence that "would be legally admissible in the highest courts," based on his extensive experience in the court system. He became so convinced from his research that he wrote a book presenting the evidence (*A Lawyer Presents the Case for the Afterlife*[62]) and has offered $1 million to anyone who can rebut the evidence we now have proving that we are eternal beings. After eight years, not one scientist, researcher, theologian, philosopher, or other professional who has examined the research has been able to, or even attempted to, rebut it. The evidence is simply incontrovertible.

Some of the vast library of research now available that proves the afterlife follows in this chapter.

Many of these descriptions are abstracted from Michael Tymn's "Distinguished researchers found evidence for survival" [63] and from Victor Zammit's *A Lawyer Presents the Case for the Afterlife*.[64]

Distinguished Scientists Become Convinced of the Reality of the Afterlife When They Study the Evidence.

A growing number of hard-nosed, skeptical scientists who have taken the time to study the afterlife and mediums seriously have become convinced of the reality of the afterlife from their encounters, often after they began their research with the goal of debunking mediums. A list of some of the scientists follows. There are, of course, many other scientists who have come to the same conclusion—this is just a small sampling of some of the most prominent. Most came to the study of mediums and the afterlife as skeptics. That makes the testimonies of their conclusions after extensive research especially credible.

Ron D. Pearson – British scientist, university lecturer and engineer in thermodynamics and fluid mechanics. Dr. Pearson wrote "Survival Physics," in which he asserts that survival of death is a natural fact of physics and that efforts to discredit evidence of survival after death are in error:

> Since survival can be shown an essential and integral part of physics, the hope must be that the efforts still being made to discredit all evidence of survival will soon come to an end. This theory has achieved publication in Russian conference Proceedings[65,66] of

1991 and 1993 respectively, and in the peer-reviewed scientific journal "Frontier Perspectives"[67] in 1997. Furthermore Prof. Peter Wadhams, Professor of Ocean Physics at Cambridge University, supported the theory during a joint broadcast on the American Radio Shows in 2001.[68]

Dr. Jan Vandersande – Physicist, holder of three patents on thermoelectric materials, consultant to NASA, manager at the Jet Propulsion Laboratory, professor at Cornell University, and president and CEO of Mountain Province Diamonds. After investigating materializations of those appearing from the afterlife for over eight years, he became convinced that the materializations are people from the afterlife and that the afterlife is a reality.[69]

Thomas Alva Edison – Inventor of the phonograph and electric light bulb. Edison was a Spiritualist and experimented with mechanical means of contacting the dead.

Sir Joseph John Thompson – Discoverer of the electron, professor of experimental physics at Cambridge, and winner of the 1906 Nobel Prize in physics. Thompson asserted that people continue to live after the body dies.

Professor Abdus Salam – Nobel Laureate and director of the International Centre for Theoretical Physics. After studying the results of investigations of the evidence of the afterlife,

> . . . he gave [Michael] Roll numerous monetary contributions from his own pocket, as well as a sizable grant from the Foundation, to help him spread the word of these exciting discoveries that verify the truth of ongoing life beyond the physical level.[70]

Sam Nicholls – Researcher into subatomic phenomena. Nicholls concluded from his studies that people in the afterlife are composed of slightly different atomic components, and that they exist in and share the same space with people on the Earth plane.

Professor Augustus De Morgan – Considered one of the most brilliant mathematicians of the 19th Century. De Morgan sought out mediums to have first-hand experiences. He concluded,

I have seen in my house frequently, various
[mediums]. . . . I am satisfied of the reality of the
phenomenon. A great many other persons are as
cognizant of these phenomena in their own houses as
myself.[71]

Dr. Robert Hare – Emeritus professor of chemistry at the University
of Pennsylvania and world-renowned inventor. Dr. Hare set out to prove
that the messages from the dead were either hallucinations or
unconscious muscular actions on the part of those present. After
extensive critical study, he concluded,

I sincerely believe that I have communicated with the
spirits of my parents, sister, brother, and dearest friends,
and likewise with the spirits of the illustrious
Washington and other worthies of the spirit world; that I
am by them commissioned, under their auspices, to
teach truth and to expose error.[72]

Professor James J. Mapes – A professor of chemistry and natural
philosophy at the National Academy of Design in New York and later at
the American Institute. After investigating many mediums in an effort to
debunk them, Mapes changed his views. Afterward, both his wife and
daughter became mediums. He concluded his study by writing,

The manifestations which are pertinent to the ends
required are so conclusive in their character as to
establish in my mind certain cardinal points. These are:
First, there is a future state of existence, which is but a
continuation of our present state of being. . . . Second,
that the great aim of nature, as shown through a great
variety of spiritual existences is progression, extending
beyond the limits of this mundane sphere. . . . Third, that
spirits can and do communicate with mortals, and in all
cases evince a desire to elevate and advance those they
commune with.[73]

Allan Kardec, Esq. – Professor of chemistry, physics, comparative
anatomy, and astronomy. After thoroughly studying many mediums, he
concluded,

Experience gradually made known many other varieties
of the mediumistic faculty, and it was found that

communication could be received through speech, hearing, sight, touch, etc., and even through direct writing of the spirits themselves – that is to say without the help of the medium's hand or of the pencil.[74]

Dr. Alfred Russel Wallace – Co-originator with Charles Darwin of the natural selection theory of evolution. Dr. Wallace was a naturalist who provided Darwin with his parallel theory, including the "survival of the fittest," before Darwin went public with their two theories. Wallace was a hard-core materialist until he began investigating mediums. He soon became one of the afterlife's greatest proponents:

> My position is that the phenomena of Spiritualism in their entirety do not require further confirmation. They are proved quite as well as facts are proved in other sciences.[75]

Sir William Crookes – Physicist and chemist who discovered the element thallium and was a pioneer in radioactivity. Crookes invented the radiometer, the spinthariscope, and a high-vacuum tube that contributed to the discovery of the x-ray. He set out to drive "the worthless residuum of spiritualism" into the "unknown limbo of magic and necromancy." However, after thorough investigations of mediums Daniel D. Home and Florence Cook, he changed his views:

> [The phenomena] point to the existence of another order of human life continuous with this, and demonstrate the possibility in certain circumstances of communication between this world and the next.[76]

Sir William Barrett – Professor of physics at the Royal College of Science in Dublin for 37 years, who developed a silicon-iron alloy important to the development of the telephone and in construction of transformers. He was knighted in 1912 for his contributions to science. His study of mediums and the afterlife brought him to this conclusion:

> I am personally convinced that the evidence we have published decidedly demonstrates (1) the existence of a spiritual world, (2) survival after death, and (3) of occasional communication from those who have passed over.[77]

Sir Oliver Lodge – Professor of physics at University College in Liverpool, England and later principal at the University of Birmingham, pioneer in electricity, the radio, and spark plug, knighted in 1902 for his contributions to science. Lodge sat in on and studied extensively the séances of Leonora Piper and Gladys Osborne Leonard. He concluded,

> I tell you with all my strength of the conviction which I can muster that we do persist, that people still continue to take an interest in what is going on, that they know far more about things on this earth than we do, and are able from time to time to communicate with us. . . . I do not say it is easy, but it is possible, and I have conversed with my friends just as I can converse with anyone in this audience now.[78]

Professor Camille Flammarion – A world-renowned astronomer, Flammarion founded the French Astronomical Society, was known for his study of Mars and was a pioneer in the use of balloons to study the stars. He investigated psychic phenomena, including mediumship, for more than 50 years and concluded,

> I do not hesitate to affirm my conviction, based on personal examination of the subject, that any man who declares the phenomena to be impossible is one who speaks without knowing what he is talking about; and, also that any man accustomed to scientific observation – provided that his mind is not biased by preconceived opinions – may acquire a radical and absolute certainty of the reality of the facts alluded to.[79]

Dr. Charles Richet – Professor of physiology at the University of Paris Medical School. Dr. Richet was considered a world authority on nutrition in health and in disease. He won the Nobel Prize in 1913 for his work on allergic reactions. He became convinced of the reality of mediumship, although he remained publicly agnostic toward survival. According to Sir Oliver Lodge, his good friend, Richet accepted survival before his death. He wrote,

> It seems to me the facts are undeniable. I am convinced that I have been present at realities [medium sessions]. Certainly I cannot say in what materialization consists. I am ready to maintain that there is something profoundly

mysterious in it which will change from top to bottom our ideas on nature and on life.[80]

Dr. Robert Crookall – Lectured at Aberdeen University before joining the staff of the Geological Survey of Great Britain, specializing in coal-forming plants. His research into the afterlife was so compelling to him that he resigned from his geological work in 1952 to devote the rest of his life to psychical research. He wrote,

> The whole of the available evidence is explicable on the hypothesis of the survival of the human soul in a Soul Body. There is no longer a "deadlock" or "stalemate" on the question of survival. On the contrary, survival is as well established as the theory of evolution.[81]

Dr. Raynor C. Johnson – A physicist who was educated at Oxford and received his doctorate from the University of London. He lectured in physics at King's College, University of London, before becoming master of Queen's College at the University of Melbourne in Australia. He studied survival in depth to judge whether it is true. He concluded,

> For myself, I can only say that my intuition, such as it is, supports [Frederic] Myers, and my attempt to evaluate the data of psychical research and form a critical judgment leads me to conclude that if survival of death is not rigorously proven, it is nevertheless established as of that high order or probability which, for practical purposes, can be taken as the same thing.[82]

John Logie Baird – Inventor of the television and infra-red camera. Baird stated that he had contacted the deceased Thomas A. Edison through a medium. He confirmed the contact: "I have witnessed some very startling phenomena under circumstances which make trickery out of the question."[83]

Dr. George Meek – Scientist, inventor, designer and manufacturer of devices for air conditioning and treatment of waste water. Dr. Meek referred to himself as a "natural skeptic" who felt originally that the talk of an afterlife just didn't make sense. To study the concept, he traveled the world interviewing top medical doctors, psychiatrists, physicists, biochemists, psychics, healers, parapsychologists, hypnotherapists, ministers, priests, and rabbis. He concluded that people are immortal, and wrote his findings in his book *After We Die What Then?*[84]

Professor Archie Roy – Professor Emeritus of Astronomy in the University of Glasgow, fellow of the Royal Society of Edinburgh, the Royal Astronomical Society, and the British Interplanetary Society, and head of the Advanced Scientific Institutes for NATO. After extensive study of psychic and medium activity, he wrote,

> I myself have been interested in psychic phenomena for
> well over 30 years and what with my personal
> experiences and my study over the years, I am
> convinced now of the reality of such phenomena.[85]

Dr. A.P. Hale – A physicist and electronics engineer. Dr. Hale conducted careful tests of electronic recordings of voices coming from the afterlife. He concluded: "In view of the tests carried out in a screened laboratory at my firm, I cannot explain what happened in normal physical terms."[86]

Sir Robert Mayer LL.D., D.Sc., Mus.D. – After studying electronic recordings of voices coming from the afterlife, he concluded, "If the experts are baffled, I consider this is a good enough reason for presenting the Voice Phenomena to the general public."[87]

Psychologists and Psychotherapists Become Convinced of the Afterlife from Their Experiences.

Psychologists have learned about the afterlife through studying mediums and through after-death communication experiences with patients.

Dr. William James – Considered one of America's foremost psychologists, Professor James wrote widely in psychology, philosophy, and religion while teaching at Harvard for 35 years. His *Principles of Psychology* (1890) became the seminal work in the field. His *Varieties of Religious Experience* is also a classic. After his investigations of the afterlife by sitting with medium Leonora Piper, he concluded,

> One who takes part in a good sitting has usually a far
> livelier sense, both of the reality and of the importance
> of the communication, than one who merely reads the
> records. . . . I am able, while still holding to all the lower
> principles of interpretation, to imagine the process as
> more complex, and to share the feelings with which
> Hodgson came at last to regard it after his many years of

familiarity, the feeling which Professor Hyslop shares, and which most of those who have good sittings are promptly inspired with.[88]

Dr. Allan Botkin – Dr. Botkin discovered, in 1995, that he could induce after-death communications (IADC™). He is very cautious about the interpretation of the source of the communication, but virtually all of his patients who have the after-death communication while sitting in his office are certain they have had communication with the deceased person for whom they are grieving. Now, over four dozen other psychologists are also inducing after-death communication in their offices around the world. A list is included on the Web site dedicated to the therapy method, http://www.induced-adc.com. In the book he and I co-authored, he wrote these words:

> I believe that if there is an afterlife, then IADCs™ are true spiritual experiences. I cannot imagine that if the afterlife is a reality, IADCs™, ADCs, and NDEs are hallucinatory aberrations produced by our brains that lead us into misunderstanding.[89]

Dr. Cesare Lombroso – Professor of psychology at the University of Turin and inspector of asylums for the insane in Italy, Lombroso was a pioneering criminologist who became known worldwide for his book, *The Criminal Man.*[90] He began investigating psychic phenomena and the intelligences behind hem in 1891 and as a result of his study concluded,

> I am ashamed and grieved at having opposed with so much tenacity the possibility of psychic facts – the facts exist and I boast of being a slave to facts. There can be no doubt that genuine psychical phenomena are produced by intelligences totally independent of the psychic and the parties present at the sittings.[91]

Dr. Bruce Greyson – Formerly a professor of psychiatry at the University of Connecticut, now Bonner-Lowry Professor of Personality Studies in the Department of Psychiatric Medicine at the University of Virginia in Charlottesville. Dr. Greyson has been researching and conducting studies on near-death experiences for over 25 years. He has written an abundance of articles on the subject for leading science and medical journals, including the *Journal of Scientific Exploration, Journal of the American Medical Association,* and *American Journal of Psychiatry.* Dr.

Greyson concluded that "the survival hypothesis is the most parsimonious explanation for the growing database of near-death experiences."[92]

Dr. Julian Ochorowicz – Professor of psychology and philosophy at the University of Warsaw who helped establish the Polish Psychological Institute in Warsaw and served as a director for the International Institute of Psychology in Paris. Dr. Ochorowicz was a firmly entrenched skeptic and critic of anyone who believed psychic phenomena and the afterlife are real. However, after an open-minded study of the afterlife and mediums, he concluded,

> I found I had done a great wrong to men who had proclaimed new truths at the risk of their positions. When I remember that I branded as a fool that fearless investigator Crookes, the inventor of the radiometer, because he had the courage to assert the reality of psychic phenomena and to subject them to scientific tests, and when I also recollect that I used to read his articles thereon in the same stupid style, regarding him as crazy, I am ashamed, both of myself and others, and I cry from the very bottom of my heart. "Father, I have sinned against the Light."[93]

Baron (Dr.) Albert Von Schrenck-Notzing – A forensic psychiatrist and member of the German aristocracy. Dr. Schrenck-Notzing became interested in psychical research in 1889. He collaborated with Richet, Lombroso, Lodge, and others in many investigations for over 30 years. While he was reluctant, apparently out of scientific conservatism, to link valid mediumship with survival, he was nonetheless convinced of the reality of mediumship.

> Finally, in the case of many phenomena, the nature and evanescence of their appearance, their flowing, changing and fantastic shapes and their mode of development until they reached their final form, argues against any possibility of a fraudulent production of them– even if one would assume that one of those present would have tried to deceive his fellow observers.[94]

One hundred well known scientists, all profoundly skeptical, and some openly hostile, declared themselves, without exception, completely

convinced of the reality of survival after having worked under the
direction of Dr. Schrenck-Notzing with his medium Willy Schneider.[95]

Dr. Carl A. Wickland – A member of the Chicago Medical Society
and the American Association for the Advancement of Science, and
director of the National Psychological Institute of Los Angeles. Dr.
Wickland specialized in cases of schizophrenia, paranoia, depression,
addiction, manic-depression, criminal behavior, and phobias of all kinds.
His wife, Anna Wickland, was a trance medium, and his direct
experiences led him to conclude that spirits on the next planes of life
communicate with and affect people on the Earth plane.[96]

Dr. Gardner Murphy – While at Harvard, Murphy accepted the
Hodgson Memorial Fund research grant. He served as president of the
American Society for Psychical Research for 20 years. He taught
psychology at Columbia University and served as chairman of the
psychology department at City College of New York. After studying the
records of medium sessions, he wrote,

> It is the autonomy, the purposiveness, the cogency,
> above all the individuality, of the sources of the
> messages, that cannot be by-passed. Struggle though I
> may as a psychologist, for forty-five years, to try to find
> a "naturalistic" and "normal" way of handling this
> material, I cannot do this even when using all the
> information we have about human chicanery and all we
> have about the far-flung telepathic and clairvoyant
> abilities of some gifted sensitives. The case looks like
> communication with the deceased.[97]

Dr. Gary Schwartz – After receiving his doctorate from Harvard
University, Dr. Schwartz served as a professor of psychology and
psychiatry at Yale University. He then became director of the University
of Arizona's Human Energy Systems Laboratory, where he conducted
extensive research with mediums. His book, *The Afterlife Experiments,*[98]
published in 2002, detailed these experiments. He concluded,

> I can no longer ignore the data [on research into the
> survival of consciousness] and dismiss the words
> [coming through mediums]. They are as real as the sun,
> the trees, and our television sets, which seem to pull
> pictures out of the air.[99]

Dr. Jon Klimo – Professor of graduate-level psychology for more than 30 years, most recently at the American School of Professional Psychology, Argosy University. Dr. Klimo has done extensive research, writing, teaching, and presentations in psychology, parapsychology, consciousness studies, new paradigm thought, metaphysics and the transpersonal domain. He concluded,

> I personally choose to believe that we do meaningfully survive death and can communicate back through mediums and channels . . .[100]

Dr. David Fontana – Professor of transpersonal psychology in Great Britain, a past president of the Society for Psychical Research and a fellow of the British Psychological Society. Dr. Fontana has done extensive survival research and is the author of many books, including *Is There an Afterlife?*[101] published in 2002. He wrote,

> Ultimately our acceptance of the reality of survival may not come solely from the evidence but from personal experience and from some inner intuitive certainty about our real nature. We are who we are, and at some deep level within ourselves we may be the answer to our own questions. If your answer is that you are more than a biological accident whose ultimately meaningless life is bounded by the cradle and the grave, then I have to say I agree with you.[102]

Dr. Brendan – Director of the Institute of Psychology Dublin. After investigating electronic voice recordings of deceased speaking to the living, he concluded,

> I have apparently succeeded in reproducing the phenomena. Voices have appeared on a tape which did not come from any known source.[103]

Carl G. Jung – The eminent psychoanalyst, contemporary of Freud, and father of Jungian psychology. Jung wrote after his own NDE,

> What happens after death is so unspeakably glorious, that our imagination and feelings do not suffice to form even an approximate conception of it. The dissolution of our time-bound form in eternity brings no loss of meaning.[104]

Professors of the Humanities Researching the Afterlife Become Convinced of It.

The same conclusion the physicians and scientists willing to study the afterlife and mediums come to has been voiced by professors of the humanities. A small number of the many who changed their views after examining the evidence follows.

Frederic W. H. Myers, Esq. (1843-1901) – Graduate of Cambridge and lecturer in classical literature while inspector of schools at Cambridge. Myers developed a theory of the subliminal self. Professor Theordor Flournoy wrote that Myers completes the triad of geniuses who most profoundly revolutionized scientific thought, with Copernicus and Darwin as the other two. After studying mediums and the afterlife, he concluded,

> I will here briefly state what facts they are which our recorded apparitions, intimations, messages of the departing and the departed, have, to my mind actually proved: a) In the first place, they prove survival pure and simple; the persistence of the spirit's life as a structural law of the universe; the inalienable heritage of each several soul; b) . . . they prove that between the spiritual and the material worlds an avenue of communication does in fact exist; that which we call the dispatch and the receipt of telepathic messages, or the utterance and the answer of prayer and supplication; c) . . . they prove that the surviving spirit retains, at least in some measure, the memories and the loves of earth."[105]

Dr. Richard Hodgson – After earning his M.A. and LL.D at the University of Melbourne, Hodgson taught poetry and philosophy at University Extension, then the philosophy of Herbert Spenser at Cambridge. He and William James decided to witness a number of séances to "discover fraud and trickery." After hundreds of sittings with medium Leonora Piper over 18 years, he concluded,

> Frankly, I went to Mrs. Piper with Professor James of Harvard University about twelve years ago with the object of unmasking her. . . . I entered the house profoundly materialistic, not believing in the

continuance of life after death; today I say I believe. The
truth has been given to me in such a way as to remove
from me the possibility of a doubt.[106]

Dr. James H. Hyslop – After receiving his Ph.D. from Johns
Hopkins University in 1887 and his LL.D. from University of Wooster,
Dr. Hyslop taught philosophy at Lake Forest University, Smith College,
and Bucknell University before joining the faculty of Columbia in 1895.
He authored three textbooks (*Elements of Logic* (1892), *Elements of Ethics*
(1895), and *Problems of Philosophy* (1905)) before becoming a full-time
psychical researcher. His research brought him to conclude,

> Personally, I regard the fact of survival after death as
> scientifically proved. I agree that this opinion is not
> upheld in scientific quarters. But this is neither our fault
> nor the fault of the facts. Evolution was not believed
> until long after it was proved. The fault lay with those
> who were too ignorant or too stubborn to accept the
> facts. History shows that every intelligent man who has
> gone into this investigation, if he gave it adequate
> examination at all, has come out believing in spirits; this
> circumstance places the burden of proof on the
> shoulders of the skeptic. [107]

Dr. Hamlin Garland – A Pulitizer Prize-winning author of 52 books,
Dr. Garland was intimately involved with major literary, social, and
artistic movements in American culture. In his book, *Forty Years of
Psychic Research,* Garland states that he was an agnostic and student of
Darwin and Herbert Spenser when he began his investigation of
mediums:

> I concede the possibility of their [spirits'] persistence,
> especially when their voices carry movingly,
> characteristic tones and their messages are startlingly
> intimate. At such times, they seem souls of the dead
> veritably reimbodied. They jest with me about their
> occupations. They laugh at my doubts, quite in
> character. They touch me with their hands.[108]

Maurice Maeterlinck, Esq. – Winner of the 1911 Nobel Prize in
literature. Maeterlinck, a Belgian, was primarily a poet, author, and

playwright, but he was also a psychical researcher. Based on his research, he concluded,

> Of all the explanations conceivable, that one which attributes everything to imposture and trickery is unquestionably the most extraordinary and the least probable.[109]

Professor William R. Newbold – Professor of philosophy at the University of Pennsylvania when he was appointed to the advisory council of the American Society for Psychical Research. Professor Newbold had numerous sittings with medium Leonora Piper. He wrote,

> Until within very recent years, the scientific world has tacitly rejected a large number of important philosophical conceptions on the ground that there is absolutely no evidence in their favor whatever. Among those popular conceptions are those of the essential independence of the mind and the body, of the existence of a supersensible world, and of the possibility of occasional communication between that world and this. We have here [in Mrs. Piper], as it seems to me, evidence that is worthy of consideration for all these points.[110]

Dr. C. J. Ducasse – The French-born American philosopher came to the United Stated as a teenager and eventually became chairman of the Department of Philosophy at Brown University. He had many sittings with mediums and lectured extensively on psychical research. He concluded,

> Some of the facts we have considered suggest that the belief in life after death, which so many persons have found no particular difficulty in accepting as an article in religious faith, may well be capable of empirical proof. That the occurrence of paranormal phenomena does appear to have such implications, is, I submit, sufficient reason to give them far more attention and study than they have commonly received in the past.[111]

Dr. Hornell Hart – Professor of Sociology at Duke University and author of several important books on social and psychological problems. Dr. Hart reviewed the literature on the afterlife and concluded,

Human personality does survive bodily death. That is
the outcome which I find emerging when the strongest
anti-survivalist arguments and the strongest rebuttals
are considered thoroughly, with passionate open-
mindedness.[112]

Colin Brookes-Smith – British engineer who joined a group to study
the afterlife and psychic phenomena. As a result of his experiences, he
stated in the *Journal of the Society for Psychical Research* that survival
should be regarded as a sufficiently well-established fact to be beyond
denial by any reasonable person. He described it as "a momentous
scientific conclusion of prime importance to mankind."[113]

Arthur Balfour – British prime minister (1902-1905), secretary of
state, and author of *A Defence of Philosophic Doubt.*[114] Balfour studied the
afterlife and mediums and felt sufficiently convinced to write elaborately
about them in the *Proceedings of the Society for Psychical Research.*

Attorneys Who Have Studied the Afterlife Become Convinced of Its Reality.

Many attorneys have changed their views about the afterlife after
examining the evidence.

Edward C. Randall, Esq. – A prominent Buffalo, New York, trial
lawyer who served on the board of directors of a number of large
corporations. Randall began studying the direct-voice mediumship of
Emily S. French. He had more than 700 sittings with French over 22
years, concluding,

Hundreds, yea thousands [of spirits], have come and
talked with me, and to many whom I have invited to
participate in the work – thousands of different voices
with different tones, different thoughts, different
personalities, no two alike; and at times in different
languages.[115]

Victor James Zammit, B.A., Grad. Dip.Ed., M.A., LL.B., Ph.D. – Dr.
Zammit is a retired lawyer of the Supreme Court of the New South
Wales and the High Court of Australia. After examining the evidence for
the afterlife, he wrote,

After many years of serious investigation, I have come to
the irretrievable conclusion that there is a great body of
evidence which, taken as a whole, absolutely and
unqualifiedly proves the case for the afterlife. . . . I am
stating that the evidence taken as a whole constitutes
overwhelming and irrefutable proof for the existence of
the afterlife.[116]

Judge John Worth Edmonds – Circuit judge, state Supreme Court
judge, member of the New York assembly, and colonel in the militia.
Confused about death and the afterlife, and with no confidence in either
the church or mediums, he launched an investigation into the activities
of mediums with a team of skeptical investigators. He and the team
visited a variety of mediums and evaluated their sessions using various
devices. As a result of his investigation, he wrote this about the voices
he heard in medium sessions:

After depending upon my senses, as to these various
phases of the phenomenon, I invoked the aid of science,
and, with the assistance of an accomplished electrician
and his machinery, and eight or ten intelligent,
educated, shrewd persons, examined the matter. We
pursued our inquiries many days, and established to our
satisfaction two things: first, that the sounds were not
produced by the agency of any person present or near
us; and, second, that they were not forthcoming at our
will and pleasure.[117]

Edward C. Randall – Distinguished lawyer and businessman from
Dunkirk and Buffalo, New York. He was one of the leading
industrialists, CEO of various companies, and president of a number of
corporations. He began as a skeptic, but after investigating the afterlife
came to accept the evidence. He heard, first hand, incredible voices that
came in the presence of direct voice and materialization medium, Emily
French. He and his wife spent twenty-two years recording sittings with
her and he became a major writer on the afterlife.[118]

Judge Dean Shuart – Prominent judge from Rochester, New York.
Judge Shuart attended the same circles Edward C. Randall did,
conducted a variety of "exacting experiments," and became equally
convinced of the reality and validity of the contacts.[119]

Dr. Aubrey Rose OBE, CBE – Leading British human rights lawyer. After empirically investigating transmissions made by one of his colleagues through direct voice medium, Leslie Flint, he stated that without doubt the voice came from the afterlife, and was that of Judge Lord Birkett, who had crossed over some time before.[120]

Clergy Become Convinced of the Nature of the Afterlife Described by Mediums, Not a Distant Heavenly Realm

Members of the clergy have an especially difficult time in voicing their convictions about the afterlife described by mediums because of the narrow views of most religions. However, those who do study the imminent afterlife become convinced of its reality as the mediums describe it, not as religion teaches it.

Dr. Isaac K. Funk – After serving 11 years as a Lutheran minister, Funk turned to editorial work and co-founded the publishing firm of Funk and Wagnalls. He was the editor-in-chief of the *Standard Dictionary of the English Language.* He wrote,

> I have the absolute assurance that when the something we call death comes, it will only mean a new and larger and more complete life. I do not expect to convince any one of the truth as I see it merely by making those statements, because I have the feeling that one must realize these things for himself; but when once such realization comes, there is thereafter no power on earth that can disturb it."[121]

The Rev. Charles Drayton Thomas – A graduate of Richmond Theological College, Thomas was a Methodist minister who served on the Council of the Society for Psychical Research in London for 19 years. Beginning in 1917, he had more than 500 sittings with Gladys Osborne Leonard, probably England's most famous medium, and concluded,

> Perhaps it will be asked what benefit may be expected from a general acceptance of this evidence for survival. I think it will do for others what it has done for me. It has supplemented and reinforced my faith, both in times of bereavement and in the prospect of old age and death. Also, it has further emphasized the value of personal religion.[122]

Father Pere Francois Brune – Catholic priest, member of the Catholic Institute in Paris and Biblical Institute in Rome, theologian, and professor in a number of leading seminaries. Father Brune wrote that the Catholic Church's attitude about communication from the afterlife is changing:

> I believe that, as several of these messages assure us, we in fact are never alone. Some deceased, once they have arrived in the Beyond, appear to have the wish of continuing their life through us, and come to sponge on us. [123]

In another statement, Brune wrote this about the changing position of the church on the afterlife:

> We do not have to do with an official change of the Church's position. But it is in fact an evolution that without any doubt is due to the realization that the phenomena exist, and that they–how complex they ever may be–indeed correspond very often to an authentic communication with our dead. [124]

Dr. Peter Bander – Senior lecturer in religious and moral education at the Cambridge Institute of Education. Dr. Bander is a psychologist and Christian theologian who began his investigation of the afterlife stating clearly that it was impossible for people who are dead to communicate with the living, that it was not only far-fetched, but outrageous to even think about it. [125] However, after participating in a study of electronic voice production (EVP), he concluded: "I noticed the peculiar rhythm mentioned by Raudive and his colleagues. . . . I heard a voice. . . . I believed this to have been the voice of my mother who had died three years earlier." [126]

Bander conducted more experiments and came to believe that the deceased communicate with the living through electronic voice devices.

A Church of England Committee Studying Mediums Concluded They Speak with Those in the Afterlife.

A committee of the Church of England studied mediumship records for two years, analyzing a great volume of the evidence on mediumship to investigate Spiritualism because it was so popular in England at the time. Its investigations included sitting with some of the leading mediums in England. At the end of that thorough investigation, seven of the ten members of the Committee—against enormous pressure—came to this conclusion: "The hypothesis that they (spirit communications) proceed in some cases from discarnate spirits is the true one."[127]

Debunkers Come to Believe the Afterlife Experiences with Mediums are Reality.

Dr. Hereward Carrington – After moving to the U.S. from Great Britain in 1899, Carrington served as assistant to Dr. James H. Hyslop at the Society for Psychical Research. His first of many books on psychical phenomena was published in 1907 and explained the fraudulent practices of physical mediums. However, Carrington came away from his investigation of Eusapia Palladino convinced of the reality of some of the phenomena. He wrote,

> I myself have observed materializations under perfect conditions of control, and have had the temporary hand melt within my own, as I held it firmly grasped. This hand was a perfectly formed physiological structure, warm, lifelike, and having all the attributes of the human hand – yet both the medium's hands were securely held by two controllers, and visible in the red light. Let me repeat, this hand was not pulled away, but somehow melted in my grasp as I held it.[128]

Dr. Harry Price – Debunker of fraudulent mediums, he came to believe in genuine psychic phenomena and founded the National Laboratory of Psychical Research, later the University of London Council for Psychical Research. About his research, he wrote,

> The fact that I have devoted many years of my life to experimentation; have studied thousands of reports dealing with the subject; have traveled thousands of miles all over Europe for obtaining first-hand experience of "phenomena"; and have spent a fortune in seeking the truth or otherwise of psychic manifestations, must surely entitle me to a sympathetic hearing. And if I were not convinced of these things, I would not waste another moment of my time or penny of my money in further research. . . . The greatest skeptic concerning paranormal

phenomena is invariably the man who knows the least about them.[129]

The Evidence Demonstrates that Mediums Communicate with Living People in the Afterlife

The mental mediums, those who receive messages from individuals on the next plane of life and convey them to people in readings, provide accurate details about people's lives. They convey them from living people on the other side, who communicate as though they were speaking through a translator. The messages mediums receive are not from a psychic knowledge about people—they are from living people who are residents of the afterlife. The conversations are animated, with questions and responses, notations about current events going on in people's lives, and even humor. The mediums and those communicating through them both assert that the living person is there communicating. Psychics don't claim that the living person is speaking during a standard reading, and if the person does come through, there is a change and clear impression such as "She's telling me . . ."

Researcher Robert Crookall Finds Accounts of the Afterlife by Mediums to Be Identical.

Dr. Robert Crookall, B.Sc., D.Sc., Ph.D., principal geologist with the Geological Survey of Great Britain, resigned from his geological work in 1952 to devote his life to psychical research. During the next nine years, he collected and analyzed medium communications from every country he could, including Brazil, England, South Africa, Tibet, Europe, India, Australia, and the Hawaiian Islands. He found that in all countries, among all cultures, people described the same characteristic accounts of out-of-body experiences, near-death experiences, and communications with the deceased through mediums. He concluded that his findings were strong evidence for the existence of an afterlife because an intellectually consistent set of statements came from many independent sources.

In 1961, Crookall wrote *The Supreme Adventure: Analyses of Psychic Communications*[130] describing the findings of his research. His descriptions of the afterlife that came from his many sources are identical to the descriptions of the afterlife that have come from direct-voice mediums before his research and since.

University of Arizona Experiments Demonstrated that the Mediums Do Receive Valid Information.

In an effort to run a controlled experiment to determine whether mediums do receive accurate information from the deceased, Gary Schwartz, Ph.D., Linda Russek, Ph.D., and Christopher Barentsen conducted a study for the Human Energy Systems Laboratory at the University of Arizona testing three talented mediums: Laurie Campbell, John Edward, and Suzane Northrop.[131]

The study did reveal that the mediums identified details about the deceased loved ones at a rate much higher than chance, leading the researchers to conclude that "The findings appear to confirm the hypothesis that information and energy, and potentially consciousness itself, can continue after physical death."

However, the statistics don't adequately show the remarkable accuracy of the mediums and the personal nature of the communications with deceased loved ones. For example, in that study, one medium, John Edward, reported that he was receiving information from a deceased grandmother for one of the people being read. He reported that the grandmother brought daisies to the person's mother's wedding, the grandmother had a large black poodle and large white poodle, and the white poodle tore up the house. Those and other details were perfectly accurate. John Edward had a 70 percent perfect hit score for that person.

But when the next person came in for Edward to read, he received a zero hit score because the grandmother of the previous person persisted in coming through, and he couldn't read for the next person. He kept hearing the songs *On the Good Ship Lollipop* and *Sabrina the Teenage Witch*.

After the zero hit reading was over, the experimenter took the person being read back to the waiting room and there was the woman whose grandmother kept coming through to John Edward, still waiting for the next medium. The experimenter asked her whether she knew anything about *On the Good Ship Lollipop* or *Sabrina the Teenage Witch*. She emotionally told the experimenter that she had curly brown hair as a child and sang and danced Shirley Temple songs with her grandmother; one of the songs was *On the Good Ship Lollipop*. Also, her name was Sabrina and when she was a teenager, some children teased her about being "Sabrina-the Teenage Witch." She would go to her grandmother for solace. John Edward knew nothing about the girl, including her name or gender.

A Second Study Also Concluded that Mediums Are Able to Identify Details About the Deceased in Readings.

A second study was performed by Gary Schwartz, Ph.D., with three other researchers from the University of Arizona Human Energy Systems Laboratory for a video-recorded HBO documentary on the afterlife. The study used five well-known mediums: George Anderson, John Edward, Anne Gehman, Suzane Northrop, and Laurie Campbell.[132]

In this study, two people were subjects for the medium sessions, one of whom had experienced six significant deaths over the previous ten years. Before the readings, each person wrote descriptions of the people who had died to provide objective data that could be compared to the mediums' readings. The mediums had no knowledge of the two people. Each subject sat behind a screen so the subject couldn't be seen by the medium giving a reading. The person was able to give only "yes" and "no" answers. Two video cameras recorded the sessions and verbatim scripts were made.

The result was that the mediums' average accuracy score was 83 percent for subject one and 77 percent for subject two. To test whether guessing could achieve the same results by chance, 68 control people were asked to guess details about the deceased loved ones of the two subjects. Their scores averaged 36 percent hits by chance. In other words, the accuracy of the mediums' details was far beyond chance guesses.

The Miraval Silent Sitter Experiment Showed the Same Accuracy by Mediums.

In the Miraval silent-sitter experiment, the mediums were Suzane Northrop, John Edward, Anne Gehman, and Laurie Campbell.[133] There were ten subjects. The study involved two parts for each reading with each subject. The first was a "silent" part in which the medium described details about the deceased without receiving any responses from the subject. In the second part, the medium was able to receive "yes" and "no" answers from the subject.

In this study, the mediums' average accuracy score was 77 percent during the silent period and 85 percent during the "yes" and "no" questioning period, showing again that the mediums were far more accurate than would be expected by chance (based on the 36 percent accuracy rating in the previous study's control group).

More Stringent Studies at the University of Arizona Yielded the Same Results.

Gary Schwartz, Ph.D., and Julie Beischel, Ph.D., of the University of Arizona performed another study[134] under even more stringent, triple-blind conditions with more mediums. It is apparent that the mediums are learning information about the deceased, but the question arises whether the medium is just using telepathy or clairvoyance to learn information from the person being read rather than really hearing from the deceased. This study added a condition to eliminate that possibility. In this later study, the subjects weren't present for the reading. Another person sat in as a "proxy sitter." The readings were conducted by phone to eliminate even the presence of the proxy sitter with the medium. Eight mediums were involved to increase the validity of the data.

Transcripts of the readings were made and the subjects whose deceased loved ones were to come through rated the readings on a scale of 0 to 6, with 0 being no accuracy and 6 being perfect accuracy on all details. They were given transcripts of both readings intended for them and readings intended for other subjects without knowing which was which to see whether they would score the reading intended for them as being more accurate than a random reading for some other person.

The result was that the average summary rating for the readings actually intended for the subject was 3.56 on the 6-point scale. The average summary ratings for the readings not intended for the person (that were actually readings for someone else) was 1.94. For three of the best-performing mediums, the summary scores were in the range of 5.0 to 5.5 out of 6, meaning they were dramatically accurate.

In other words, the study showed that mediums in controlled conditions that included not even speaking on the phone with the person being read resulted in communication with the deceased.

A list of recommended, legitimate mediums, some of whom do phone readings, is at http://youreternalself.com/chapter2.htm.

The British Admiralty Acknowledged a Medium's Abilities.

The fact that mediums receive information from those who have crossed over to the other side was acknowledged by British government officials startled by the truth of the information.

Helen Duncan was a Scottish medium in the twentieth century who gave hundreds of séances, with those attending describing them using superlatives such as "astonishing." In January 1944, while World War II was raging, Helen Duncan held a séance at 3:30 p.m. one afternoon in Edinburgh, Scotland. Brigadier Firebrace, who was the chief of security in Scotland, happened to be at the séance. During the séance, Duncan, in a mediumistic trance, reported that the British ship HMS Hood had been sunk that day in the North Atlantic. No one could have known that at the time. Immediate announcements of calamities in televised newscasts didn't exist and there was great secrecy about military movements and events during wartime.

When Firebrace returned to his office that afternoon, he called the British Admiralty saying he had heard a rumor that the HMS Hood had been sunk, asking whether that was true. The British Admiralty denied that the HMS Hood had been sunk, possibly not even knowing it themselves. However, later that day, as Firebrace was leaving his office, he received a telephone call from the Admiralty confirming the sinking occurred at 1:30 p.m., just two hours before the séance.

The astonishing revelation worried the British Admiralty. They could find no explanation for it. Then six months later, at another séance, a young man materialized saying he had been severely burned and died in the sinking of another British warship, the HMS Barham. The editor of *Psychic News*, Maurice Barbanell, was at the séance. He called the British Admiralty after the séance, asking why information about the loss of the HMS Barham had not been divulged to the parents and families of those who had perished. The British Admiralty admitted that, in fact, the HMS Barham had been sunk, but that they had kept it secret because they feared that its loss would have had a serious impact on public morale.

After the two uncanny revelations of information Duncan couldn't have known, the alarmed British Admiralty had her arrested and charged with witchcraft under a law dating to 1735. She was imprisoned for nine months. Prime Minister Winston Churchill was outraged, calling the conviction "tomfoolery." The ancient law against witchcraft was not repealed until 1951. In spite of an effort in 1998 to have her posthumously pardoned, the British government refused to pardon her—implying the British government still maintained that Helen Duncan had been performing witchcraft.

> [At her trial], some forty-one witnesses with the highest credibility, including a Royal Air Force Wing Commander, stated in court on oath that Helen Duncan

was a genuine materialization medium, explaining in
detail their psychic experiences with her. . . . Not one of
[these] defense witnesses was "broken" in cross
examination.[135]

The British Admiralty did not suggest that she had received the
information from the enemy or another Earthly source. They resorted to
silencing her using a 1735 law against witchcraft until the war was over.
Unwittingly, the British government had provided official
acknowledgement that Helen Duncan was communicating with the
spirits of people who had passed away.[136]

Medium Readings Have Revealed Information that Could Not Be Known by the Person Being Read.

It is very common for medium readings to include information
unknown to the observers or the person being read. The information is
later verified to be true, showing that the medium is receiving
information about the deceased and it is not coming from reading the
living people's minds.

In one account, an extended chess game was played by a living
grand master (Viktor Korchnoi) and a deceased chess master (Maroczy)
through medium Robert Rollans. At one point, the researcher decided to
ask the deceased Maroczy about a detail he had researched to verify that
it really was the deceased chess master coming through. He found an
article stating that Maroczy had played a match against a player listed as
Romi in 1930. With that information, at the next séance the researcher
asked Maroczy through the medium whether he had defeated an Italian
named Romi in a match. Maroczy replied through the medium that he
didn't recognize that name, but he did defeat a man named Romih
spelled with an "h" on the end of the name. The researcher delved
further and found an actual program from the match. The name was, in
fact, Romih, not Romi.[137]

Family Members Have Verified that Medium Readings are Genuine Conversations with the Deceased Loved One.

In the thousands of séances that are on record between a living
person and a deceased loved one with a genuine, verified medium, the
living person is always adamant that the person with whom he or she

communicated was the deceased. Three of the thousands of examples on record today will serve as illustrations.

A deceased young man who gave his name as Peter William Handford Kite came through at a Leslie Flint séance asking that his parents be contacted at an address he gave and invited to come to a séance. The parents were contacted and did come to a second séance at which their son came through and spoke for nearly forty minutes. The parents confirmed that it was Peter's own voice. During the séance, he told them many facts that his parents confirmed to be true, such as the following:

- He had made a joke before he died about buying an Alsatian.

- His mother had put a photograph of him and photographs of his grave in Norway in her bag that morning.

- He liked the cherry tree in the memorial garden they had planted for him.

- His bedroom had not been changed in the six years since he died.

- He had not liked the wallpaper in his bedroom.

- His father was still driving his car although it was a too small for him.

The young man's parents both affirmed emphatically that they had a conversation with their son.[138]

A young man named David Cattanach, who died at age 18, made many visits to the Leslie Flint séances over a period of 10 years, speaking with his mother at several of them. Gordon Smith, who knew the mother personally, wrote this about her and the séances:

> I know her personally and she is someone I would
> describe as very astute, someone who would not easily
> be fooled, especially when it came to her son, and she
> had no doubts that she was hearing his voice.[139]

A man named Michael Fearon, killed during WWII, was also a frequent visitor to the Leslie Flint séances, at which he often spoke with his mother. You can hear the conversation between him and his mother at http://youreternalself.com/chapter2.htm. The British Broadcasting Corporation arranged a broadcast during which they played a tape of a séance in which Mrs. Fearon was speaking to her son. After the tape played, the moderator asked her, "Mrs. Fearon, as Mike's mother, what makes you so sure that it's your son's voice that you hear?" She answered, "Well, Mike was twenty-seven when he died and I'd been with him all that time . . . and I ought to know at the end of that, oughtn't I?"[140]

Rigorously Tested Physical Mediums Have Been Shown to Be Speaking to the Deceased

Since the nineteenth century, when mediums could hold séances without fear of retribution, a number of capable mediums have held thousands of séances. The most talented attracted the greatest attention, of course, and as a result were the most tested by skeptics and debunkers. That provides for us a vast storehouse of records of rigorous, repeated testing and testimonies by credible witnesses, many of whom were avowed skeptics before the testing. There have been frauds, just as there have been fraudulent doctors, counselors, police officers, and stock brokers. As Allen Spraggett wrote,

> Many people judge this aspect of Spiritualism [physical mediumship] harshly, but if one stops to consider the number of bad popes and charlatan evangelists, perhaps Spiritualism has not done so badly after all.[141]

However, the fraudulent mediums were winnowed from the genuine, and the result is a list of highly talented mediums who were found to be speaking to the eternal selves no longer using bodies.

Following are brief summaries of a small number of mediums' accomplishments and results of their testing by credible witnesses, including government officials, scientists, and royalty. Enough is included, with citations, to demonstrate that they communicated with eternal selves living on the next plane of life and that rigorous, repeated testing found no fraud or deception in their activities. The people they were communicating with are alive, just not using bodies.

Gladys Osborne Leonard

For over forty years, Gladys Osborne Leonard's mediumship was studied exhaustively by members of the Society for Psychical Research. The tests always confirmed that her communication was with the deceased. In none of the many tests was there a hint of fraud.

The Rev. Charles Drayton Thomas, a Wesleyan minister and member of the British Society for Psychical Research (SPR), sat with her over 100 times to test her abilities. Thomas' own father came through and offered to assist in the tests. Drayton Thomas had an extensive library. The deceased father told the son, through Mrs. Leonard, to go to the lowest shelf in his library and take the sixth book from the left. On page 149, three-quarters down, he would find a word conveying the meaning of falling back or stumbling. When Drayton Thomas went home, he located the book, found page 149, and looked at the words three-quarters down. There, he found the words, ". . . to whom a crucified Messiah was an insuperable stumbling-block."

Over a period of 18 months' experimentation, the deceased father was able to pick up more and more words and numbers even more accurately, both in his own library and in a friend's library. The words were all verified.

They decided to try having Drayton Thomas' deceased father provide information from newspapers and magazines not yet printed. On January 16, 1920, the junior Thomas was told to examine the *Daily Telegraph* the following day and to notice that near the top of the second column of the first page the name of the place Thomas was born, Victoria Terrace on Victoria Street in Tuanton. When Thomas checked the paper the following day, he found the word "Victoria" exactly where his father said it would be.

Mrs. Leonard was able to satisfy every test she was subjected to, and the researchers were convinced she was indeed speaking with the living individuals who were simply not using a body anymore.[142]

Leonora Piper

Leonara Piper was a nineteenth-century medium who was also tested repeatedly by a wide range of skeptical observers. The Society for Psychical Research conducted several thousand sittings over two decades with carefully controlled environments to preclude fraud. The sittings were remarkably accurate and those who knew the deceased acknowledged that the contacts were with their loved ones, based on the unmistakable content and detail.

Piper was studied repeatedly by Richard Hodgson, one of the leading members of the Society for Psychical Research. He started out as a skeptic determined to expose Piper as a fraud. In the end, he had no doubts that she was speaking to eternal selves living on the next plane of life. His report is 300 pages long, with detailed descriptions of the controls he used to prevent fraud. Leonora Piper was never caught in trickery and her achievements were described as "baffling."[143]

One of the many case studies of her remarkable mediumship follows. [144] It was experienced and recorded by Hodgson.

George Pelham, a lawyer and acquaintance of Hodgson, died in an accidental fall at age 32. Pelham had followed Hodgson's work with Piper and was skeptical about the afterlife, calling it inconceivable. But he told Hodgson that if he died, he would try to contact Hodgson. Five weeks after his death, Piper sat in a séance with John Hart, a close friend of Pelham, and Hodgson. She announced that George Pelham was there to speak.

The spirit of George Pelham provided a long list of details about himself, his early life, his friends, and his family that could be researched and verified to prove he was indeed George Pelham, still alive on the other side of life. For example, when Pelham had died, his father had sent his friend John Hart (who was sitting in this séance), some shirt studs of Pelham's to keep as a memento. Hart happened to be wearing the studs that evening and Pelham, through the medium, identified the studs Hart was wearing as formerly his. He also told Hart how his mother had chosen the studs and how Pelham's father delivered them to Hart.[145]

In another sitting, Pelham told Hodgson he had seen his (Pelham's) father take a photograph of the deceased Pelham to an artist to have it copied. After the séance, Hodgson contacted Pelham's mother to see whether that had been true. She said that, in fact, Pelham's father had taken a photograph to an artist to be copied.[146]

This is what happened as a result:

> Pelham's father eventually wrote to Hodgson, "The letters you have written to my wife giving such extraordinary evidence of the intelligence exercised by George in some incomprehensible manner over the actions of his friends on earth have given food for constant reflection and wonder. (My) preconceived notions about the future state have received a severe shock."[147]

In another sitting with family members who verified that the communication was with their loved one still living in the afterlife, Mrs. Piper was asked by the Reverend and Mrs. S.W. Sutton if she could communicate with their recently deceased little girl. The account of the séance is now in the archives of the Society for Psychical Research. This is Victor Zammit's record of what happened:

> Mrs. Piper was able to establish contact between the Suttons and their very much-loved little girl from the afterlife. The information left no doubt whatsoever that the little girl was actually communicating from the afterlife with her mother and father still living on the earthplane.
>
> She confirmed that she used to bite buttons. She identified her Uncle Frank and a friend who had died with a tumor and made reference to her brother by his pet name. She made reference to her sore throat and paralyzed tongue and that her head used to get hot before her death. She referred to Dinah her doll, to her sister Maggie, and to her little toy horse. She also sang two songs, the same songs she had sung immediately before she died. The Suttons had no doubt that they had made contact with their little girl and were especially happy when she reassured them: "I am happy . . . cry for me no more."[148]

Dr. James Hyslop, a professor of logic and ethics at Columbia University, initially a skeptic, was converted to accepting the afterlife after he studied Mrs. Piper, who repeatedly produced high quality evidence of the afterlife. In *Life After Death*[149] he wrote,

> I regard the existence of discarnate spirits as scientifically proved and I no longer refer to the skeptic as having any right to speak on the subject. Any man who does not accept the existence of discarnate spirits and the proof of it is either ignorant or a moral coward. I give him short shrift, and do not propose any longer to argue with him on the supposition that he knows anything about the subject.[150]

Rudi Schneider

Eugene Osty, MD, was the director of the Metaphysic Institute in Paris. Intent on understanding the remarkable abilities of a young medium named Rudi Schneider, he set up controlled conditions and was able to produce genuine physical phenomena without fraud. During Schneider's séances, people on the next plane of life would move objects placed on tables while the room was dark. Osty tested whether Schneider's spirits could move objects placed on a table by setting up a sophisticated arrangement of infra-red rays and cameras to "catch" any human that touched objects during the séance. This is how Hereward Carrington, a British spiritualist and investigator of psychic phenomena, described the experiment:

> Dr. Osty placed the objects to be moved upon a small table. Across the top of the table he passed a beam of infra-red rays. These were, of course, invisible to the eyes of those present, but the apparatus was so designed that if any solid object was interposed in the path of the rays, cutting off as much as thirty per cent of them, a battery of cameras would be exposed, flashlights ignited and the pictures taken of the tabletop at that moment. This would happen if any material thing tried to move the objects — say a human hand. A series of photos would at once reveal the fraud.
>
> In the sittings that ensued objects were moved on numerous occasions, flashes were set off, and the plates developed. What did they show? Nothing — that is, nothing abnormal. They just showed the table top. But something had nevertheless been moving about over the table because the beam of infra-red rays had been interfered with and the objects had been displaced.[151]

Osty also set up controlled conditions to see whether the researchers could detect changes in the atmosphere that would show that some entity was present. This is Carrington's description of the experiment:

> The second stage was to locate and identify the presence of the intelligence. To do this the experimenter devised an apparatus, a galvanometer, by means of which it would be possible to register the oscillation or the vibration rate of the intelligence once the experiment commenced. As soon as the experiment commenced, the intelligence began to move things around indicating that he was present; then something quite spectacular

happened — the galvanometer began to register the "pulsation" of the invisible intelligence. As Carrington states: "It was somewhat like taking the pulse of an invisible being standing before them in space!"[152]

Eileen Garrett

Eileen Garrett was a medium who held séances in the early twentieth century. One séance was interrupted by a man who identified himself as Flight Lieutenant H.C. Irwin of the Airship R101. Those at the séance later learned that Airship R101 had crashed three days before, but the government had not revealed it to anyone yet.

During the séance, the deceased Irwin described the airship's destruction in great detail. The account was presented to the Air Ministry Intelligence, who were startled and impressed at the accuracy and the details they had not known that were revealed in the séance. They were sufficiently convinced of the authenticity of the source for Major Oliver Villiers, of the Air Ministry Intelligence, to arrange seven additional séances with Garrett to hear the deceased Irwin describe more details about the crash. The major learned about technical subjects Garrett could not have understood, using technical vocabulary such as "useful lift of the airship," "gross lift," "disposable lift," "fuel injection," "cruising speed," "cruising altitude," "trim," "volume of structure," and other jargon.

Irwin also described top-secret information about a classified experiment the ministry had been engaged in. They had been attempting to use a mixture of hydrogen and oil in airships, but the information was strictly protected. The ministry officials agreed that the information that came from Irwin through Garrett was completely accurate, even to the town the airship passed over before it crashed and the locations of hidden diaries crew members had kept that revealed their fears about the secret project.[153]

Shirley Bray

Direct-voice mediums have voices come from the air around the medium and at various places in the room. The room must be darkened, so skeptics have devised tests to ensure that the voices are not coming from the medium. Such tests were used to authenticate the voices that were recorded during séances with Australian medium, Shirley Bray.

The voices of three people on the next plane of life who regularly manifested through her were tape recorded. These taped voices were then put through the high tech voice-recognition machine used by the British police. It was the same technology used in the investigations of serial killers. This is the account of the results:

> The voice machine can measure variables such as pace, rhythm, accents etc. The machine showed that all taped voices from the medium Shirley Bray were those of totally different individuals. Scientists stated in unequivocal terms that because the machine registers the person's breathing pattern while speaking it would not have been possible for one person to produce the three voices on the tape. This is because the voice pattern-vibration for each individual is just like a fingerprint — different from person to person.[154]

Elwood Babbitt

Another ingenious test of medium authenticity was devised by a history professor named Charles H. Hapgood. He tested medium Elwood Babbitt. Babbitt was a trance medium, meaning the medium would go into trance and those on the other side would take over the medium's body, speaking through it using the mediums vocal apparatus. The skeptic would suggest that the trance medium is simply disguising his or her voice and making up information. Hapgood tested Babbitt using an electroencephalograph (EEG) to measure changes in brain-wave patterns when Babbitt was "taken over" by deceased people during trances. Hapgood measured the brain wave patterns when Babbit was out of trance and during the trances. If the EEG patterns were the same in both instances, it would indicate that Babbitt was consciously creating something resulting in the voices. These were the results:

> Hapgood took EEGs of Babbitt while three different intelligences were allegedly in control of the medium. The EEGs of each of the three were found to be completely different from each other and from the EEG of Babbitt not in trance. An EEG expert, Dr Bridge, noticed that the EEG's were characteristic of people of

different physical age and could not belong to one person.[155]

Daniel Dunglas Home

D. D. Home (pronounced like "hume") was a well-known medium of the middle of the nineteenth century. His mediumship demonstrates the reality of communicating with those on the next plane of life because the feats were attested to by well-known people who experienced them. In 1855, his mediumship was witnessed in France by Prince Murat, Napoleon III, and the Empress Eugenie. This is an account of the séance with Prince Murat, Napoleon, and the Empress:

> . . . Napoleon followed every manifestation with keen and skeptical attention and satisfied himself by the closest scrutiny that neither deception nor delusion was possible. His and the Empress' unspoken thoughts were replied to and the Empress was touched by a materialized hand in which, from a defect in one of the fingers, she recognized that of her late father. The second séance was still more forceful. The room was shaken, heavy tables were lifted and glued down to the floor by an alteration of their weight. At the third séance a phantom hand appeared above the table, lifted a pencil and wrote the single word "Napoleon" in the autograph [handwriting] of Napoleon I. As Prince Murat related later to Home, the Duke de Morny told the Emperor that he felt it a duty to contradict the report that the Emperor believed in spiritualism. The Emperor replied:
>
> "Quite right, but you may add when you speak on the subject again that there is a difference between believing a thing and having proof of it, and that I am certain of what I have seen."[156]

As a result of the hundreds of carefully controlled examinations researchers conducted without finding a hint of deception, even skeptics unsympathetic to mediumship were forced to acknowledge that nothing fraudulent could ever be found in Home's medium sessions.[157]

Leslie Flint

Leslie Flint conducted séances in which thousands of people spoke to deceased loved ones and the deceased responded in normal conversations. The people whose loved ones came through all expressed with certainty that the voices were their loved ones' and that they had had conversations with the real, living person, although they had been dead, at times for decades.

Flint had the remarkable ability of having people from the next plane of life speak audibly using a voice box they created in the air from a substance that came from the medium's body (ectoplasm). They did not use their own voice boxes because they were moldering away in the ground somewhere or reduced to ashes stored in a funeral urn. The voices, however, were clear and authenticated by people who knew the speakers, especially their immediate families who carried on conversations with the deceased during the séances.

Flint was described as the most tested medium in all of history. In one instance, to ensure he hadn't been doing the speaking, he placed a volume of pink water in his mouth so he couldn't speak without spitting it out, and on top of that, his mouth was sealed by an adhesive strip. During the ensuing séance, voices came from nowhere, as usual, and spoke with those assembled. After the séance, the intact tape was removed from his mouth and he returned the entire volume of pink water into a glass, demonstrating that he had not created the voices.[158]

Even after such rigorous testing that proved he was not producing the voices, Flint was repeatedly subjected to more elaborate tests. The creativity of his testers was remarkable. In one test, he wore a throat microphone to detect any possible vibrations in his vocal organs. In still another, he was observed through an infra-red viewer to see if he was taking the tape off of his mouth.[159]

A report of the stringent tests performed on Flint appeared in the *Psychic News*, February 14, 1948:

> . . . one experiment where he conducted a séance with elastoplast pressed over his lips, bandages over the elastoplast and his hands and legs tied to a chair. The observers concluded that in spite of the above restrictions the voices were soon speaking with their usual clarity, even shouting. Some twelve persons in the room all heard more than enough to convince the most

obdurate skeptic that the sealing of Mr. Flint's lips in no
way prevented the unseen speakers from saying
anything they wished. At the conclusion of the
experiment they found the plaster and the cords intact
and undisturbed.[160]

At no time during any test did sound come from his mouth. In none
of the hundreds of demanding tests by qualified, skeptical scientists, was
anything found to be fake or deceptive.

The voices continued to come through in all circumstances: hotel
rooms, halls, apartments—anywhere Flint would sit and wait for the
voices to come. William R. Bennett, professor of electrical engineering at
Colombia University in New York City, tested Leslie Flint at length.
After completing his exhaustive investigation, he thoroughly vouched
for Flint's authenticity:

> My experience with Mr. Flint is first hand; I have heard
> the independent voices. Furthermore, modern
> investigation techniques not available in earlier tests
> corroborate previous conclusions by indicating that the
> voices are not his. But to be thorough, one should
> consider the possibility of live accomplices. This
> suggestion became untenable for me during his visit to
> New York in September 1970, when, in an impromptu
> séance in my apartment, the same voices not only
> appeared but took part in conversations with the
> guests.[161]

You can hear some of the audio recordings of people in the afterlife
speaking during Leslie Flint séances by clicking on the links at
http://youreternalself.com/chapter2.htm.

David Thompson

David Thompson is now conducting séances in Australia with voices
of the deceased coming through in the séances and materializations of
those in spirit in the presence of a variety of people with careful, rigid
controls. One of those is Victor J. Zammit, lawyer and author of *A Lawyer
Presents the Case for the Afterlife.*

Montigue Keen was head of the Parliamentary and Legal
department of the National Farmers Union of England and Wales,
journalist, magazine editor, and secretary of the Society for Psychical

Research Survival Research Committee. Keen investigated David Thompson's physical medium abilities on October 25, 2003, using tight controls that prevented the medium from uttering a sound or moving. In spite of the strict controls, the medium was transported, with the chair to which he was taped, to a different part of the room, the medium's cardigan was reversed on his body while the straps binding him were intact, and four distinctive voices were heard. These were Keen's conclusions:

> The voices themselves could not have come from the gagged medium. The only other "regulars" on whom suspicion might rest were Bianca, his wife, Paul the leader who was seated next to me, and whose voice and location would have clearly identified him, and DF, the host, who was seated at the opposite end of the room from the medium. Any of these possibilities would have easily and immediately detectable by those present, as well as likely to be defeated by listening to the tape recording.[162]

You can hear some of the audio recordings of people in the afterlife speaking during David Thompson séances by clicking on the links on the page at http://youreternalself.com/chapter2.htm.

The Scole Experiments

For six years, a group in Norfolk, England, conducted experiments of contact with the afterlife. The following professionals participated in the experiments: Dr. David Fontana, Professor Arthur Ellison, Montague Keen, Dr. Hans Schaer, Esq., Dr. Ernst Senkowski, Piers Eggett, Keith McQuin Roberts, Dr. Rupert Sheldrake, and Professor Ivor Grattan-Guiness. A group of NASA scientists participated, as well as professionals from the Institute of Noetic Sciences.

The experiments resulted in communication with a variety of deceased people, revelations of information that nobody but the deceased could know about, appearance of objects that came from nowhere, voices of the deceased heard by all experimenters in attendance, and materialization of people who were deceased. Rolls of film were placed in locked boxes by experimenters and images appeared on them. Video cameras recorded the appearance of deceased people.

A scientific report titled "The Scole Report" was produced by the Society for Psychical Research based on the experiments. The conclusion was, "None of our critics has been able to point to a single example of fraud or deception."[163]

A stage magician, James Webster, was brought in to see if any magic tricks could produce the phenomena. Webster had more than fifty years experience in psychic research, applying his knowledge of magic tricks to such phenomena. On three occasions he attended sittings with the Scole group and published this conclusion in an English newspaper in June 2001: "I discovered no signs of trickery, and in my opinion such conjuring tricks were not possible, for the type of phenomena witnessed, under the conditions applied."[164]

Studies of the Material from Mediums that Forms Voice Boxes Shows Weight Loss in the Medium When It Appears

The mediums and those in their circles explain that a substance called ectoplasm comes out of mediums and sitters in the séance to form voice boxes and manifestations. Since it comes out of the medium and sitters, it would be reasonable to expect that the medium and sitters would lose weight when the ectoplasm was outside of the body. Studies were conducted to see whether that was true.

Professor W.J. Crawford, a lecturer in mechanical engineering at Queen's University Belfast, conducted meticulous studies of the mediums and ectoplasm. He set up controlled circumstances in which the weight of the medium was measured during the entire séance. At the times when the ectoplasm was creating a spirit materialization, the medium's weight dropped from 120 pounds to 66 pounds, in itself a remarkable occurrence.[165]

George Meek, 1991 award winner for contribution to new sciences by the International Association for New Science, found that during a materialization séance, there is a temporary weight loss from both the medium and the sitters as a substance is withdrawn from their bodies. Fifteen physicians, psychologists, and others made up the research team. The researchers found a shared weight loss of 27 pounds among the medium and physicians, psychologists, and others who made up the research team.[166]

Materializations of Deceased People Have Been Seen and Verified by Observers

Perhaps the most remarkable evidence of the continuation of life after the body dies is the materializations that have been observed and verified by a large number of professionals, royalty, scientists, and others whose testimony is above question. These are not "ghosts," without personality or identity. They are full appearances of real people who carry on conversations and are hugged by their loved ones. One example follows, from Victor Zammit's book, *A Lawyer Presents the Case for the Afterlife*,[167] describing materializations with a Brazilian materialization medium named Carlos Mirabelli:

> At a well-attended séance in Sao Vicente the chair on which the entranced Mirabelli was sitting rose and floated in the air two meters above the floor. Witnesses timed its levitation for 120 seconds. On another occasion Mirabelli was at the da Luz railroad station with several companions when he suddenly vanished. About fifteen minutes later a telephone call came from Sao Vicente, a town ninety kilometers away, stating that he had appeared there exactly two minutes after he had disappeared from da Luz.
>
> At a séance conducted in the morning in full daylight in the laboratory of the investigating committee in front of many people of note including ten men holding the degree of Doctor of Science [the following happened]:
>
> - The form of a little girl materialized beside the medium.
>
> - Dr. Ganymede de Souza who was present confirmed that the child was his daughter who had died a few months before and that she was wearing the dress in which she had been buried.
>
> - Another observer, Colonel Octavio Viana also took the child in his arms, felt her pulse and asked her several questions which she answered with understanding.

- Photographs of the apparition were taken and appended to the investigating committee's report.

- After this the child floated around in the air and disappeared, after having been visible in daylight for thirty six minutes.

- The form of Bishop Jose de Camargo Barros who had recently lost his life in a shipwreck appeared in full insignia of office.

- He conversed with those present and allowed them to examine his heart, gums, abdomen and fingers before disappearing.

At another séance conducted at Santos at half past three in the afternoon before sixty witnesses who attested their signatures to the report of what had happened [the following events occurred]:

- The deceased Dr Bezerra de Meneses, an eminent hospital physician, materialized.

- He spoke to all of the assembled witnesses to assure them that it was himself.

- His voice carried all over the room by megaphone.

- Several photographs were taken of him.

- For fifteen minutes two doctors who had known him examined him and announced that he was an anatomically normal human being.

- He shook hands with the spectators.

- Finally he rose into the air and began to dematerialize, with his feet vanishing first followed by his legs and abdomen, chest arms and last of all head.

- After the apparition had dematerialized Mirabelli was found to be still tied securely to his chair and seals were intact on all the doors and windows.

- The photographs accompanying the report show Mirabelli and the apparition on the same photographic plate.

At another séance under controlled conditions Mirabelli himself dematerialized to be found later in another room. Yet the seals put upon his bonds were intact as were the seals on the doors and windows of the séance room.[168]

Helen Duncan is one of the best-known materialization mediums of all time. She reunited thousands of people with their deceased loved ones. These are some of the accounts verified by witnesses and the families of the deceased (cited in Victor Zammit's book[169]):

- Nurse Jane Rust testified on oath . . . that she, through Helen Duncan, actually met a loved one again—her husband who materialized from the afterlife and kissed her. "I have never been more certain of anything in my life before," she said. She stated that she had been enquiring for 25 years as a skeptic but it was only when she met Helen Duncan that she was able to actually meet her loved ones including her mother who had passed on.

- A high ranking Air Force officer, Wing Commander George Mackie, stated on oath that through Helen Duncan's materialization gifts he actually met his "dead" mother and father and a brother.

- James Duncan (no relation), a jeweler, testified that both he and his daughter had seen his wife materialize on eight different occasions, in good light. Duncan had seen her close up at a range of 18 inches and they had talked of domestic matters including a proposed emigration to Canada that they had previously kept secret. He had, he said, not a shadow of a doubt that the voice was that of his wife. He also claimed to have seen materializations of his father, who was about his own height and bearded, and his mother.

- Mary Blackwell, president of the Pathfinder
  Spiritualist Society of Baker Street London, testified
  that she had attended more than 100 materialization
  séances with Helen Duncan at each of which
  between 15 and 16 different entities from the
  afterlife had materialized. She testified that she had
  witnessed the spirit forms conversing with their
  relatives in French, German, Dutch, Welsh, Scottish
  and Arabic. She claimed that she had witnessed the
  manifestation of ten of her own close relatives
  including her husband, her mother and her father all
  of whom she had seen up close and touched.[170]

Some years later a team of magicians headed by William
Goldston—founder of the Magicians Club—carried out
an experimental sitting with Helen Duncan. Goldston
and his colleagues were astounded when their dead
friend, the magician "The Great Lafayette," materialized
and spoke to them in his own voice. Goldston wrote a
report on the event for *The Psychic News* in which he
confirmed that Helen Duncan's mediumship was
genuine and that no magician could possibly duplicate
the phenomena that he and his fellow magicians had
witnessed.[171]

Dr. Elisabeth Kübler-Ross was an internationally renowned
physician, author, speaker, and expert on death and dying. She was
listed as one of the 100 most important thinkers of the century by *Time*
magazine in 1999, and received 20 honorary degrees for her
achievements. She published 20 books on death and dying, and her
book *On Death and Dying*[172] was named one of the 100 most influential
books of the century. She was included in the International Biographical
Centre's list of the foremost women of the twentieth century.

In her renowned book, *On Life After Death*,[173] Dr. Kübler-Ross
described her visitation in a physical form by someone who had passed
away two years earlier:

I was at a crossroad. I felt I needed to give up my work
with dying patients. That day, I was determined to give
notice and leave the hospital and the University of

Chicago. It wasn't an easy decision because I really loved my patients.

I walked out of my last seminar on death and dying towards the elevator. At that moment, a woman walked towards me. She had an incredible smile on her face, like she knew every thought I had.

She said, "Dr. Ross, I'm only going to take two minutes of your time. If you don't mind, I'll walk you down to your office." It was the longest walk I have ever taken in my life. One part of me knew this was Mrs. Schwartz, a patient of mine who had died and been buried almost a year ago. But I'm a scientist, and I don't believe in ghosts and spooks!

I did the most incredible reality testing I've ever done. I tried to touch her because she looked kind of transparent in a waxy way. Not that you could see furniture behind her, but not quite real either. I know I touched her, and she had feeling to her.

We came to my office, and she opened the door. We went inside, and she said, "I had to come back for two reasons. Number one, I wanted to thank you and Reverend Smith once more for what you have done for me. But the real reason why I had to come back is to tell you not to give up your work on death and dying. Not yet."

I realized consciously that maybe indeed this was Mrs. Schwartz. But I thought nobody would ever believe me if I told this to anybody. They really would think I had flipped!

So my scientist in me very shrewdly looked at her and said, "You know, Reverend Smith would be thrilled if he would have a note from you. Would you terribly mind?" You understand that the scientist in me needed proof. I needed a sheet of paper with anything written in her handwriting, and hopefully, her signature.

This woman knew my thoughts and knew I had no intention to ever give her note to Reverend Smith. However, she took a piece of paper and wrote a message and signed it with her full name. Then, with the biggest smile of love and compassion and understanding, she said to me, "Are you satisfied now?"

Once more, she said, "You cannot give up your work on death and dying. Not yet. The time is not right. We will help you. You will know when the time is right. Do you promise?" The last thing I said to her was "I promise." And with that; she walked out.

No sooner was the door closed, I had to go and see if she was real. I opened the door, and there was not a soul in that long hallway![174]

People with Medium Abilities Have Spoken and Written in Languages They Could Not Know

Dr. Neville Whymant, a British professor of linguistics, was a specialist in languages who knew 30 languages. He attended a séance at the home of William Cannon, a New York City lawyer and judge, performed by medium George Valiantine. In the séance, a man came through speaking ancient Chinese. Whymant knew modern Chinese and knew the literature of ancient China, so he was able to interpret it as perfect ancient Chinese. He learned that the speaker was Confucius, whose writings Whymant knew well. He asked the speaker, in Chinese, about poems people had puzzled over for centuries that Confucius had written. Before Whymant could finish the poems, the spirit spoke the remaining words. Confucius then explained the errors in copying that had occurred after his death, solving the puzzles.[175]

In another case, reported by Dr Morris Neterton, a blond, blue-eyed eleven-year old boy, under hypnosis, was audio taped for eleven minutes speaking an ancient Chinese language he could have no knowledge of. When the recording was given to a professor in the Department of Oriental Studies at the University of California, he identified it as a recitation from a forbidden religion of Ancient China.[176]

Dr. Ian Stevenson, director of the Division of Perceptual Studies and head of the Department of Psychiatry at the University of Virginia, reported the documented case of a 37-year-old American woman who, under hypnosis, experienced a complete change of voice and personality into that of a male. She spoke fluently in the Swedish language—a language she did not speak or understand when in the normal state of consciousness.[177]

In 1931, a young English girl named Rosemary began to speak in an ancient Egyptian dialect under the influence of the personality of Telika-Ventiu who had lived in approximately 1400 BCE. In front of Egyptologist Howard Hume she wrote down 66 accurate phrases in the lost language of hieroglyphs and spoke in a tongue unheard outside academic circles for thousands of years as verified by Howard Hume. The accounts are in the files of the Society for Psychical Research.[178]

Pearl Curran, a medium from Saint Louis who was barely literate, began to write in astonishingly accurate Middle English. Under the guidance of a spirit entity, she produced sixty novels, plays and poems, including a 60,000 word epic poem.[179]

Proof the Mediums Are Speaking to Living People on the Other Side of Life

Mediums are clearly not doing psychic readings. In other words, they are not getting information from a vast storehouse of information about life and people in the greater reality. The people who converse are personalities, alive and fully functioning. They carry on dialogues.

Psychic readings contain very different information. As far as I know, 100 percent of the psychics say they're getting psychic information, not communication from the deceased, and 100 percent of the mediums say they're getting information from the living people on the other side, not simply psychic information. You would expect that some psychics would feel confusion or doubt about the source of their information, and some mediums would similarly express doubt about whether these are real people they're talking to. But neither the psychics nor the mediums have any doubt about their different sources of information.

Most importantly, relatives of the deceased attest to the fact that they have been speaking with their deceased loved ones. This statement was made by Professor James Hyslop, Columbia University, after speaking with his deceased relatives:

I have been talking with my (dead) father, my brother, my uncles. . . . Whatever supernormal powers we may be pleased to attribute to (the medium) Mrs. Piper's secondary personalities, it would be difficult to make me believe that these secondary personalities could have thus completely reconstituted the mental personality of my dead relatives.[180]

Cross Correspondences

More objective proof that the mediums are speaking to living people in the afterlife comes from the research called "cross correspondence" that has been carried out to ensure that the information mediums receive isn't simple psychic knowledge. In cross correspondence, a series of messages are given by someone in the afterlife to different mediums in different parts of the world. Individually, the messages are not meaningful. Together, however, they have a clear message. That means a single medium couldn't be receiving psychic information. Instead, the deceased has carefully planned to give the messages to a number of mediums. That requires a living person in the afterlife to plan and execute the communication.

The Myers Cross-Correspondence is the best known example of such a study.[181] Frederick W.H. Myers was a Cambridge Classics scholar and writer in the nineteenth century who was one of the founders of the Society for Psychical Research. He originated the concept of cross correspondence.

After Myers died in 1901, over a dozen mediums in different countries began receiving incomplete scripts through automatic writing that were all signed by Frederick Myers. The scripts were all about obscure classical subjects (that would be known to Myers, a Classics scholar at Cambridge). When all the scripts were assembled, like a jig-saw puzzle, they formed a complete message. Frederick W. H. Myers, living in the afterlife and communicating through the mediums, had planned and executed the writings so they proved no single medium was receiving psychic knowledge rather than communication from a deceased person.

Later, two other leaders of the Society for Psychical Research died: Henry Sidgwick and Edmund Gurney. Soon after each of their deaths, fragments of messages came to mediums around the world from them, and the Myers "study" was replicated successfully. Over the next thirty years, more than three thousand such scripts were transmitted to mediums around the world, some as long as 40 typed pages. They now fill 24 volumes of 12,000 pages. As investigators involved in the research died, they joined the study on the other side by communicating incomplete messages through a number of mediums around the world that formed complete wholes when brought together.[182]

Hundreds of other accounts of such cross correspondence are recorded in the *Proceedings of the Society for Psychical Research*.[183]

Proxy Sittings

Another proof that the contact in medium readings and séances is with the actual, living person on the next plane of life comes from "proxy sittings." In a proxy sitting, someone comes to the medium reading or séance for a reading for someone else, not for himself or herself. The proxy sitter knows only the name of the deceased and the name of the person wanting to have contact with the deceased. That decreases the likelihood that the medium is just doing a psychic reading of the person, without really receiving communication from the loved one speaking from the next plane of life.

The Reverend Charles Drayton Thomas, a Methodist minister, repeatedly acted as a proxy sitter investigating the mediumship of Gladys Osborne Leonard for the Society for Psychical Research. For example, from 1936 to 1937, Thomas went to four sittings with Leonard as a representative for a woman about whom he knew only her name, Emma Lewis, and that she wanted to contact her father, Frederick William Macaulay. With those two pieces of information, Leonard provided seventy items of information, which Thomas recorded and conveyed to Emma Lewis. She confirmed, beyond a doubt, that they came from her father because of the unique content only he would have known.[184]

In another example of such proxy sittings, Professor Eric R. Dodds, a Regius Professor of Greek at Oxford University and president of the Society for Psychical Research, supervised a series of proxy sittings with medium Nea Walker. He concluded, "The hypothesis of fraud, rational inference from disclosed facts, telepathy from the actual sitter, and co-incidence cannot either singly or in combination account for the results obtained."[185]

Near-Death Experiences Reveal
the Reality of the Afterlife

> The only word I seem to be able to use to talk about that
> place is beautiful. . . . As I stood there in the middle of
> this lush green field, I could see animals, flowers, and
> trees. . . . I saw children playing. God, it was beautiful.
>
> *– from Kenneth G's near-death experience* [186]

Today, medical science is able to revive people who are nearly dead, with little or no brain functioning. When they come back from the brink of death, many have remarkable accounts of feelings of calmness and peace, moving upwards through a tunnel, meeting deceased loved ones, encountering a being of light, experiencing a life review, and feeling a return to the body, often very reluctantly. These are near-death experiences (NDEs). The data indicating that the NDE occurs when the mind separates from the body were presented in Chapter 1. The information in this chapter focuses on the data showing that the NDE is evidence of the afterlife.

Dr. Fred Schoonmaker, a cardiologist from Denver, conducted a survey of over 2,000 patients who had suffered cardiac failure, many of whom reported other-worldly experiences. He suggests that up to 60 percent of those who experience a cardiac arrest will report an NDE. [187]

Those who have studied NDE accounts conclude that the phenomenon cannot be explained as a purely physical event. Cardiologist Dr. Michael Sabom at the Emory University School was skeptical about the NDE experience. With an associate, Sarah Kreutziger, he interviewed patients in his own hospital. The results were, "Having been on both sides of the argument, I now believe that the near-death experience is not simply the result of misfires within the dying brain, but that it is a spiritual encounter." [188]

Michael Schroeter-Kunhardt, MD in psychiatry, conducted an extensive study of near-death experiences. He concluded, "The large body of NDE data now accumulated point to genuine evidence for a non-physical reality and paranormal capacities of the human being." [189]

Dr. Sam Parnia, leader of a research team studying near-death experiences at London's Hammersmith Hospital, has come to this conclusion:

To be honest, I started off as a skeptic but having
weighed up all the evidence I now think that there is
something going on.

It's not possible to talk in terms of "life after death." In
scientific terms we can only say that there is now
evidence that consciousness may carry on after clinical
death. Our work will prove one way or the other
whether a form of consciousness carries on after the
body and brain have died.[190]

One of the most compelling pieces of evidence that the near-death
experience is real is that the people insist they experienced a real-life
event, not a hallucination or dream. They say they could tell the
difference between a real occurrence and a dream, and what they
experienced was as real to them as any waking event. NDE experiencers
who have also been in comas at some time say what happened during
their comas was quite different. The NDE was a real-life event; the
visions or hallucinations going into or coming out of a coma were clearly
hallucinations. As a result, they say emphatically that the NDE changed
their views of life and death.[191]

Experiencers sometimes learn information about deceased loved
ones they could not have known if they had not encountered them while
in the NDE. Dr. Bruce Greyson, formerly a professor of psychiatry at the
University of Connecticut, now Bonner-Lowry Professor of Personality
Studies in the Department of Psychiatric Medicine at the University of
Virginia in Charlottesville, described the following case at the Esalen
Center for Theory & Research Conference on Survival of Bodily Death,
February 11-16, 2000:

The author Maggie Callanan in her 1993 book, *Final
Gifts*, wrote about an elderly Chinese woman who had
an NDE in which she saw her deceased husband and her
sister. She was puzzled since her sister wasn't dead, or
so she thought. In actuality, her family had hid her
sister's recent death from her for fear of upsetting her
already fragile health.[192]

In another study, the researchers recorded the account of an NDE
case with information the patient had no knowledge of and didn't
understand until ten years later. During an NDE, a patient reported that
he saw his deceased grandmother. Standing next to her was a man he

didn't recognize who was looking at him full of love. More than ten years later, he learned that he had been born out of wedlock, fathered by a Jewish man during WWII. This man was deported and killed. When the patient was shown a photo of his biological father he recognized him as the man he had seen ten years before during his NDE.[193]

Purely Physiological Explanations for the NDE Accounts Have Been Shown to Be Insufficient to Account for Them.

People who insist the mind is in the brain and the afterlife doesn't exist have advanced a variety of physical explanations for the accounts given by near-death experiencers. However, all have been demonstrated to be implausible. The most prominent suggestions and the reasons they have been found to be invalid follow.

Why NDEs Could Not Be Caused by Medication

People who have near-death experiences report being hyper-alert, often remarking, "I saw clearer than I've ever seen." They remember in great detail things that happened around them and in adjacent rooms while their brains showed no activity. They report having conversations with deceased relatives and seeing scenes very clearly. The reports are of sensations and consciousness that are more lucid than normal, an effect opposite to that of a brain clouded by drugs.

Michael Sabom, a cardiologist on staff at Northside and Saint Joseph's Hospitals in Atlanta, Georgia, studied the experiences described in NDEs and concluded that they are quite different from hallucinations induced by drugs.[194]

Melvin Morse, M.D., associate professor of pediatrics at the University of Washington, came to the conclusion, after an extensive study of seriously ill children, that drugs were not related to NDEs:

> In the case of the suggestion that mind-altering medication causes the NDE, Melvin Morse has produced a study where a group of one hundred and twenty-one children were seriously ill, but had less than a five per cent chance of dying, and yet none had an NDE [because they had not been near death]. Of another thirty-seven children who had received many forms of mind-changing drugs, again, there were no NDEs. However, in another group of twelve children who had suffered a

cardiac arrest, eight of these recalled having an NDE. A considerable amount has been written by medical professionals that demonstrates that medication cannot be the cause of the NDE.[195]

Why NDEs Could Not Be from Loss of Oxygen to the Brain

For a short time, there was an explanation prominent among skeptics that the near-death experience was due to oxygen deprivation. That explanation was never given credence by anyone who knows anything about the brain's functions. When the brain doesn't receive sufficient oxygen, the condition is termed anoxia or hypoxia. Anoxia or hypoxia result from smoke or carbon monoxide inhalation, being in high altitudes with thin oxygen, strangulation, anesthetic accidents, poisoning, or dying. The result is that the victim is stuperous or comatose, with very poor or no brain function.

However, people experiencing NDEs describe their senses as being more acutely aware than they had ever been. They describe calm and confidence, not stupor. When they are revived, they have vivid memories of the experience, unlike people who suffer from oxygen deprivation who are unable to remember anything of the experience.

In addition, some who have NDEs are being administered oxygen at the time and thus are not suffering from anoxia. Dr. Fred Schoonmaker, a cardiologist from Denver, had by 1979 carried out investigations of over 2,000 patients who had suffered cardiac arrests, many of whom reported NDEs. His findings showed that NDEs occurred when there was no deprivation of oxygen. In fact, in a cardiac arrest, the patient is actually supplied with oxygen, and any anesthetic being used is stopped, meaning this cannot be the cause of the NDE in such cases.[196]

Why NDEs Could Not Be Due to a Dying Brain

There has been a suggestion that the NDE is a hallucination from a dying brain. However, that explanation is not viable. Dr. Ian Stevenson of the University of Virginia, and his colleagues, wrote in *The Lancet*[197] that if the physical brain were really necessary for all thought, one would expect the trauma of the dying brain to result in impaired cognition. However, in NDEs quite the opposite is true. The person is more aware than normal.

The researchers also noted these factors showing that the NDE could not be from a dying brain:

1. In the cases where brain disturbances were evident on the patients' EEG scans, NDEs were less common. [The brain was active but not functioning well, unlike the conditions during NDEs when brain functions stop.]

2. In delirium, the person tends to see events occurring at a distance, whereas, in NDEs, experiencers are close to many parts of what is experienced.

3. The effects of delirium brought on by trauma vary widely in content, but NDEs are remarkably consistent across virtually all experiencers regardless of age, nationality, religious background, and all other demographics.[198]

Marshall, Lazar, and Spellman wrote in the journal, *Brain*, that brain physiology is such that many parts of the brain must be coherent for lucid experiences to occur. A disorganized, dying brain couldn't produce the experiences described by near-death experiencers:

> Cerebral localisation studies have indicated that complex subjective experiences are mediated through the activation of a number of different cortical areas, rather than any single area of the brain. A globally disordered brain would not be expected to support lucid thought processes or the ability to "see," "hear," and remember details of the experience. Any acute alteration in cerebral physiology leads to confusion and impaired higher cerebral function.[199]

Dr. Peter Fenwick, a British neuropsychiatrist and fellow of the Royal Academy of Psychiatrists, explains that the NDE experience could not be the result of a dying brain because a dying brain has confusional and paranoid thinking:

> Cerebral damage, particularly hippocampal damage, is common after cardiac arrest; thus only confusional and paranoid thinking as is found in intensive care patients should occur. The paradox is that experiences reported by cardiac arrest patients [during NDEs] are not confusional. On the contrary, they indicate heightened awareness, attention, and memory at a time when consciousness and memory formation are not expected to be functioning.[200]

Michael Sabom, MD, a cardiologist in Atlanta, Georgia, monitored the brain waves of his patients using an electroencephalograph (EEG) and was able to show that some who had reported NDEs had been clinically dead, meaning they registered no electrical activity in their brains. A lack of EEG activity is accepted as constituting death in many places in the Western world, including America.[201] In other words, the NDE occurred after the brain had already passed the dying experience.

Why NDEs Could Not Be Created by the Other Physiological Problems Advanced as Possible Sources

Other physiological explanations have been advanced for NDEs. However, none are viable. Dr. Michael Sudduth, professor of philosophy at the University of Hartford, St. Michael's College, Calvin College, and San Francisco State University, explains why none of these are viable:

> NDE type experiences induced in these ways involve several qualities not present in putative NDE cases.
>
> 1. Release of endorphins relieves pain for a longer period of time than NDEs.
>
> 2. Temporal lobe seizures produce various illusions, hideous hallucinations, and feelings of despair. The overall negative experiences are not consistent with positive NDEs.
>
> 3. Brain Hypercarboa (high doses of carbon dioxide) tends to produce a sense of bodily detachment, perception of bright lights, revival of memories (much like NDEs). However, they also produce perceptions of geometric figures, animation of fantasized objects (e.g., musical notes floating by), a compulsion to solve mathematical puzzles, and horrifying images. The latter are not compatible with NDEs.
>
> 4. Brain Hypoxia (produced by deprivation of oxygen to the brain) tends to produce greater degrees of impairment of cognitive faculties, mental lethargy, and mental confusion. This seems inconsistent with the clarity of perception in NDEs.[202]

Psychological Explanations for the NDE Accounts Have Been Shown to Be Insufficient to Account for Them.

Some skeptics have suggested that the NDE experience results from psychological abnormalities: mental instability, psychiatric pathology, attempts to cope with the experience of dying, hallucinations, or religious or cultural expectations being fulfilled. These have been shown to be unsatisfactory explanations for NDEs.

Why NDEs Could Not Result from Mental Instability

To learn whether people who describe NDEs are less mentally stable than the general population, Gabbard and Twemlow administered a psychological test called the Profiles of Adaptation to Life (PAL) to NDE subjects. They found that the NDE subjects were actually significantly healthier than psychiatric inpatients or outpatients, and somewhat healthier than college students.[203] The authors didn't explore whether the NDE had anything to do with the greater mental health.

Melvin L. Morse, MD, formerly physician in pediatrics at Seattle Children's Hospital, summarizes the research and commentary about whether NDEs represent psychiatric pathology:

> There is little evidence or reason to believe that these experiences represent psychiatric pathology or dysfunction, according to German psychiatrist Michael Schroeter.[204] They can be easily distinguished from hallucinations of schizophrenia or organic brain dysfunction.[205,206] NDEs are predominantly positive and lack the paranoid ideation, distortions of reality, negative imagery, olfactory elements, and aggressive and hostile elements of drug-induced hallucinations or other transient psychoses.[207,208] They represent an acknowledgment of reality, whereas intensive care unit psychosis usually represents a denial of reality.[209] They occur to people in excellent mental health, who have a similar capacity for fantasy, as well as similar repressed anxieties as the typical population.[210] To explain NDEs as depersonalization or regression into the psychologic state before ego differentiation ignores the clinical experiences of the subjects, which are experienced with intact ego identity.[211]

Why NDEs Could Not Be a Defense Against
the Trauma of Feeling One is Dying

Another common explanation is that the NDE occurs because of depersonalization, meaning it is simply a self-defense mechanism as the person is confronted with non-existence. But this conflicts with the feeling of the enhanced self-identity that invariably occurs in an NDE. Furthermore, if the event is only a physical-brain reaction, it would have to be in a dream-like state where finer details are missing, but the NDE is marked by the absolute clarity.

Also, the traumatized patients often don't realize they are in a life-threatening situation and enter unconsciousness suddenly, without considering whether they're dying.

Why NDEs Could Not Be Hallucinations

Addressing the frequent suggestion that NDEs can be accounted for as hallucinations, Dr. Bruce Greyson, Bonner-Lowry Professor of Personality Studies in the Department of Psychiatric Medicine at the University of Virginia, stated three reasons they could not be hallucinations:

1. Incredibly accurate and verifiable information results from the NDE that would not result from a hallucination.

2. People on drugs who have NDEs actually see fewer deceased relatives when they travel out of body. This suggests that people who do see relatives are clear-minded, not hallucinating.

3. People see deceased relatives but not living relatives in their NDEs. In some cases, children see dead relatives whom they had never met or seen pictures of. That could not result from a hallucination.[212]

Michael Sabom, MD, and Kenneth Ring, MD, independently studied NDEs and determined that they cannot be accounted for as hallucinations:

> Turning to the question of whether the NDE was a hallucination (the most common skeptical argument), they [Sabom and Ring] both noted that a hallucination is accompanied by heightened brain activity. But their studies produced data showing that NDEs happened

more often when neuroophysiological activity was reduced, not increased. Sabom also found that NDEs were more likely when the person was unconscious for longer than 30 minutes; Ring found that the closer people were to physical death, the more extensive the NDE.[213]

Why NDEs Could Not Result from Religious Expectations

The phenomenon is not a result of some religious expectations. If it were fulfilling the experiencer's expectations of what dying is like, we would expect that only people who believed in and expected a near-death experience would have one, not suicides who anticipate annihilation, fundamentalists who expect only to see God, or agnostics and atheists who would not believe in an NDE phenomenon at all. In fact, that is not the case. Carol Zaleski wrote in her book, *Otherworld Journeys,* describing NDEs, "Suicide victims seeking annihilation, fundamentalists who expect to see God on the operating table, atheists, agnostics and carpe diem advocates find equal representation in the ranks of the near-death experiencers."[214]

Why NDEs Could Not Come from Cultural Expectations

Studies in widely differing geographic locations at different times in history within different cultures have produced remarkably similar findings, showing they're not dependent on expectations in any culture. Victor Zammit lists the variety of studies of NDEs in various countries:

> Margot Grey's study of NDEs in England[215]; Paola Giovetti's study in Italy[216]; Dorothy Counts' study in Melanesia[217]; Satwant Pasricha and Ian Stevenson's study in India.[218] More studies are coming out from different countries on a regular basis, and historical examples show that the experience has been remarkably consistent over time (see Plato's example of Er's NDE in *The Republic*).[219]

Suggestions that Descriptions of the Trauma Scene Come from Other People Are Not Viable.

People who have had NDE experiences often describe the trauma scene, conversations, and equipment in great detail, even though they were unconscious and their brains were not functioning when the events occurred. Skeptics suggest that the experiencers must have been told about the events by healthcare workers afterward or they overheard things during the event. These explanations are not viable, however, as the evidence below demonstrates.

Why NDE Reports of What Happened During Their Resuscitations Could Not Result from Descriptions of What Happened Given after the Trauma by Medical Personnel

Some suggest that NDE accounts come from descriptions given by medical personnel right after the event that the experiencers simply recount for the interviewers. However, Michael Sabom, MD, explains why that isn't a tenable explanation:

> Sabom found this unlikely for two reasons: doctors and nurses don't normally furnish resuscitation victims with descriptions of their resuscitation as detailed as those recounted by NDE survivors; and in several cases, NDE patients recounted the details to medical personnel shortly after being revived and before their own doctors could have told them anything.[220]

Why Accounts of What Happened During the Near-Death Experience Couldn't Be from Remarks Made During the Resuscitation Effort

Skeptics who don't believe that near-death experiences originate from the mind outside of the brain suggest that the person's accounts of what happened during the resuscitation effort while they were unconscious came from simply hearing bits and pieces of what went on as they floated in and out of consciousness. However, Michael Sabom, MD, examined six cases on record that included visual descriptions and discovered that the reports included visual details the patients could not have observed in their unconscious state, and some details were, in fact, outside of their visual fields, even in other rooms.[221]

This study by Sabom also eliminates the possibility that experiencers could be recalling descriptions of the procedure they happened to have read at some time during their lives. The accounts given by NDE experiencers include details relevant only to the specific event that caused the person to be near death.

Another Indication NDEs Are Real Experiences: Children Describe Their NDEs Matter of Factly.

A child under the age of two has no concept of death, and from two to five years, the child has a limited understanding that death is when the body stops moving. However, NDEs are described as occurring to infants and young children who have a different concept of death and have not yet experienced ego differentiation. Pediatric nephrologists from Massachusetts General describe a childhood NDE in which the child suffered a cardiac arrest from renal failure at 8 months of age and began to articulate her NDE at age 3. She described going into a tunnel and seeing a bright light.[222]

Melvin Morse, Associate Professor of Pediatrics, University of Washington School of Medicine, Seattle Children's Hospital, presents another report of an NDE involving a child described by Gabbard and Twemlow.[223]

> Todd was age 2 years 5 months when he bit into an electric cord from a vacuum cleaner. Medical records document that he was in ventricular asystole with no spontaneous respirations for approximately 25 minutes. After his resuscitation, he slowly recovered cortical and neurologic functions over the next 4 to 6 months. At age 33 months, he was playing in the living room when his mother asked him about biting into the cord. He stated: "I went into a room with a very nice man and sat with him. (The room) had a big bright light in the ceiling. The man asked if I wanted to stay or come back with you." He then looked up at his mother and stated: "I wanted to be back with you and come home." He then smiled and went back to playing with his toys. This occurred in 1972, before the publication of [Raymond] Moody's book [naming and describing near-death experiences].[224]

Conclusions about Near-Death Experiences

Carl Becker, Ph.D., professor of comparative thought at Kyoto University, a recognized scholar in bioethics, death, and dying, studied NDEs in Japan and the United States. He determined that NDEs are real, verifiable, objective events because of four characteristics:

- The experiencers have precognitive or clairvoyant knowledge they could not have known that is later verified to be true.

- The near-death experience is the same across cultures and religions.

- Experiencers all state that the NDE experience is different from their religious expectations, so they don't fit with what someone would imagine or fantasize.

- In some circumstances, a third party observes the visionary figures, indicating that they are not merely subjective hallucination.[225]

Peter Fenwick and Elizabeth Fenwick studied 300 near-death experiences.[226] Elizabeth Fenwick explained that her intention was to find a materialistic, non-spiritual, brain-based explanation for the phenomena. After the study, she concluded,

> While you may be able to find scientific reasons for bits of the Near-Death Experience, I can't find any explanation which covers the whole thing. You have to account for it as a package and skeptics . . . simply don't do that. None of the purely physical explanations will do. They [Skeptics] vastly underestimate the extent to which Near-Death Experiences are not just a set of random things happening, but a highly organized and detailed affair.[227]

Induced After-Death Communications Demonstrate the Reality of the Afterlife

In 1995, Dr. Allan Botkin, a psychotherapist at a Chicago VA hospital, was startled when one of his patients described having an after-death communication while sitting in his office. The procedure Dr. Botkin was using to help reduce the man's grief was eye movement desensitization and reprocessing (EMDR). In EMDR, the psychotherapist has the patient move his eyes back and forth rapidly as he would in REM (rapid eye movement) sleep. The patient then closes his eyes and usually experiences profound breakthroughs in understanding. No one is quite sure how it works, but it has been proven to be one of the most powerful therapeutic tools the discipline of psychology has ever discovered. To date, 30,000 psychotherapists have been trained to use it and it has been endorsed by many psychological and health organizations, including the American Psychological Association and United States Veterans Administration.

The Vietnam combat veteran Dr. Botkin was working with had been experiencing devastating grief for decades from intrusive memories of a young Vietnamese orphaned girl he had come to love as a daughter, but who died in his arms from a bullet wound. During a normal EMDR therapy session, Dr. Botkin's combat vet said that while his eyes were closed, he saw the girl he had come to love in Vietnam as a beautiful young woman, not the child he had known. That matches what the mediums describe happening when children die—they grow up in the afterlife. The combat vet's experience healed his grief instantly, and he was certain the girl was alive in the afterlife.

Over the next few weeks, 15 percent of Dr. Botkin's patients experienced similar after-death communications. He named the experience an induced after-death communication (IADC™).

In the next months, Dr. Botkin learned how to use the therapy method intentionally and had a 98 percent success rate with grieving patients at the VA hospital. In the next several years, he trained over 50 psychotherapists in how to administer the therapy, and thousands of patients have now had after-death communications. In virtually every case, they alleviate the experiencer's grief almost immediately. Most emphatically state that they have had a real communication with their deceased loved ones, and they view the afterlife differently, even those patients who started the therapy as atheists.

Dr. Botkin and I describe the therapy method and present 84 cases in the book, *Induced After-Death Communication: A New Therapy for Grief and Trauma.*[228] The Web site describing the therapy method and listing contact information for therapists who use the method is on the Web at http://www.induced-adc.com.

Remarkably, in many of the sessions, the patients learn things they aren't expecting to learn and couldn't know. In other words, the source must be the deceased. Five such cases from among the 84 in the book follow. In each case, the person experiencing the IADC™ was given EMDR eye movements and then sat quietly with eyes closed. The IADC™ unfolded naturally without prompting from Dr. Botkin. He didn't learn about it until the experiencer opened his or her eyes and described it to him.

In the first case, a reporter had a session with Dr. Botkin as part of her interview of him. She reported having an induced after-death communication with a deceased friend in which she saw him playing with a dog. The deceased friend told the reporter that the dog was his sister's dog. The reporter said to Dr. Botkin that she didn't know her friend's sister had a dog. After the session, she called her friend's sister and asked whether she had a dog. She said, "Yes, I had a dog, but he died." She then described the dog and it was the same breed and color as the one the reporter had seen in the after-death communication.

Dr. Botkin also explained that the reporter looked remarkably like an old friend he had known years ago. He kept having flashbacks to his old friend as he was talking to the reporter. During the induced after-death communication, the reporter told Dr. Botkin that her deceased friend said, "That was a long time ago Dr. Lil." She didn't understand what that meant. Dr. Botkin knew immediately, however. His patients called him "Dr. Al," so that is what the reporter was actually hearing, but she didn't hear correctly his nickname that was used by patients only. The deceased friend knew what Dr. Botkin was thinking about the reporter's resemblance to his old friend, "a long time ago."[229]

In another case, during the therapy session in Dr. Botkin's office, the patient's deceased father had a conversation with him during the IADC™. His father said to the patient, "Forgive me for being so cold when we adopted you." That made no sense to the patient because he remembered his father as always being warm and close to him. That evening, he asked his mother, "Was Dad cold to me when I was young?" His mother gasped and said, "Yes. How could you have remembered that? You were only a tiny baby." She explained that his father had been cold to him when he was adopted as an infant and wouldn't hold him, but after a few months, everything was fine and the patient grew up to have a very close relationship with his father. He had learned something in the after-death communication he couldn't have learned from any source other than his deceased father.[230]

In a third case, a blue-eyed Swede Vietnam combat vet asked Dr. Botkin to help him have an after-death communication with a black soldier in his platoon who had died in a firefight. There had been racial tension in his platoon, but in spite of that, he said he was experiencing some grief over the black soldier's death. Dr. Botkin agreed and induced an after-death communication. The patient closed his eyes and sat for a couple of minutes. Then he opened his eyes, shaking his head and looking perplexed. "The guy saw right through me," he said. He then explained to Dr. Botkin that he just wanted to find out the black soldier's name so he could put the name on paperwork that would get him additional money for the grief he would claim he was suffering. The VA gave money monthly to vets who could prove they had some trauma that was causing them grief. But when he asked the black soldier for his name while in the after-death communication, the soldier said, "Why do you want my name now? You didn't want it then." The vet muttered again, "The guy saw right through me" and never brought the issue up again in the therapy sessions.

The deceased black soldier said what Dr. Botkin's patient was not expecting, a statement that could only have come from another living person who was not willing to cooperate with the subterfuge.[231]

In a fourth case, during a normal EMDR session, not an IADC™ session, a combat vet wanted therapy to reduce his consuming anger with his commanding officer over sending him into combat without a rifle. Since he believed the commanding officer was alive after Vietnam, Dr. Botkin couldn't do an IADC™ to communicate with the commanding officer about the anger. So Dr. Botkin did a normal EMDR session to work on the anger.

But when the vet closed his eyes after the EMDR eye movements, he was surprised to see the commanding officer with whom he had conflict standing before him in his mind. The commanding officer said he was very sorry for what he had done, and he realized the problems that it caused for the vet in later life. "He looked like he really meant it," the vet said. "I believe him." With that forgiveness, the anger resolved itself for the first time in 31 years. But Dr. Botkin was surprised to see that a living person came through in an IADC™ session.

The next day, the vet checked the lists of everyone who died in Vietnam. He discovered that his commanding officer had died soon after the vet left Vietnam.[232]

The final example is a very touching story of a man named Jim who had an IADC™ with Dr. Botkin to resolve grief over the death of his friend, Simon. He had been very close to Simon and his wife, Darlene. In the after-death communication, Jim first saw Simon and talked with him. After he opened his eyes and told Dr. Botkin what had happened, he said, "I feel he's OK. But you know, I was really hoping to have a message for Darlene. She's not doing well at all." Dr. Botkin induced another after-death communication so Jim could ask Simon for a message for Darlene, but this time, Jim saw only two hands: a broad and masculine hand over a feminine hand. He felt they were Simon's and

Darlene's hands, but there was no message. Jim was disappointed that he didn't have something for Darlene, but elated at the contact with his friend.

After the session, Jim went to Darlene's home and told her he had a communication with Simon, but was disappointed that he didn't have a message to give her from Simon. He said he just saw Simon's hand on top of her hand. She began to cry, smiling and nodding her head. She said, "Last night I had a dream. It was so clear it didn't seem like a dream. I felt, really felt, Simon holding my hand. Jim, he did give you a message from him to me. He was saying that it really was him holding my hand last night." [233]

These experiences are connections with the living person who has never gone very far and is just not using a body any more. The IADCs™ occur when the psychotherapist helps the patient set aside anger, guilt, shame, and other negative emotions using the powerful EMDR therapy method. That leaves only the deep, underlying sadness. The psychotherapist then takes the person into that sadness, plumbing its depths until the person has experienced the most painful reaches of it. The person, most often in tears, then closes his eyes and remains open to whatever will happen.

When all negative emotions and the deep sadness are out of the way, what is left is the compassion and love that created the sadness, and that compassion and love drops the veil between the Earth plane and the afterlife; the after-death communication occurs. Then the loved one, who has always been alive, well, loving, and caring, is able to communicate. The results are rich, inspiring, loving reunions that heal grief.

Those we love and feel compassion for are never far from us. We just can't quiet the noise of the Earth plane to communicate with them. The IADC™ psychotherapy method does that.

The Universe Was Uniquely Made for Us

The universe in which our eternal selves exist was made uniquely for us. That would stand to reason. The universe is made up of three eternal elements: energy, matter, and us (our eternal selves). The energy and matter are the scenery in which we have experiences and learn lessons. Thus, we would expect that this combination of matter and energy would fit a human being's needs for survival and growth, both intellectually and spiritually. In fact, it does more than simply fit. It is so perfectly matched to our needs that even minor deviations from the carefully engineered design would have rendered life in the universe impossible. It is matched to us in ways that are far beyond chance.

The fact that the universe is so remarkably matched to us inspired Dr. Stephen Hawking, the renowned theoretical physicist, to coin the term "Anthropic Principle" for it. He wrote, "The odds against a universe like ours emerging out of something like the Big Bang are enormous. I think there are clearly religious implications whenever you start to discuss the origins of the universe. There must be religious overtones. But I think most scientists prefer to shy away from the religious side of it."[234]

The odds against the existence of a universe that has produced and sustained life like ours are immense. These are some of the remarkably precise conditions the universe has that, if any one fluctuated a small degree one way or the other, wouldn't allow humanity to live on Earth:

- If the strong force that acts on the quarks, neutrons, and protons of the atomic nucleus were just slightly *weaker*, the only element that would be stable would be hydrogen. No other elements could exist, and humankind couldn't live.

- If the strong force that holds the nucleus of atoms together were just a bit *stronger*, then the universe would be made up of atomic nuclei containing just two protons, so hydrogen would not exist to create water and the stars and galaxies would have evolved in ways that wouldn't support life.

- If gravity were just a little *stronger*, the average star would have only 10 to 12 times the mass of the sun and could exist for only a year, not enough time for humankind to live and grow.

- If gravity were just a little *weaker*, then matter would not have assembled into stars and galaxies, and the universe would be cold and empty.

- "Entropy" is the second law of thermodynamics. Things disintegrate—they fall apart over time. But that means our universe began with order and is gradually becoming less orderly. No one knows why there was order at the beginning and not chaos.

- At the "big bang," the initial rate of expansion would have had to have been chosen very precisely for the rate of expansion still to be so close to the critical rate needed to avoid re-collapse. This means that the initial state of the universe must have been very carefully chosen if the hot big bang model was correct right back to the beginning of time. It would be very difficult to explain why the universe should have begun in just this way, except as the act of a God who intended to create beings like us.[235]

The gravity pull of the Sun and Moon perfectly stabilize the Earth's tilt of the rotation axis that results in a stable climate. The moon's size is just right to cause ocean tides that mix nutrients from the land and oceans to make life possible. The Earth is just far enough from the Sun so water can stay liquid and temperatures can be such that human beings can live. The Earth is just the right size to have an atmosphere. [236]

The Earth is set up remarkably precisely to provide the water and oxygen the planet needs to support life. It has what amounts to an "oxygen machine," as explained by researchers in the journal *Nature*. Large amounts of oxygen are stored in a mineral called "majorite" deep within the earth. Some of the majorite is continually rising to the surface on convection currents. As it rises, pressure and temperature decrease and the oxygen is released. That gives the Earth oxygen, and may be responsible for some of the water so necessary for life. Then, the Earth's magnetic field is set precisely so it helps keep the water and oxygen-rich atmosphere from being blown away by solar winds.[237] It's a remarkable piece of engineering.

Another indication that the Earth has been set up specifically for us is that evolution doesn't explain the emergence of life from chemicals. The emergence of life by accident would have required that amino acids, the building blocks of life, be joined together in chains of hundreds of thousands of units to form proteins, and then proteins would have had to have combined into the single-celled creatures we call "life." But evolution works through mutations of cells, by accident, resulting in the fittest surviving and passing along their mutations as adaptations. So the cells would have had to have existed first to have such evolution, and they couldn't evolve by themselves without some intelligent design. Work in a laboratory to produce the amino acids required to sustain life has not been successful:

> When, in 1953, Stanley Miller, then a graduate student at
> The University of Chicago, produced a few amino acids
> through purely random reactions among chemicals
> found naturally throughout the universe, the scientific

community felt the problem of life's origin had been solved. Far from it. Subsequent experiments have failed to extend his results. Thermodynamics favors disorder over order. Attempting to get those amino acids to join into any sort of complex molecules has been one long study in failure. The emergence of the specialized complexity of life, even in its most simple forms, remains a bewildering mystery [to the Darwinian evolutionists].[238]

The same kinds of remarkable engineering are present in galaxies. For human beings to be able to live in a particular galaxy, it would have to have exactly the right mass, type, age, and allotment of heavy elements. Our Milky Way Galaxy has that fine tuning. [239]

The earth is also uniquely situated with distinct properties that allow conscious beings to discover how the universe works. That fact is explained by the authors of *The Privileged Planet: How Our Place in the Cosmos is Designed for Discovery*.[240] Our universe is set up not only to allow human beings to exist, but also to allow us to have maximum opportunities to make discoveries about it.

The authors explain that the moon is just the right size, is just the right distance from the Earth, and is moving in just the right orbit to cover the sun precisely so we can have perfect solar eclipses—the moon exactly covers the sun from where we're standing. As a result, we've made discoveries about the sun's corona and the warping of light by gravity that couldn't have been made without this incredible set of matched conditions.

We're also situated perfectly so we can observe and make discoveries about the universe. We have front-row seats. There's very little dust where we're located to absorb light from nearby stars and distant galaxies so we can see the remarkable images such as the Hubble image on the cover of this book. We're far enough from the center of the Milky Way Galaxy, and the galaxy disk is flat enough that it doesn't excessively obscure our view of the distant universe. We can see a wonderful diversity of nearby stars and other galaxy structures.

Look at the cover of this book. You'll see spirals and flattish circles and ovals among the stars; those are galaxies hundreds of millions of light years away, each containing up to 100 billion stars. Our position in our own galaxy allows us to see them. And because of where we're situated, we can see the unique cosmic microwave background radiation that led us to realize the fact the universe is expanding and finite in age.[241]

All of that is engineered with such precision that it would be impossible for it to occur by chance as a result of an explosive expansion 13.7 billion years ago. These precise placements are within a universe with vast expanses of space where the Sun, Earth, and Moon could have been formed anywhere by chance when the solar system was born 4.5 billion years ago. One analogy is that expecting to get our uniquely designed living environment out of an accidental explosive expansion in the universe is like expecting to get a dictionary out of an explosion in a printing shop.

The impossibility of all of these factors coming together accidentally to produce the scenery for our eternal selves has led an increasing number of scientists to suggest "intelligent design." They are quick to point out that this concept doesn't suggest a God, especially the God envisioned as a big old man in the sky. It simply means that some intelligent organization seems to be necessary for the universe to exist as it does to support human beings:

> The sudden appearance of the correct biocentric
> parameters "out of nothing" is essentially tantamount to
> a miracle because there is evidently no other way to
> account for this perfect life-giving format by random
> processes alone.[242]

Charles Townes, co-inventor of the laser and the Nobel Prize winner, wrote that the discoveries of physics "seem to reflect intelligence at work in natural law." Francis Collins, director of the Human Genome Research Institute, declared, "A lot of scientists really don't know what they are missing by not exploring their spiritual feelings." Michael Turner, astrophysicist at the University of Chicago Fermi Lab, wrote, "The precision is as if one could throw a dart across the entire universe and hit a bull's-eye one millimeter in diameter on the other side."[243]

The scenery has been created for us so the dramas that are our eternal lives can play out, and we can grow spiritually.

Your Eternal Self Defies Evolution and Entropy

Darwinian Evolution asserts that organisms evolve to become more sophisticated because they experience chance mutations that result in favorable adaptations. So, lungs developed because aquatic creatures were more likely to survive if they could get oxygen from the air during droughts. Sometime along the way, around 400 million years ago, the swim bladder of a fish opened to the air and enabled the fish to gulp air and gain oxygen through its membrane. That was a mistake in the fish's physiology that actually gave it an advantage over other fish that couldn't take in oxygen from the air during droughts. As a result, it and its descendents thrived.

This is the principle of "natural selection" described by Charles Darwin. Natural selection favors the fit, strong, clever, self-seeking, and ruthless. Those who are fit, strong, clever, self-seeking, and ruthless will be more likely to live and bear progeny, perpetuating the adaptations they experience that made them more fit.

However, the evolution in spirituality we are seeing actually takes people out of the physical realm so they're less able to compete in the world. They aren't fitter, stronger, cleverer, more self-seeking, and more ruthless. They are, in fact, willing to give up their own possessions, be transparent and honest, focus on others, and give without reservation. We would expect that Darwinian evolution would squash such weak creatures.

Large numbers of people are becoming increasingly compassionate and other-centered, even as society remains self-absorbed and materialistic. Spiritual growth, in other words, is not the result of a genetic mutation; it is a result of the fact that we are spiritual beings having a physical experience, and our true natures are overpowering physical realm instincts as we reduce their influence over us. Spirituality defies Darwinian evolution. It seems that the design of the universe is such that we are evolving toward spiritual maturity, not toward physical prowess that dominates through force and not toward intellectual self-centeredness that dominates through devious cleverness. We're evolving to have unconditional love.

Darwin would roll over in his grave if he were there; but he's not.

The Mystics and Sages Have Known About This Spiritual, Eternal Self for Millennia

The people most able to understand the inner self are those intent on understanding it with their minds. Scientists focused solely on matter and energy can't understand the self—it's beyond their reach because they aren't open to studying it.

So, we can look to the mystics and sages who have identified the eternal self for millennia. This quotation is from the Upanishads, part of the Hindu scriptures dating from around 600 BCE:

> The Self is one. Unmoving, it moves faster than the mind. The senses lag, but Self runs ahead. Unmoving, it outruns pursuit. Out of Self comes the breath that is the life of all things.
>
> Unmoving, it moves; is far away, yet near; within all, outside all. The Self is everywhere, without a body, without a shape, whole, pure, wise, all knowing, far shining, self-depending, all transcending; in the eternal procession assigning to every period its proper duty.[244]

Materialists dismiss the insights of the mystics as imprecise, unprovable ramblings. However, they miss the wisdom that is beyond the physical realm. The mystics have told us we're eternal beings and not to be so preoccupied with acquiring and consuming in this temporary, physical period of our lives. But humankind hasn't listened.

Then What Are We?

We're eternal beings having an Earthly episode in our eternal life. The eternal self exists apart from energy and matter. It's outside of the body and outside of the Earth, meaning consciousness (the mind) is elemental. It exists independent of matter and energy.

That explains how we can know things before they happen. It explains how I'm able to sit in my office and see things on a stranger's table hundreds of miles away. And why Yeshua ben Yosef and other luminaries were so certain that death is only a transition into another part of our eternal existence. We have an immense amount of knowledge that we are eternal spirits and no rebuttal of it!

Knowing that to be true is important to your spiritual growth. If you believe you are limited in time and space to this short lifetime and you are the bag of flesh you see in a mirror, then you will be less interested in loving others, being a servant to others, listening to the Higher Power, feeling your inner self has worth, and conserving nature. You'll try to get all you can get because life is short and you have only one time around. Knowing that you are an eternal being having an Earth episode of your eternal existence is critical to spiritual growth. And if everyone has that knowledge, then society as a whole will grow spiritually as well.

How Long Will the Spiritual You Live?

Forever. We know that, not just because those spiritual teachers who have their ear to the universe have told us that; we know it because of what we know about science and the mind. Matter and energy are eternal, and the mind is outside of matter and energy; it continues unaffected when matter and energy change form, so regardless of what happens to the universe, our minds will remain whole and alive, watching the show.

Unlike matter and energy, the mind doesn't disintegrate; it doesn't decay—it always grows and matures. Whatever might happen to the physical universe, our eternal selves will continue, happily and contentedly, looking forward to the wonderful eternal future.

Then even if there were a big crunch in which the universe collapsed into itself, or a big chill when the universe ran out of heat, our minds, which are one with the Higher Power, would not be affected. Every sentient being in the universe would just start evolving on another plane in another universe. Like matter and energy, our minds are eternal, and wouldn't be squashed in the big crunch or frozen in a big chill.

Those in the afterlife tell us that there are millions of different planes and spheres where people are living and growing at different levels. Some are so advanced in their spiritual growth that we could never understand them. We could understand as much of them as a bullfrog could understand about quantum mechanics. We aren't in the same plane of existence. But becoming that advanced is in our spiritual futures. There's no rush; we have an eternity to get there.

What are you? You are an eternal self having a physical period of your eternal life.

You can learn more at http://youreternalself.com/chapter2.htm.

3

What Is Your Relationship to Other People?

"Relationship" is a good word to include in the title of this chapter because it implies some family connection such as brother or sister. In fact, the luminaries and members of many religions use "brother" and "sister" in referring to each other. We are eternal beings having a physical experience together, with the closeness family members share. We know we're of the same family because our minds are intimately connected, even though we're in separate bodies on the physical plane of existence; our minds are always joined. This chapter explains the evidence we have today that our minds are one.

Minds are Linked Outside of the Brain

You would think that since the mind is outside of the brain, someone should spot it traveling down the road or pick it up on Channel 3. Actually, what we need in order to know whether the mind is outside of the brain is for one person's mind to be able to communicate with another's without speaking, signaling, or even being in the same room, building, or country.

That's exactly what happens. A large number of studies have now shown that minds are linked and we can pick up thoughts from someone else simply by intending to know those thoughts, even over great distances. That means that someone can know instantly what someone else is thinking or experiencing several hundred miles away, even though the brain is still encased in a rigid cranium and the sensory organs leading into it aren't involved in the knowing.

Hundreds of Experiments Have Proven that Our Minds Are Linked.

The most famous experiments showing that telepathy links people's minds have been done successfully thousands of times. They are called the "ganzfeld" experiments. A receiver relaxes quietly in a comfortable chair with half ping-pong balls over each eye to eliminate visual stimuli. Earphones are placed over the receiver's ears with white noise playing through them. The receivers, in other words, have outside stimuli and distractions blocked.

A sender is in another room isolated from the receiver. The sender randomly selects an image (painting, drawing, movie clip, film strip, or cartoon), looks at it, and attempts to send a mental picture of it to the receiver relaxing in the other room. The receiver speaks about any images or thought processes that come to her during the time period. What the receiver says is recorded by an experimenter.

Afterwards, the receiver is shown a set of four pictures and is asked to select which seems to be the image the sender was looking at. If the receiver picks the right picture, that is a hit. In some versions of the ganzfeld experiments, the receiver doesn't pick a picture. Instead, the descriptions the receiver speaks are sent to independent judges who decide whether the receiver was describing the image the sender was looking at.

Since there are normally four images, guessing (chance) would result in 25 percent correct on average. In the thirty years since the first test, this experiment has been performed in over 3,100 sessions, in dozens of laboratories. The findings have been that the receivers usually choose, on average, 32 percent to 34 percent of the pictures the senders are looking at. That's quite a large percentage when chance guesses would result in only 25 percent hits. The odds against the 32 percent success rate happening by chance are 1,000,000,000,000 (a trillion) to one.[1]

Another analysis of 28 studies performed by 10 researchers, done by Charles Honorton, director of the Division of Parapsychology and Psychophysics at Maimonides Medical Center in New York, showed the same percentage of hits. His analysis showed that the odds against the receivers of the telepathy guessing what the senders were looking at were ten billion to one.[2]

Honorton then improved on the method with Marilyn Schlitz, Ph.D., vice president for research and education at the Institute of Noetic Sciences and Senior Scientist at the Complementary Medicine Research Institute at the California Pacific Medical Center. Honorton and Schlitz conducted ganzfeld experiments using a computer to select the images the sender saw, eliminating all possibility that another human being could be involved in the telepathy. These experiments were called "autoganzfeld" experiments.

Eighty still pictures and eighty short audio and video segments were used as the targets. Senders viewed one chosen at random by the computer, with no human intervention in the selection. The receivers were placed into steel-walled, sound-proofed, electromagnetically shielded rooms to isolate them from any influence, even electromagnetic signals. In addition to the psychologists involved, two magicians oversaw the study: Ford Kross, an officer of the Psychic Entertainers Association, and Cornell University psychologist Daryl Bem, a professional mentalist.

These were the results:

> All together, 100 men and 140 women participated as
> receivers in 354 sessions during the six-year
> autoganzfeld research program. The participants
> ranged in age from seventeen to seventy-four; and eight
> different experimenters, including Honorton, conducted
> the studies. The program included three preliminary
> and eight formal studies. Five of the formal studies

employed only "novices"—participants who served as the receivers in just one session each. The remaining three formal studies used experienced participants.

The bottom line for the eleven series, consisting of a total of 354 sessions, was 122 direct hits, for a 34 percent hit rate. This compares favorably with the 1985 meta-analysis hit rate of 37 percent. Honorton's autoganzfeld results overall produced odds against chance of forty-five thousand to one.[3]

In one autoganzfeld experiment, the target image was that of a fire-eater. These were the subject's responses:

I find flames again. . . The fire takes on a very menacing meaning. . . . an image of a volcano with molten lava inside . . . Molten lava running down the side of the volcano. . . . Suddenly I was biting my lip, as though lips had something to do with the imagery. . . . The lips I see are bright red, reminding me of the flame imagery earlier.

The subject mentioned the words fire or flame a remarkable 29 times.[4]

The ganzfeld studies have been replicated by a number of scientists with the same results, showing that people are able to receive the thoughts of another person. These are some of the professionals who replicated the results:

- Dr. Kathy Dalton, Department of Psychology, University of Edinburgh
- Dr. Robin Taylor, post-doctoral research fellow, University of Edinburgh
- Dr. Dick Bierman, Department of Psychology, University of Amsterdam
- Dr. Daryl Bem, Department of Psychology, Cornell University
- Dr. Richard Broughton, Rhine Research Center
- Dr. Adrian Parker, the University of Gothenburg, Sweden
- Dr. Rens Wezelman, Institute for Parapsychology, Utrecht, the Netherlands[5]

Some people are better able to link with another person's mind than others. Honorton and Schlitz did a study with 20 music, drama, and dance students from the Juilliard School in New York City. It is generally known that creative people are more attuned to the minds of others and to knowledge from psychic sources. Overall, these students acting as receivers achieved a hit rate of 50 percent, one of the highest hit rates ever reported for a single sample in a ganzfeld study. The musicians were particularly adept: 75 percent successful identifications of the targets, where 25 percent would be by chance.[6]

Dr. Schlitz described one of the sessions in which she was the sender (watching a video) and a Juilliard student was the receiver, sensory deprived by being shielded in a Faraday cage in another room without being able to hear or see anything. The student had half ping-pong balls over his eyes so his vision gradually turned to black blankness because of sensory deprivation. He had earphones on with white noise blocking out any external sounds. The student was instructed to simply describe impressions of what he "saw" or experienced in his mind, without focusing on anything or trying to imagine anything.

This is Dr. Schlitz' description. The sound from the receiver's room was transmitted to the sender's room so she could hear the receiver's reactions, but no sound could come into the receiver's room.

> One of the Juilliard School students, Dustin, was the receiver. I was the sender. I was looking at a film clip from the film, *Altered States*. Dustin was sitting in a soundproof, electromagnetically shielded room, a Faraday cage. I was in an acoustically shielded room some distance away, so it was not possible to have any sensory exchange between us. I had a one-way feed of sound from his room so I could hear him, but he couldn't hear me at all. As I was watching the film clip of the hell scene, I heard Dustin saying "Red, red, everything's red." At the same time, the whole scene I was watching was tinted red because it was the descent into hell. And then he said, "I see crucifixes, a corona sun," just like the scene I was seeing. And then, to my amazement, he said, "I see this giant lizard opening and closing its mouth." At exactly that moment, I was watching a giant lizard on the screen in front of me opening and closing its mouth.[7]

In the interview, Dr. Schlitz also described a female student's ganzfeld session in the same study:

> She described a hot air balloon, yellow colors, a wizard, a dog, a black female night-club performer, and the cityscape of New York. She also said other things that weren't correct. As it turned out, the video clip was from The Wiz and it was the scene where they're walking across the Brooklyn Bridge out of New York. The scene had the cityscape of New York behind them and it was all yellow because they were on the yellow-brick road. In the scene was Diana Ross as Dorothy, the scarecrow, the lion, and the dog. And over the city, there was a hot-air balloon.[8]

Studies of Telepathy between Subjects Have Demonstrated Repeatedly that People's Minds Are Linked.

Extensive experiments have been carried out at the Rhine Research Centre to determine whether people can communicate telepathically. In their book, *Extra-Sensory Perception After Sixty Years,*[9] the researchers reported that by 1940, 33 experiments had been done to see if "receivers" could get telepathy messages from "senders." The studies involved almost a million trials, with a variety of different setups to make sure the effects occurred under different conditions. They had the senders and receivers at great distances from each other for some studies, and in others had the receivers describe the image the sender would see before the computer even selected it to show to the sender. Twenty-seven of the 33 studies produced statistically significant results showing that the senders' and receivers' minds were linked.

Other Experiments Measuring Involuntary Responses Show that People's Minds Are Linked.

Other experiments eliminated the need for the receiver to try to identify images a sender was looking at. Instead, the studies measured the receiver's brain waves as the sender was being subjected to periodic light flashes.

This is the description of a study by Russell Targ, physicist at the Stanford Research Institute, and Harold Puthoff, a physicist who was director of the CIA/DIA-funded SRI International research agency:

The receiver was placed in a sealed, opaque and electrically shielded chamber, while the sender was in another room where he or she was subjected to bright flashes of light at regular intervals.

Electroencephalograph (EEG) machines registered the brain-wave patterns of both. As expected, the sender exhibited the rhythmic brain waves that normally accompany exposure to bright flashes of light. But, after a brief interval the receiver also began to produce the same patterns, although he or she was not exposed to the flashes and was not receiving sense-perceivable signals from the sender.[10]

Jacobo Grinberg-Zylverbaum, at the National University of Mexico, wanted to find out whether two people could link their minds just by intending to do so. He put pairs of subjects together inside self-contained box-like enclosures and asked them to meditate together for 20 minutes. The enclosures, called "Faraday cages," are tightly sealed, soundproof, and electro-magnetic radiation-proof. In other words, no signal and no sound could get in or out of the enclosures.

Then he placed the subjects in separate Faraday cages and connected each to EEG machines to measure their brain-wave patterns. He knew that if the brain wave patterns changed in the same way for both, at the same time, the two would be connecting through their minds, even though they couldn't possibly have any sensory input from each other.

One was the "sender" and the other the "receiver." The sender was subjected to flashes of light, sounds, or intense but not painful electric shocks to the index and ring fingers of the right hand. The sudden stimuli occurred at random intervals and all involved (sender, receiver, and experimenter) had no idea when they would happen. The receiver stayed relaxed, with his or her eyes closed focusing on feeling the "presence" of the sender without knowing anything about the sender's being stimulated. One hundred stimuli were applied to the senders in each pair of subjects. The EEGs of both subjects were taken continually, with times for all the records so they could be compared.

After the test, they compared the brain wave patterns, second by second, for the sender and receiver. When nothing was going on with the sender, the brain wave patterns of the two subjects were both random, not showing any correspondence with each other. But, the moment the sender was subjected to flashes of light, sounds, or intense

but not painful electric shocks to the fingers, the receiver's brain waves
showed a reaction in around 25 percent of the cases.[11]

He performed more than fifty experiments over five years with the
same results.

Very interestingly, when the EEG electrodes were attached to a
young couple who were deeply in love, the brain wave patterns showed
them to be closely synchronized constantly, throughout the experiment,
even when there were no stimuli. Their minds were linked continually.
The couple also reported that they had a sense of "a deep oneness" with
one another in their lives. Their intuition fits with the data.

As further proof that the subjects' minds were linked, he found that
when a receiver showed reactions to the sender's shocks in one
experiment, the receiver usually showed them in other types of
experiments with that sender as well.[12]

The same links between minds were found by Fred H. Thaheld, a
physicist from Folsom, California, who studied whether people's minds
communicate without being in the same room or talking. He put two
people into two separate chambers shielded from electromagnetic
energy in Faraday cages so there was no way for them to see each other,
communicate, or even exchange energy. Both were hooked up to EEG
machines to record their brain wave patterns. When one person was
shown a rapidly alternating pattern (called a visual pattern-reversal
stimulus), that person's EEG responded showing the brain was receiving
the stimulation with a particular pattern of brain waves. At the same
time, the brain of the person in the other Faraday cage responded with
similar brain waves, even though the second person saw nothing.[13]

Charles Tart, Ph.D., instructor in psychiatry in the School of
Medicine of the University of Virginia and professor of psychology at the
University of California at Davis, had two subjects at a time meet and
agree they intended to maintain mind contact when they were separated.
He then had them separated a long distance so they couldn't see or
communicate with each other. To evaluate whether they were
communicating, he set up the experiment to measure the receiver's body
stress when the sender was put under stress. When people are stressed,
they sweat more. When the person has more sweat on the skin,
electricity passes over it more quickly, so researchers can tell in an
instant whether someone is sweating more by measuring whether a tiny
current passes between the electrodes on the skin at different speeds. It
shows when a person's stress level has suddenly increased. That's why
these tests are used as lie detectors. Lying puts a person under stress;

telling the truth leaves the person calmer. Two technical terms for the method are "skin resistance response" (SSRs) and "galvanic skin resistance" (GSR).

Tart put electrodes on each of the subjects, attached to two fingers, to measure skin resistance to find out if there were any changes in stress. In addition, he monitored blood volume and heart rate. The common name for this more complete test is a "polygraph test." Pens attached to arms swing over a paper that rolls across a surface and the times the movement occurred are recorded on the paper. The resulting pen marks show changes in skin resistance (sweating), blood volume, and heart rate.

Tart then gave mild electric shocks to one subject, the sender. The result was that the receiver's skin resistance response, blood volume, and heart rate reacted each time the sender was shocked. The receiver wasn't consciously aware of these physical changes he or she was experiencing.[14]

The studies are strong support for the assertion that people's minds are one. The separation we see in bodies doesn't seem to be there in our minds.

People Influence Each Other Using Their Minds.

In another set of experiments, people were able to influence other people's minds and physiology by focusing on them, even when they were separated from one another by great distances. These experiments have been replicated several times with the same results: Braud & Schlitz, 1983[15]; Braud & Schlitz, 1989[16]; Schlitz & Braud, 1985.[17]

In these studies, one person (the receiver) sat in a comfortable room with electrodes attached to two fingers to measure tension or relaxation. A computer did the measurements so there was no person involved. In a separate, distant room, another person (the influencer) also had electrodes attached to two fingers to see when that person was under stress. Records were produced second by second showing how each person's body was reacting.

The influencer attempted to either make the receiver feel calm or agitated during ten 30-second periods. The times and whether the influence was calm or agitated were chosen at random so the receivers couldn't know when the influencers were trained on them and couldn't know the type of influence being applied.

During calming attempts, the influencer relaxed, calmed himself or herself, and gently thought of wishing the subject would become calm, while visualizing the receiver being in a relaxing, calming setting. During agitation attempts, the influencers tensed their bodies and wished for the receiver to become more active, while visualizing the receiver in energizing or arousing situations.

During the time between the influencing attempts, the influencers worked at keeping their minds off of the receivers and the experiment, thinking about unrelated things. In other designs, the influencers just closed their eyes and visualized the entire experiment being successful, without focusing on a calming or agitating scene. Both strategies to shut down the influence turned out to work, based on the skin resistance measurements.

The researchers performed 15 of these experiments, with the number of pairs of influencers and receivers in each experiment ranging from 10 to 40. In all, there were 323 sessions with 271 different subjects, 62 influencers, and 4 experimenters. The experiments showed that in 57 percent of the individual sessions, receivers were measurably affected by the influencers' thoughts.

They replicated the study with 32 new subjects and had similar results.[18] The researchers concluded that ". . . an individual is indeed able to directly, remotely, and mentally influence the physiological activity of another person through means other than the usual sensorimotor channels."[19]

In a similar set of studies, Engineer Douglas Dean at the Newark College of Engineering, psychologist Jean Barry, Ph.D., in France, and psychologist Erlendur Haraldsson, Ph.D., at the University of Utrecht, all observed significant changes in receivers' finger blood volume when a sender, located thousands of miles away, directed emotional thoughts toward them. [20]

Healers' Intentions to Link with a Receiver of the Healing Register in the Receiver's Body Instantly.

Healers have been known to have a positive effect on people who are ill, both when in the same room and from great distances. The intentions of the healers to connect with those who are the focus of the healing (receivers) were studied by measuring whether the receivers had changes in MRIs of their brains at the moments the healers focused on them. Jean Achterberg, Ph.D., professor of psychology at Southwestern

Medical School and the Saybrook Institute, studied 11 pairs of healers and receivers of the healing intentions. Before beginning the MRIs of the receivers' brains, each healer was asked to try to connect with the receiver in any ways they used in their own healing traditions: sending energy, prayer, having good intentions, or thinking of the receiver and wishing the highest good for him or her.

The receiver was in the MRI machine and completely isolated from the healers and the experimenters. The healers were asked to send their prayers or thoughts for two minutes at irregular times determined by tosses of a coin. The study is considered "blind" because the receivers in the MRI did not know when the distant intentions were being sent.

The results of the study were highly significant. MRI scans of the brains of 9 of the 11 receivers showed major significant changes in brain function each moment the healers began praying or thinking about them, even though they did not know when they were receiving the attention. Their brains, according to Dr. Achterberg, "lit up like Christmas trees."[21]

Measures of Brain Waves Show People in the Same Room Synchronize Their Brain Waves.

People commonly describe a feeling of a group unity among people assembled for a meeting, discussion group, or support group. That phenomenon was studied by Dr. Nitamo Montecucco, professor at the University of Milan Centro di Medicina Olistica e Psicosomatica. His research with up to twelve subjects in a room showed a synchronization of the brain waves of the entire group.[22]

Experiments Show that Groups of Meditators 200 Kilometers Apart Can Synchronize Brain Waves.

In another study by Dr. Nitamo Montecucco, on May 20, 2007, eight subjects meditated in Tuscany and eight subjects meditated in Milan, 200 kilometers away, focusing on linking their minds. EEG measurements of the two groups were taken using computerized instruments synchronized up to a hundredth of a second using a global positioning system. The results showed that their brain waves displayed synchronization at levels far beyond chance.[23]

Dream ESP Experiments Show Minds Are Linked.

Another demonstration that people's minds are linked has come from studies of dreams. It has been widely known that someone may have a dream and the next day find out a family member or friend was involved in the very activity about which they dreamed. This phenomenon was studied by Stanley Krippner, professor of psychology at Saybrook Graduate School, fellow in three American Psychological Association divisions, president of two divisions, director of the Kent State University Child Study Center, and director of the Maimonides Medical Center Research Laboratory. Krippner and his colleagues at the Dream Laboratory of Maimondes Hospital in New York City had volunteers spend the night at the laboratory to study their dreams. They were the receivers, who were to sleep and see whether they dreamed of an image a sender was looking at.

When they arrived at the Center for the study, each receiver met a sender and the experimenters explained the procedure to them so both the sender and receiver knew they would be trying to merge their minds during the receiver's dream state that night. The receiver was led to a room with a bed, where electrodes were attached to the receiver's head to monitor brain waves and eye movements. The receiver was then left alone in the room to sleep.

After the receiver was situated, one of the experimenters threw dice that, in combination with a random number table, gave a number that corresponded to a sealed envelope containing an art print. This envelope was given to the sender, who went into a private room in another part of the hospital, distant from the receiver's room. When the sender arrived at the private room, he or she opened the envelope and spent the night concentrating on the print.

The experimenters watched a monitor connected to the receiver's electrodes to see when the receiver was in a dream state, called an REM or "rapid-eye-movement" state. When a REM state ended, the experimenters woke the receiver by intercom and the receiver was asked to describe any dream he or she might have had before awakening. The experimenters recorded the comments and the receiver was permitted to go back to sleep. The next morning, the receiver was interviewed and asked to describe the remembered dreams again. The interview was conducted double blind—neither the receiver nor the experimenters knew which art print had been selected the night before.

A series of these experiments was conducted between 1964 and 1969, producing 62 nights of data for analysis. The result was that the receiver's descriptions showed significant correlations with the art print the senders were focusing on.[24]

These experiments provided yet another verified indication that people's minds are linked outside of the brain.

People Share Induced After-Death Communications.

Dr. Allan Botkin was a psychotherapist at a Chicago Veterans Hospital when he discovered that he could induce an after-death communication in patients while they were seated in his office. He used a protocol called EMDR in which the patient is guided in moving his or her eyes back and forth, as people do in REM sleep, the dreaming state of sleep. At the VA hospital, 98 percent of patients with whom he performed the procedure had some form of after-death communication with the person for whom they grieved. Some involved entire conversations with the deceased. Since then, he and over 50 colleagues have induced thousands of these communications, called induced after-death communications (IADCs™).

One remarkable phenomenon occurred during some of the sessions demonstrating that people's minds are linked.[25] In the first session in which this occurred, an observing psychologist learning the procedure was in the room with Dr. Botkin and the patient. While Dr. Botkin induced the after-death communication with the patient, the observing psychologist closed his eyes and performed the eye movements on himself to relax. Images appeared in the psychologist's mind: a vivid scene of a swampy area with cattails, a pond, and a willow tree. He felt as though he were lying on the grass with the pond at eye level. It made no sense to him so he simply opened his eyes and continued to observe Dr. Botkin and the patient. The patient had not yet begun speaking, so the psychologist had no knowledge of what the patient was experiencing during the IADC™.

When the patient opened his eyes after experiencing an IADC™, he said he saw the swamp on his deceased uncle's farm. He felt like he was lying in the grass looking at the swamp. The psychologist in training was surprised at this coincidence and asked, "Did you see cattails?" The patient said, "Yes," not expecting that to be an unusual statement since he had said it was a swamp. The psychologist then said, "Did you see a pond and a willow tree?" The patient was clearly surprised. "Yes," he said. "How did you know that?" The observing psychologist explained what he too had just seen.

Dr. Botkin and the observing psychologist were very intrigued by this phenomenon, so they experimented with eight other patients who agreed to participate. This time, the observing psychologist wrote down everything he experienced before the patients reported what happened during their IADCs™. In every instance, the psychologist's accounts matched the patients' IADCs™ with great accuracy.

Another psychologist who heard Dr. Botkin's explanation wanted to replicate the effect by seeing whether she could share the after-death communication with a patient herself. In a session with a combat veteran, after she finished the IADC™ eye-movement protocol and the patient closed his eyes, she performed the protocol on herself and closed her eyes. She experienced very vivid scenes of a soldier in a peaceful, green valley coming toward her. He was saying, "It's all right. It wasn't your fault." She opened her eyes, and when the patient opened his eyes, he explained that he saw the soldier he had been grieving about and the soldier said to him that it wasn't his fault. The psychologist was stunned.

She asked the patient to describe what he saw, and he said "It was a beautiful lush, green place with slight rises on either side like a valley." That was the scene the psychologist saw.

Another psychologist tried to replicate the experience with a forty-year-old mother of two whose husband had died. After the IADC™ protocol, the patient closed her eyes and the psychologist performed the protocol on himself, then closed his eyes. He saw a clear image of a man in a bright white shirt, looking young and healthy, holding his hand over his heart. After the patient opened her eyes, she said she had a visual image of her husband wearing a very bright white shirt. She said he looked younger and completely healthy. He was holding his hand over his heart.

These experiences, reported by three psychotherapists across 11 patients are going to be studied further. However, the most obvious conclusion is that it is possible for a psychotherapist to share the mental event of a patient who is silent with his or her eyes closed. They link minds.

Subjects Mentally Experienced the Same Fantasy Reality.

Charles Tart, MD, instructor in psychiatry in the School of Medicine of the University of Virginia and professor of psychology at the University of California at Davis, had two graduate students at the University of California, Anne and Bill, mutually hypnotize each other. He had Anne hypnotize Bill and after he was hypnotized, he had Bill hypnotize Anne. In this state, Anne and Bill experienced the same fantasy images, without attempting to create the fantasy. This is the account of what they said immediately after they had the experience with their eyes closed:

> When they opened their eyes they reported that everything seemed grey. Then the greyness was replaced by the vision of a beach whose sand glowed like diamonds, whose rocks were crystals pulsating with a beautiful internal light, and whose waves were great bubbles of unearthly beauty. . . .

> Tart quickly realized that Bill and Anne were actually experiencing the *same* "hallucinated" reality. They found themselves together in this Paradise, walking hand in hand, or swimming together in the marvelous sea, exploring their new world. . . . In their shared reality they were talking to each other . . .

> In session after session, the two constructed and shared various realities, all involving all five senses, and all as real as the world in which they left Tart behind. They discussed details of their shared experiences for which there was no verbal hypnotic stimulus. They felt that they must actually have been in the places they experienced together.[26]

Students Spontaneously Imagined the Same Images without Communicating About Them.

Raymond Moody, M.D., Ph.D., professor of psychology and chair in Consciousness Studies at the University of Nevada, taught courses in perception and consciousness. As part of the courses, he invited students in groups to do "gazing" experiments in which they stared into mirrors with the lights dimmed. After a while, many began to project into the unclear, darkened mirror images from their subconscious, much as one would do in a Rorschach ink blot test. At times, they saw personal memories that had been buried by the conscious mind. At other times, what they saw startled them because they perceived things that should have been impossible to find out from simply staring into a mirror.

Dr. Moody reports in his book, *Reunions: Visionary Encounters with Departed Loved Ones,*[27] what happened on more than one occasion demonstrating that the students' minds were linked:

> In one class seven students described the same vision from different parts of the room. Why seven out of thirty people saw a man in a turban I can't begin to answer. Another time, two students at different tables saw a ballet dancer in their speculum [mirror]. Another time, a man saw the vision of an inflamed tooth. When he told the class what he had seen, the woman next to him gasped and said that she was having an infected tooth pulled in the morning. [28]

In none of these cases, Dr. Moody explained, was there any prompting or discussion beforehand that would have led to these images.

People Know When Someone Is Staring at Them.

A significant number of researchers have completed studies showing that people really do have a feeling when someone is looking at them. Between 68 and 94 percent of the population report having experienced the sense of being stared at.[29]

Rupert Sheldrake, a British biologist well known for his research on the mind, studied the sense of being stared at. In a series of trials, he had "looker" look or not look at subjects in a random sequence determined by tossing a coin. In each trial, the people being looked at were asked to guess whether or not during this trial they were being looked at. The results showed they were correct on average 56.9 percent of the time. We would expect 50 percent correct by chance. This positive effect was highly significant statistically, with the odds of it being by chance of one in 3 million. In one school in Germany in which students known to be sensitive to such impressions were tested repeatedly, 71.2 percent of the guesses were correct, and two of the students were right about 90 percent of the time. Sheldrake duplicated the study in more than 15,000 trials involving more than 700 subjects with the same results.[30]

In an effort to eliminate any possibility that the person being stared at might receive cues about when the looker was looking at them, Richard Wiseman, professor of public understanding of psychology at the University of Hertfordshire, a practicing magician, and Marilyn Schlitz, Ph.D., vice president for research and education at the Institute of Noetic Sciences, decided to improve on the study methodology. They put a looker in one room looking at a monitor, while the person being stared at (the stare receiver) was in another room with a video camera trained at the back of his or her head.

The stare receiver had electrodes attached to the first and third fingers of the hand to measure changes in skin resistance that would reveal subtle tension in the body. When people actually see someone staring at them, their tension increases, and that tension, it was supposed, would show up on the skin resistance test if the stare receiver sensed that someone was staring at him or her.

The stare receiver sat alone in the room with the door shut and no possible contact with anyone outside of the room. The looker watched the person on the monitor only when told to do so. The times were recorded along with the stare receiver's finger skin resistance changes. The result was that the stare receiver often reacted when being stared at from the other room just as they had when Sheldrake did the studies with both people in the same room.[31]

The study was replicated by Dean Radin, senior scientist at the Institute of Noetic Sciences, Dick Bierman, Ph.D., a professor at the University of Amsterdam, and Robert Morris, Ph.D., at the University of Edinburgh. They achieved the same results. Many subjects' bodies reacted when they were stared at from another room.[32]

William Braud, Ph.D., University of Houston psychology professor, co-director of the William James Center for Consciousness Studies, and director of research at the Mind Science Foundation, replicated the studies in 1990 and 1993.[33]

This sense of being stared at is happening between minds, without physical contact between the two people involved.

Siblings' Minds Are Linked.

We would expect that the minds of people who are close to one another and love one another would be even more closely linked. We've all experienced a sense of knowing what's going on with a person we love or knowing what they're thinking or even finishing their sentences.

To learn whether the minds of people close to one another actually are linked, studies have been done with children in the same family. One test performed under the intense scrutiny of television cameras was performed in 1997 on a program titled *Carlton TV's Paranormal World of Paul McKenna*. The subjects on this occasion were Elaine and Evelyn Dove.

Elaine sat in the studio in front of a large pyramid. Evelyn was in a separate room sealed off from all communication from outside the room, with electrodes attached to her fingers to measure her stress level. She went through some relaxation exercises and her polygraph showed that she was nicely relaxed.

Meanwhile, in the other room, sealed away from Evelyn, Elaine continued watching the pyramid. Suddenly, without warning, the pyramid exploded in a burst of sparks, flashes and colored smoke, startling Elaine and giving her a considerable shock. At exactly that moment, Evelyn's polygraph pen recorded a huge swing, with one pen running off the top of the paper. Without trying to communicate with her sister, Evelyn automatically picked up her distress. When asked whether she felt or sensed anything, Evelyn said she experienced nothing out of the ordinary. Her mind outside of the body had communicated to the body and bypassed the brain entirely.[34]

Twins' Minds Are Linked.

It is widely known that twins communicate telepathically, and when something happens to a twin, the other very often feels the same emotions or pain in exactly the same way even though they can be separated by thousands of miles. A well-known, extensive review of the studies was written by Guy Lyon Playfair.[35] The conclusion of the review of the studies was that here is powerful evidence that twins are joined telepathically through shared emotions, thoughts, tactile sensations, and even physical manifestations such as bruising or burning.

The journal *Science* published a study by two physiologists who reported finding significant correlations in brain waves between isolated identical twins. These sorts of studies came to be known as Distant Mental Intention on Living Systems (DMILS).[36]

A demonstration of this link between twins was shown before a vast audience on January 10, 2003. Richard Powles and Damien Powles, identical twins, were invited to a television studio to participate in a telepathy experiment to be shown later that day on a chat show named *Channel 4's Richard and Judy Show.*

Richard Powles was taken to a soundproof room in the television studio and was asked to sit before a bucket of ice-cold water. In another studio well out of sight and earshot, his identical twin brother Damien was sitting quietly connected to a polygraph machine. Sitting beside Damien was polygrapher Jeremy Barrett, who was monitoring his respiration, abdominal muscles, pulse, and skin conductance. Barrett and Damien had no idea what Richard, in the other room was about to do.

When told to do so, Richard plunged his arm into the bucket of near-freezing water, giving a gasp as he did so.

At the exact moment of Richard's sharp gasp caused by the freezing water, there was a sudden blip on the line monitoring Damien's respiration rate. It was as though he too had gasped, but he actually hadn't. The effect was so obvious that Barrett pointed to it with his thumb to indicate that he knew something had happened to Richard.

They continued the experiment with the twins on the same show. Richard was asked to open a cardboard box placed before him. He did, excitedly, expecting to find something nice (preferably edible) in it. Instead, a huge rubber snake shot out of it at him, giving him a fright. His twin Damien's pulse rate, indicated by the pen on the polygraph, shot up at the same moment.[37]

The ability of twins to link telepathically is a commonly known phenomenon. What is important is that they couldn't link if their minds were confined to the brain. They feel the emotions and pain their twin feels without using any part of the body to receive the feelings. That is further evidence that our minds outside of the body are one.

People in Groups Develop a Collective Sense Greater Than the Individuals

Ralph Waldo Emerson, the well-known American writer, described the collective sense or "group soul" that is commonly experienced in groups:

> In all conversation between two persons tacit reference
> is made, as to a third party, to a common nature. That
> third party or common nature is not social; it is
> impersonal; is God. And so in groups where debate is
> earnest, and especially on high questions, the company
> become aware that the thought rises to an equal level in
> all bosoms, that all have a spiritual property in what was
> said, as well as the sayer. They all become wiser than
> they were. It arches over them like a temple, this unity
> of thought in which every heart beats with nobler sense
> of power and duty, and thinks and acts with unusual
> solemnity. All are conscious of attaining to a higher self-
> possession. – *Ralph Waldo Emerson*[38]

When people in groups come together in peace, with the intention of connecting, a new presence is created among them. People in intimate groups even refer to this new presence using the pronoun "it," feeling that it exists with its own properties and integrity. The experience is commonly known among people who work with groups. Chris Parish, who has been studying the dynamics of groups for two decades, describes the characteristics of such groups:

> The fascinating thing is that the actual quality between
> everyone . . . is that there's no gap between them. It's a
> strange thing because people will say something like,
> "It's one voice." One of the qualities is that when anyone
> speaks, it could be oneself speaking. Because as this
> higher consciousness emerges . . . there seems to be a
> sense of deep communion, of oneness, of non-
> separation. And yet at the same time, everyone feels
> more independent than they did before. People often
> remark that they feel more deeply themselves, more a
> release to express themselves, in a freer way. . . . That
> becomes a quality between people.[39]

What that means is that those working with groups have a clear sense that they together form a being they are part of but that is greater than the sum of their individualities. They feel a oneness, a unity of thought and feeling, and an outpouring of compassion and love. From this chalice flows an experience that changes them and places them as a group on a higher plane of being.

Data Show We Are Part of a Larger Mind.

In the literature, this overarching oneness in a group is called "collective consciousness" or "group soul." There are data showing that it in fact exists.

Data Show the Group Has a Collective Mind

One study cited previously showed that two people in love had the same brain wave patterns when together. [40]

In another, the Princeton University Engineering Anomalies Research laboratory conducted studies with pairs of people who knew each other to see whether they together could influence the numbers produced by a random-number generator. In 42 experimental series with 15 pairs and 256,500 trails, many produced results that exceeded the effect of either person alone.[41] Couples who were in a relationship had six times the power to influence the machine than did the individuals.[42] Their minds, linked, apparently have a combined effect more powerful than individuals have alone.

Experiments referred to earlier, with up to twelve subjects in a room, showed a synchronization of the brain waves of the entire group.[43]

Successful sports-team members refer to a "sixth sense," empathy, and an ability to "anticipate the moves of the other."[44] They may refer to a "shift in communality," an almost audible change in which sports participants "react as a . . . unit, rather than as an aggregate of individuals."[45]

Robert Kenny, an internal consultant at the International Center for Integrative Studies, notes that sports participants anticipate each other's movements ahead of time, so they may be communicating mentally between team members. Kenny suggests that, in the end, extrasensory communication may be somewhat ordinary instead of extraordinary.[46]

Additionally, the heartbeats of people in a group synchronize with each other, called entrainment.[47] Kenny describes it this way:

> Although the number of subjects is still too small to reliably generalize, researchers at HeartMath have found that the heart rates of people who have a close living or working relationship, and who generate feelings of appreciation for each other while sitting four feet apart (and being blind to the data), can become entrained. This entrainment apparently also occurs during sleep,

between couples that have been in long-term, stable and loving relationships. Their heart rhythms can converge and can simultaneously change in the same direction.[48] Another study found that the heart rates of married couples, who were skilled at empathizing, became synchronized and tracked each other during empathetic interactions.[49] Despite some methodological problems, several studies have suggested that entrainment may also occur during empathetic interactions between therapists and clients.[50]

Data Show This Collective Mind Even Affects People Not in the Group

The result of this higher or collective mind the group shares is that when a group of people is meditating in calm and peace, the minds of large groups of people in the geographical area seem to be influenced, even though they have no knowledge of the meditation:

> A 1993 study found that, when 4,000 people meditated together, violent crime in Washington, D.C., declined 23% over the course of the experiment, in contrast to its rising in the months before and after. The results were shown not to be due to other variables, such as weather, the police, or anti-crime campaigns. The predicted effect had been posited with an independent review board, which had participated in the study design and monitored its conduct.[51]

The data were compelling, but especially so when the same findings were replicated in a study of 24 U.S. cities:

> A similar effect was shown in a study of 24 U.S. cities, in which 1% of the urban population regularly practiced TM [transcendental meditation]. A follow-up study demonstrated that the 24 cities saw drops of 22% in crime and 89% in the crime trend, compared to increases of 2% and 53%, respectively, in the control cities.[52]

Another study was performed in Israel using a transcendental meditation group:

> During a two-month period in 1983 in Israel, on days when a TM-Sidhi [meditation] group equaling the

square root of 1% of the surrounding population meditated, independently published data showed that war-related deaths in Lebanon dropped 76%, and conflict, traffic fatalities, fires and crime decreased. In Israel, the national mood increased, as measured by a blinded content analysis of the emotional tone of the lead, front-page picture story in the *Jerusalem Post*, and the stock market increased. Other potential causal variables were controlled for.[53]

What Is Your Relationship to Other People?

This chapter began by asking, "What is your relationship to other people?" The answer is that even though we have different bodies on Earth, our minds are one.

"Love your neighbor as yourself." The admonition is echoed in words spoken by all the spiritual luminaries since the Axial Age. It doesn't mean people are separate and we must put up with having to love others as ourselves even though we find them despicable. It means the others are ourselves. We are not separate. Our minds are one with each other.

That has profound implications for our spiritual growth and behavior. The differences we seem to see according to age, gender, race, nationality, religious affiliation, and even bodies are illusions. They are artifacts of the physical realm where suffering, anger, conflict, war, insensitivity, and cruelty result from the ignorance that suggests because our bodies are separate, we are separate. We aren't. We are one.

Who are we? We are the mind that uses the body to have experiences.

Where are we? We're outside the brain, everywhere and nowhere, because we are the conscious mind that is above and aside from the material world.

What are we? We are eternal beings having a physical experience. We are in the world, but not of it. The physical realm is the scenery in which we participate in this drama called life, but when the curtain falls, we walk out of the theater arm in arm with our loved ones and go on to another play.

What is our relationship to other people? We're participating in this life drama as one mind, learning and growing together within the scenery that is the physical realm. But in reality, we're also sitting in the audience, intently watching, feeling ourselves at one moment the protagonist in the drama, at the next moment, a watcher sitting beside those we love, and at the next moment, the only watcher in the universe because we are all that: ourselves, our loved ones, and the Higher Power, all at once.

You can learn more about your relationship to other people at http://youreternalself.com/chapter3.htm.

4

What Is the Relationship of Your Eternal Self to the Physical Realm?

Since your eternal self is aside from the body, what is the relationship of the body to the eternal self? The eternal self isn't a "spark" or a "soul" that is embedded in the body somewhere, such as in the heart or the pineal gland. Instead, your body self and your eternal self are one when you are using the body, and your eternal self changes as the body self changes. When you drop off the body, the eternal self simply continues. In other words, the body only stands in for you as the real you has experiences in the physical realm.

But the body and brain aren't you.

The eternal self, then, influences the way the body self develops and functions. In medical science, that has come to be known as the "mind/body" connection, and some will only refer to the "mind/body," not the mind or the body separate from each other.

Your Mind Becomes the Experience

The mind isn't in the physical world; it has no matter or energy in it, and it isn't in any matter or energy. When your mind experiences something in the physical world or remembers an experience, the mind is doing the experiencing. The brain takes the same form that it had when the experience was first experienced, so it seems the brain is generating the experience—it isn't. The mind had the thought before the brain became active with it. We know that because the experience happens whether the brain is active or not, and people remember the experience even when the brain isn't functioning (see Chapter 1).

When you intend to remember something—say a room in the house in which you grew up—your mind instantly has the memory, and your conscious self forms the brain's areas of sight, hearing, taste, smell, touch, emotion, and sense of movement to take on the same form the mind and brain had when you first had the experience. But the memory comes from outside of the physical realm, and your self that is outside of the body has the experience. You feel the same physical sensations and emotions you felt when you first had the experience, just as though the sense impressions were coming from your eyes, ears, nose, tongue, or skin.

We know that stimulating parts of the brain can cause the mind to re-experience a segment of a memory,[1,2] but we also know the mind is outside the brain (see Chapter 1). It appears that just as a person can change a channel in the television to get another image from the signal outside of the television, stimulating the brain results in some different images being experienced in the mind. However, we don't yet understand fully how the brain is involved in having an experience that has already registered in the mind outside of the brain.

The body and brain, then, are much like a television that starts up, registers activity when it receives a signal, and seems to have Larry King in it speaking. But we know Larry King isn't in the television, just as the mind and memories aren't in the brain. The signal with Larry King in it was created before the television fired up to display the image. The television takes on the form in its complicated electronic parts required to make Larry King's picture and voice come to you, but Larry King is quite apart from the television. If this television stops working, you can pick up the same signal from another television or even directly to your mind with no television involved at all; you can travel to meet and speak to Larry King personally and eliminate the television altogether. You,

Larry King, and I aren't affected by changes in the television. If you drop the television, smashing its component parts so it no longer receives sound or pictures, you and Larry King aren't affected at all. That's the way it is with the brain; it can be damaged while the mind, which cannot be damaged, isn't affected.

You and I are one in that realm outside of the physical realm where our minds are, but we are also the individuals we know ourselves to be. We're together right now having this experience as you read the words I wrote. We're watching the show, just as we would if we were sitting together watching the television. We're one mind.

The Mind Can Influence Healing of the Body That Is in the Physical Realm

A great number of studies now demonstrate that when people "intend" for others to have a positive outcome from medical problems, the people's bodies respond positively. In other words, prayer, even from distant locations, influences physical bodies to heal. These are references to a sampling of the many studies that have now been done.

Larry Dossey, M.D., former chief of staff of Medical City Dallas Hospital and co-chair of the National Institutes of Health's panel on mind/body interventions, wrote *Healing Words: the Power of Prayer and the Practice of Medicine* in 1993 describing how prayer in virtually all its forms influences patient recovery, even when the person prayed for didn't realize he was being prayed for, and the people praying knew little about the person for whom they were praying.[3]

Dr. William S. Harris studied whether having people remote from the patients pray for coronary patients would have an effect on the patients. The results were significant improvements in the group prayed for over the control group.[4]

Dr. Fred Sicher, Elisabeth Targ, Dan Moore, and Helene S. Smith studied efforts by distant people to heal people with advanced AIDS. The results were evidence of healing among those prayed for.[5]

The laying on of hands, even without actual touch, resulted in those treated having positive outcomes in four studies.[6,7,8,9]

John A. Astin, Elain Harkness, and Edzard Ernst published their examination of 23 studies of prayer healing, non-contact therapeutic touch, and distant healing in the *Annals of Internal Medicine 2000*. Positive effects on patients occurred in 57 percent of the studies.[10]

Wayne B. Jonas and Cindy C. Crawford examined 13 randomized studies of spiritual healing by healers who simply intended to heal. Their finding, published in the journal *Alternative Therapies*, was that 46 percent showed healing results that could not have been obtained by chance.[11]

Robert N. Miller, Ph.D., had eight healers focus on healing 96 hypertensive patients. Neither the doctors nor the patients knew which patients were the focuses of the healing. He reported a statistically significant reduction in systolic blood pressure for patients who received distant healing from eight healers when compared to control patients not receiving healing; diastolic pressure, heart rate, and body weight showed no such effects. Four of the healers had a 92.3 percent improvement ratio in their total group of patients compared with a 73.7 percent improvement for the control group.[12]

LeShan,[13] Goodrich,[14,15] and Winston[16] found significant influences upon people focused on by healers at distant locations when healers used meditation to produce feelings of merging with or being "at one" with the people being healed.

In 1988, cardiologist Randolph Byrd, M.D., published a study in the well-respected, peer-reviewed *Southern Medical Journal*, in which he studied the effects of prayer on cardiac patients' healing. Over ten months, 192 patients in the Cardiac-Care Unit at the San Francisco General Medical Center, chosen at random from those admitted, were prayed for by people outside of the hospital. At the same time, another 201 patients also chosen at random were in a group not prayed for. Neither the patients nor their evaluating physicians were aware of which patients were receiving prayer. The prayed-for patients showed significantly superior recovery compared to controls. The prayed-for patients were five times less likely than control patients to require antibiotics and three times less likely to develop swelling or fluid in the lungs. None of the prayed-for patients required a tube inserted into the windpipe to aid in breathing, whereas 12 controls required this support. Fewer prayed-for patients than control patients died, but the difference in this area was not statistically significant. The design and the results of the Byrd study were considered very impressive, and even skeptical commentators seemed to agree on the significance of the findings.[17]

Neil C. Abbott's article in the *Journal of Alternative and Complimentary Medicine* explains that 10 of 22 studies the authors examined showed significant positive effects of healing as a therapy for human disease.[18]

These are two accounts illustrating the many remarkable healings on record:

1. A patient with lung cancer refused treatment and instead had his church congregation pray for him. A year later, his medical examination showed him to be completely free of lung cancer.[19]

2. Rita Klaus developed multiple sclerosis in her early 20s and the disease progressed steadily, as expected. As the disease prevented her from walking, the tendons in her legs were surgically cut to enable her to hobble short distances with the aid of braces. Then, she took part in a church healing service that she described as leaving her with "a feeling of absolute love like I'd never felt, coursing through me." She heard a voice one night inviting her to be healed. As she sat in her wheelchair the next day, she felt unusual sensations in her legs. When she looked, she saw that her twisted, deformed legs had regained normal appearance. She was able to stand, then walk. She tested her recovery by running up a flight of steps and then went on a joyous celebratory romp through the nearby woods. Upon examination, her doctor found no trace of her disease. The permanent damage to her body had also disappeared, a physiological change that should be impossible.[20]

The findings show that people can influence other people's health without touching them, being in the same area, or even knowing anything about them. Minds can create changes in physical bodies.

The Mind Has Been Shown to Influence Other Growth and Healing in the Physical Realm

A great variety of studies involving many different living organisms have demonstrated that the mind has a pervasive influence on the physical realm.

To find out whether prayer would affect body cells even when they were apart from a living person, one study used blood platelets taken from healthy human volunteers. Blood platelets were put into a number of flasks. Some were designated to be treated by a healer, who used the mind to try to influence the blood platelets by increasing the amount of an important enzyme in blood platelets (monoamine oxidase). Another group of flasks wasn't targeted by any healer. They were the control group. The result was that the healers successfully influenced the activity of monoamine oxidase in the designated flasks while the control flasks remained unchanged.[21]

In a similar study, human blood was placed in test tubes with some saline solution. The effect of the saline solution is to make the blood cells break open. A group of 32 healers were asked to use their minds to try to prevent the blood in a specific group of the test tubes from being damaged by the saline solution. At the same time, a control group of test tubes prepared in the same way was not given such attention. The finding was that the blood in the test tubes focused on by the healers showed significantly slower deterioration from the saline solution.[22]

Other studies have shown that the mind's intention to have positive effects has an impact on a variety of living organisms: health and physical condition of mice,[23,24,25,26,27,28,29,30] growth of fungus,[31,32] growth of bacteria,[33] growth of seeds,[34] and growth of yeast.[35]

The importance of showing the range of organisms that the mind can influence is to illustrate that the mind affects organisms in the physical realm in a great variety of ways. These are just the organisms measured. We can assume that our minds, individually and collectively, must have a similar effect on all living organisms we come into contact with.

Data Show the Mind Affects the World Around Us

William A. Tiller, Ph.D., Stanford University Professor Emeritus in physics, performed experiments to discover whether conscious intention influences the material world. In carefully controlled experiments, people were asked to focus on specific things in the material world, trying to influence their composition. The focused attention of subjects had these effects on the physical world of matter and energy:

- The acidity (pH) of water was intentionally raised or lowered by one pH unit.

- The activity of a human liver enzyme was increased by 15% to 30%.

- The larval growth rate of a fly was increased by 25%.[36]

The results measured were highly significant; the possibility of occurrence by chance was less than one in 1000.

Tiller's experiments had one other finding that showed how the mind affects physical reality. The spaces in which the experiments were conducted seemed to become increasingly conducive to enhancing the experimentation the more they were used. People's minds were able to influence things in the space more strongly and more quickly as time went on; the space was conditioned by the minds of the people involved. Even when no people were involved in the experiments, just magnets, the spaces were more conducive to having effects. As Tiller put it, in those spaces, the laws of physics no longer seem to apply.[37] People's minds had changed the matter in the physical realm in a positive way.

Dr. Dean Radin, of the Institute of Noetic Sciences, tested this effect to see whether the mind's intention to heal would change a space so that healing occurred more strongly there when it was used repeatedly for healing. He placed flasks of living human brain cells into a space to see whether the brain cells could be influenced by healers' intentions to make them grow strongly there. He also placed an inanimate object in the space, a random-number generator, to see whether the healer's mind influenced the numbers it produced. A random-number generator creates a stream of numbers at random. If the numbers start to show some order, then that means something has influenced the machine.

Some flasks of brain cells and a second random-number generator also were set up outside of the space where there was no healing intention to see whether they would change just by sitting for a period of time. This was the control.

A healer focused on the brain cells and the random-number generator in the "healing space," trying to make the brain cells grow more strongly and give the numbers produced by the random-number generator some order. As expected from the hundreds of other experiments done with healers and random-number generators, the brain cells grew more strongly when the healer focused on them, and the random-number generator started showing ordered numbers, not the random numbers it was programmed to produce. The control group showed no change. Minds had influenced matter.

But more interestingly, as the experiment progressed and the healer kept focusing on making things happen in that space, the cells grew even more strongly and even more ordered numbers came from the random-number generators. That showed that, over time, the space became more conducive to healing.[38]

We can imagine the differences in healing energy and sense of wellbeing between the office space of a physician who genuinely loves and cares for her patients and the office of a physician who holds disdain for patients, treats them harshly, and just wants to collect fees from them.

Experiments Have Shown that Minds Can Intentionally Influence Random-Number Generators

Other studies have been performed to see whether people can intentionally influence random-number-generators. Robert Jahn, former director of the PEAR Lab, and psychologist Brenda Dunne reported on experiments in which people separated from random-number-generators by several thousand miles attempted to influence the machines. The finding was "small but replicable and statistically significant" changes.[39]

Minds can influence inanimate machines.

Random-Number-Generator Studies Show that Events Significant to People Affect the Machines

Other studies of the influence of minds on random-number generators have measured whether an event that affects large numbers of people can influence changes in the numbers being produced, even though people aren't trying to influence the machines. That would show that the entire environment, across large geographical areas, is being influenced when many minds are thinking and feeling something.

In the studies, random-number generators around the world were examined after events that affected great numbers of people to see whether the numbers began to show some order during the events. During widely televised events that have captured the attention of many people, such as Princess Diana's death and the 9/11 tragedies, the combined outputs of sixty random-number generators around the world showed changes at the exact moments of the announcements of the events, changes that could not be due to chance.

To add control to the studies, researchers identified an event they knew was about to happen that would have an impact on large numbers of people and set up a study to measure the effects on random-number generators in different parts of the world. Dean Radin and Roger Nelson of the Institute of Noetic Sciences, and University of Amsterdam professor Dick Bierman, decided to run random-number generators in each of their labs on October 3, 1995, the day that the O.J. Simpson murder trial verdict was to be read. If the results were dramatic, they could test their hypothesis that something significant would happen in the minds of many people that would affect random-number generators in the physical world. The random-number generators might show a sudden order, meaning they were "disturbed" by the mass of minds hearing or watching the verdict.

Dean Radin describes the results in *The Conscious Universe*. He uses "RNG" to stand for "random-number generators." "Order" in the numbers means the machines were being affected in some way because they were not generating entirely random numbers.

> . . . around the time that the TV preshows began, at 9:00 AM Pacific Time, an unexpected degree of order appeared in all the RNGs. This soon declined back to random behavior until about 10:00 AM, which is when the verdict was supposed to be announced. A few minutes later, the order in all five RNGs suddenly peaked to its highest point in the two hours of recorded data precisely when the court clerk read the verdict. [40]

What happened was that millions of minds were united in their sentiments. We know they affected the random-number generators because we have recorded factual data from computers evaluating the numbers. But more importantly, that means the collective minds affected trees and mountains and buildings—and people. Influences on other things just can't be measured, but must be there as well. In other words, when an event of great significance occurs, many minds react to it together and that collective mind then affects inanimate objects such as computers.

We are all one with each other and with the material realm.

Experiments Have Shown that Minds Can Influence Patterns in Random Noise (White Noise)

Another experiment by the Princeton Engineering Anomalies Research Laboratory used white noise to see whether minds could affect the physical world. "White noise" is just random noise, such as the noise we hear when an alalog television isn't connected to a station and we see fuzz on the screen. The noise is raspy and constant because it's made up of random vibrations in the air.

Since 1998, about 50 computers around the world have been constantly recording and analyzing white noise generated from devices much like the television set when there's no signal. If the noise suddenly had some organization to it that wasn't random, we would say it was affected by something. The effect wouldn't be audible to the human ear, but the computer could identify it and let the researchers know something just happened.

These 50 or so computers measuring white noise since 1998 have shown some very remarkable findings. At the time of the terrorist attacks on the World Trade Center, white noise from the computers around the world showed that something dramatic had happened.[41] More interestingly, the computers measuring changes in the white noise showed that the global consciousness had been alert at 4 a.m., five hours before the first airplane crashed (8:45) and six-and-a-half hours before the second airplane crashed (10:30). That would have been around the time the hijackers started to put their plan into action. The events had not occurred, and whether these men were going to be successful in their plan could not have been known in any ordinary sense, but our collective minds knew what was going to happen, and our shock registered on inanimate devices around the world.[42]

The same effects on the white noise have resulted during dozens of other such incidents that affected the minds of many people, such as floods, bombings, tsunamis, house votes, acquittals of figures, earthquakes, and plane crashes. The randomness of the white noise changed with each event. The chances that these reactions in inanimate machines occurred coincidentally at those times are less than a million to one. The data on the other events are available from the Princeton University Web site. The link is at http://youreternalself.com/chapter4.htm.

The minds of millions of people were affecting inanimate computers in the physical world, meaning they also were affecting all organic and inorganic things. We just don't know to what extent.

Crystals in Frozen Water Form Differently Depending on the Attitudes of People

Dr. Masaru Emoto[43] has conducted thousands of experiments with water crystals showing that the mind's attitudes affect how water crystallizes when frozen. In one experiment, for example, Dr. Emoto put water from the same source into two bottles. He wrote the words "You fool" on a label and taped it to one of the bottles. He wrote the words "Thank you" on a second label and taped that label to the second bottle.

Dr. Emoto then froze water from each bottle and photographed the crystals that were formed using a microscope and camera. The result was that the crystals formed from water taken from the bottle with "You fool" on it were grotesque and misshapen. The crystals formed from water taken from the bottle with "Thank you" written on it were beautiful and symmetrical, like snowflakes.

We must assume it wasn't the printed words that influenced the water; it was the minds of the people who wrote and read the words. We know that because the symbols on the labels are just ink stains on a flat surface with no meaning except to people; the writer's and reader's minds created meaning from the ink marks.

These experiments have now been performed many times using different sources of water and different treatments. In all circumstances, when a loving, compassionate, gentle attitude or melodious sound is focused on the water, beautiful crystals form when the water is frozen. When harsh, demeaning, hateful, dehumanizing attitudes or cacophonous sounds are focused on the water, the frozen crystals are misshapen and grotesque.

When tap water is frozen, it doesn't form clear crystals; the forms are disorganized. But when the same water is prayed for, the water crystallizes into beautiful, delicate crystals.

When a sample from a Japanese city reservoir's water (Fujiwara Dam) was frozen, it showed misshapen crystals, but when a prayer was offered before the reservoir, samples of its water formed beautiful crystals when frozen.

Water exposed to heavy-metal music formed grotesque crystals. Water from the same source exposed to Bach's melodious "Goldberg Variations" froze into exquisite, beautiful crystals.

You can see the photographs of water crystals at Dr. Emoto's Web site. The link is at http://youreternalself.com/chapter4.htm.

Dr. Emoto's results have been replicated by Dean Radin, senior scientist at Institute of Noetic Sciences, in double-blind experiments performed by a team that included Dr. Emoto.[44]

We know that people's minds influence the composition of water in the physical realm, but that was the only effect that Dr. Emoto was measuring. The effects on water mean the prayers and the words likely were influencing those people thinking "You fool," those people reading "You fool," other people in the area, the room in which the experiments occurred, and everything else in the environment that simply wasn't measured. We certainly know that these attitudes affect our bodies, which are between 55 percent and 69 percent water.

We Know Our Minds Are Influencing the Physical World

The data from these studies show that our minds are influencing the physical realm, but we have no idea how wide-ranging and pervasive this influence is. We can see the effects only in computer-measured random white noise and numbers, water crystals, rates of healings, and growth of cells. However, we must assume that the effects aren't limited to the small number of things we measure; there is no reason not to believe that our collective minds are influencing every living and nonliving thing in the same way, with lasting effects, just as spaces are conditioned to be more conducive to healing.

When we have constant arguments in the home, feel anger toward co-workers at the office, feel road rage in our cars, we know we're influencing the makeup of our minds to be more angry and frustrated — we're becoming the anger. However, it appears that we may also be influencing the makeup of our bodies, the physical spaces where these attitudes are displayed, the other people around the space, and anyone who later comes into the space to be with us. Because we know that healing thoughts enhance the healing qualities of a space and the properties of water, it is reasonable to expect from the data that a space in which there is much love will become more conducive to loving; conversely, perhaps an angry space will more likely encourage angry feelings. If that is true, then the more loving people are, the more the world will be conducive to loving.

The world is scenery finely tuned by the Higher Power for our dramas as we mature spiritually. The data seem to indicate that even the scenery is influenced by our minds. Those on the other side of life tell us that when they come down to the Earth plane to communicate, it's like trying to penetrate a deep, dark fog because of the violence, self-centeredness, hostility, and separation that permeates the Earth plane. We possibly are forming crystals in all of life that are misshapen and deformed by thinking "You fool" or "You make me sick." Those in the afterlife say that these thoughts have created disease and deformity — neither were intended for the physical realm, and both, they explain, will be eradicated when our collective minds are more loving and compassionate.

As we grow spiritually as a species, we can expect that the Earth will have an essence that is symmetrical and beautiful, just as the crystals of frozen water become when "Love" or "Thank you" are taped to bottles of water, or when the water is prayed over. Our minds are creating the inner reality we live in as we interact with people and the world, but it appears likely that our minds are also affecting the physical realm.

We Are One with Nature

The facts that our minds are one and our minds influence the physical realm means that we are one with nature as well as each other. When we inflict harm upon another living creature, the trauma will be felt by our minds, the minds of others, and the physical world of nature itself. Killing animals in experiments or for recreation and teaching children to enjoy killing animals for any reason are likely creating an environment that is damaging to humankind and the world in which we live because of the violence, hostility, and disregard for other living creatures that it displays. Destroying the environment with pollution and self-centered over-consumption are likely creating an essence that generates more pollution, discontent, anger, and self-absorption.

We are one with the physical realm and are creating a world that is shaped by the spiritual beings that we have grown into. All of us, together, are bearing fruit from the trees that we are, every moment of our lives. Together, our world has available for us only the fruit we have all created. If we live in a world of anger, self-absorption, tragedy, suffering, and violence, it is because we have created it.

You can learn more about our relationship to the physical realm at http://youreternalself.com/chapter4.htm.

5

What Are You to Do with Your Eternal Life?

You are an eternal being having an Earth phase of your eternal existence. Knowing that, what are you to do with your life on Earth?

The mystics and those on the next planes of life tell us that the purpose of life is to grow spiritually, to help others grow spiritually, and to evolve humankind so all societies on the Earth plane enjoy peace, brotherhood, love, and compassion. Bliss, confidence in our eternal natures, loss of all fears, elimination of disease, peace, elimination of all violence, and love and brotherhood among all people will follow as natural consequences. They are the fruit. Spiritual maturity is the tree.

As we grow spiritually, we come to know that all others are one with us and with the Higher Power. We become energized and empowered by the Higher Power in ways we now don't understand and aren't open to yet. That will change us and humankind.

The Earth is a school, and we are the students. Our purpose is to learn in this school so we progress spiritually and help humankind progress spiritually.

What Those on the Next Planes
Describe as Our Purpose in Life

Some religions and individuals suggest that our purpose in life includes considerations other than those described by people now in the afterlife. We have clear descriptions of eternal life and the afterlife now in recordings of people on the next plane of life speaking and in the descriptions given to mediums. We know what is true now and what has come from the imaginations of people through the centuries. The most prominent assertions taught by religions and individuals that are not supported by those in the afterlife follow.

Those speaking from the afterlife do not describe our purpose in life as becoming perfected so we merge into a super-consciousness or ground of all being. They describe themselves as being exactly the same after death as they were before, progressing through eternity in spiritual development as the individuals they were on Earth, but on a vast number of unique spheres that the individual enters according to his or her state of mind. They do describe group souls and developing into higher planes of being, but they always maintain their individuality. During some of the periods of their eternal lives, they explain, they may have experiences as other individuals to grow and mature spiritually, but the core person remains. Loved ones stay with them and they have access to both those who have gone into the afterlife before and those still alive on the Earth plane, even though they can't freely interrupt the lives of people still engaged in learning lessons on the Earth plane.

Those in the next planes of life do not describe the purpose of life as progressing individually in spirituality without progressing with a community. None suggest asceticism or becoming a hermit as desirable means of growing spiritually. They speak of simultaneous development in individual spiritual maturity and in brotherhood and peace in humankind. We are to love and be loved in a spiritual community.

They do not describe the purpose of life as becoming increasingly adept at withdrawing mentally into an altered state. Meditation seems to be useful in helping some people learn about the self and become open to inspiration, but the purpose of life isn't to lose the Earthly realm or remove the self through a meditation practice. The descriptions of life by those on the next planes of life are of eternal life continuing in a form just as it is now, with us and our loved ones growing in love, peace, and brotherhood as we live ordinary, everyday lives. We are not to withdraw from life and eradicate the self.

However, it is true that in the process of growing spiritually, we need to give up on the assumptions about ourselves, life, existence, and the Higher Power that we were taught by society in the physical realm. That physical-realm self is filled with illusions about whom we are. To grow beyond it into love, compassion, and wisdom, we must give up on the Earthly self we grew into from childhood. When it is removed, we will know our eternal self that we will grow into more perfectly over time.

Those speaking from the afterlife clearly state that the truth of the universe comes from within, and luminaries such as Yeshua ben Yosef describe the path people can take to their own, individual spiritual maturity. They speak about Yeshua often, with great reverence, as the teacher whose insights will help people grow spiritually.

The mystics and those on the next planes of life do not talk about a hell or Divine judgment. Those are simply primitive tribal myths. Our purpose in life is not to get into heaven and avoid hell. You can read more about that at http://youreternalself.com/chapter5.htm.

Preparing for the Next Stages of Life

By growing in spiritual maturity, we are also preparing for the transition to the next plane of life. In our society today, most who cross over to the next plane are completely unprepared for what happens to them. Many are bewildered and have difficulty adjusting. Often, they have left unfinished business behind on the Earthly plane because of our backward attitude towards death. People feel they need to be confident in a miracle cure, so they don't speak openly with the dying about their deaths. Many are uncomfortable with talking about death, so they whisper comments out of earshot of the dying person and try to "wear a happy face" when with them.

People need to understand the death transition well before the time they experience it. Death is only a doorway into the next phase of eternal existence. It should be talked about openly, with sadness at the temporary separation, but also with confidence and anticipation. Death will be a time of wonderful reunions and leaving behind pain and suffering. It will be a new beginning, with new experiences.

We Are to Help Begin the Development of Heaven on Earth for Our Descendents

As we grow spiritually, we participate in helping humankind evolve into a compassionate community with people who are servants to all others and who love unconditionally. This community will be a heaven on Earth where people support and aid each other without judgment or condemnation. We cannot have that society in our lifetimes; humankind is too far from it. However, we can begin the slow, steady movement toward this future kingdom by growing spiritually as far as we can now.

In that way, we will be helping our descendents enjoy a heaven on Earth. Year by year and century by century, they will become more blissful, loving, peaceful, free of the need to deceive, free of anxiety, fear, and worry, and free of the fear of death. But we must begin the journey.

In a few generations, all of our descendents will know without reservation that they are eternal beings having an Earth period of their eternal lives. There will be no conflict, violence, deceit, mistrust, wars, fear of death, self-centeredness, or exclusion because of race, creed, or nationality. Instead, there will be unconditional love of people for one another, a profound feeling of brotherhood with an international spirit, the desire for peace, and a deeply felt desire to be a servant to everyone else. In that idyllic society, no one will feel unloved or excluded. All will be welcome in all circumstances. When tragedy strikes, everyone—family, community members, and strangers—will rush to serve and help. There will be no need for insurance; everyone will contribute to recreate what was lost. There will be no need for money or bartering. All will give freely what they have. There will be no lawyers. Everyone will live in harmony. Every person will be a humble servant; no one will be a king.

That is the heaven on Earth that is in humankind's destiny.

Then What Are You to Do During This Earth Phase of Your Eternal Life?

The answer to the question of what you are to do during this Earth phase of your eternal life is to learn the lessons that will enable you to grow to be as spiritually mature as you can be, help everyone you meet to grow as well, and help all of humankind develop toward the heaven on Earth that is in humankind's future. You can learn more about our purpose in life at http://youreternalself.com/chapter5.htm.

6

What Is Spirituality?

Your mind is spiritual. The body is just a temporary overcoat of flesh; it can't be spiritual. The part of you that is spiritual is that part that thinks, feels, and decides how to act. It is the part of you that loves, feels compassion, and longs for peace and brotherhood. That part of you is your mind. When the body is no longer useful at death, it's cast off like a tattered overcoat you no longer need or want; but the mind continues.

This chapter explains that spirituality is a process, not a destination, and that growing spiritually means changing the mind.

Spirituality Is Who You Are, Not What You Do

The physical realm is the world of beginnings and endings, creation and destruction. Matter and energy change forms as ceaselessly as the ocean's surface rises and falls from frothy wave to wave. Trees, mountains, buildings, and human bodies are all temporary. They're just the scenery, and when a drama is finished, the scenery is torn down to make room for another set that can contain another play. Only we, the players, are real and eternal—our minds are spiritual, and our minds are entirely separate from the brain and physical realm.

Since only what is in the mind is spiritual, then St. Peter's Basilica in Rome is no more spiritual than your town's public library. The priest or minister is no more spiritual than a bartender. Going to church is no more spiritual than going bowling on Saturday night. Giving money to the church is no more spiritual than spending money in a casino.

If your mind is composed of assumptions and perspectives that allow your natural love and compassion to come through, then you will feel love for more people in more circumstances. Ultimately, you will not need to forgive because you will feel no offense. You will not need to think of loving because you will love before the thought of loving arises. Your nature will be compassionate. You will be love.

Loving, compassionate, forgiving sentiments don't require actions to be spiritual. The spiritual mind was inside you before you even felt compassion for a homeless person. You felt compassion because your mind was already such that you were going to feel compassion when you saw that person—that state of your mind is spiritual. Whether you stop and speak to that homeless person or give money or buy her a meal isn't spiritual. Those are just things that happen in the physical realm, and nothing in the physical realm is spiritual. But they are the inevitable result of who you are in your mind. Who you are is spiritual. Because you love, you show compassion and give to others.

Feeling, thinking, or acting with love and compassion are the fruits that appear in the physical realm, but the spiritual you is the tree:

> Do people pick grapes from thornbushes, or figs from
> thistles? Likewise every good tree bears good fruit, but a
> bad tree bears bad fruit. A good tree cannot bear bad
> fruit, and a bad tree cannot bear good fruit.
>
> – *Yeshua ben Yosef*

Your eternal self is the tree in the spiritual realm. The fruit is the natural outgrowth of your spiritual state that appears in the physical realm. But unlike the tree, you have free will and you can grow yourself into the tree you want to be. We and God are the only beings who have free will. The reason is so that we can grow in spiritual maturity.

The assumptions and perspectives aren't infused in your mind. They're constantly changing, and the spiritual person you are today is a different person from whom you'll be a year from now, 20 years from now, and a thousand years from now. You will mature spiritually by bringing to awareness your assumptions and perspectives, by comparing them with whom you want to be based on your understanding of your place in the universe, by changing them so you think, feel, and act differently, and by seeing the results in yourself and in others' reactions to you.

You have free will to change your mind to be what you want it to be. Your spiritual mission in life is to change your mind to be loving and compassionate. All the rest of the spiritual goals the luminaries have defined through the millennia will follow naturally as you fulfill that mission. You grow spiritually by changing your mind one assumption at a time. And as you change your mind, you change your nature.

"Metanoia, for the kingdom of heaven is at hand," Yeshua ben Yosef is reported to have said (in Aramaic). The Greek "metanoia" was mistranslated "repent," but it actually means "change your mind"; that was Yeshua's meaning. Yeshua was saying the kingdom of heaven is already here; it's within you. To enter it, just change your mind.

We Were Reared to Believe That Having Things and Money Is All That's Important in Life

Most people rearing children today teach them, by action and example, that the only important qualities in life are wealth, material success, achieving pleasure, and doing what someone requires. That's what people learned as children and they never abandoned those beliefs.

Children learn that love is conditional—"I will love you if . . . you obey me, you take care of me, you don't get me angry, you get good grades . . ." The child who obeys will be rewarded with "good boy" or "good girl." The words for the disobedient child are "bad boy" or "bad girl." But in both "good" and "bad" remarks, the child hears, "I will love you only if . . ."[1]

Schools are intended to help children "be successful in life"—in other words, conform to the requirements of society and the business world. There's no talk of spiritual development or growing into a unique person in the schools. The assumptions that are taught and reinforced are those resulting in obedience, without critical thinking; children are taught to be preoccupied with the desire to acquire and consume. In other words, they are initiated into the cult of materialism through the pervasive influence of schools and other organizations they're forced to attend.

During those early years, we develop minds full of fears, anxieties, worries, and desires. The fears a child feels that she isn't loved, doesn't belong, and is otherwise inadequate aren't created by the atoms and molecules in the world and aren't part of natural maturation like becoming taller and growing facial hair. The fears are taught by the people who rear the child and unfortunate experiences. Today, as we go through our days, we create realities based on the childhood assumptions, and they result in fear, anxiety, worry, and frustration.

But as adults we can change the realities—that is free will.

Anyone who refuses to change the assumptions and perspectives that formed their mind as they were growing up remains a prisoner of childhood. Intellectually and physically they are adults, but spiritually, they are infants.

To grow spiritually, you must abandon the assumptions you learned in childhood and take on the assumptions true to your eternal self. You must break out of prison.

What Do We Really Want to Become?

Having broken out of prison by being willing to deny the assumptions with which you were reared, you need spiritually mature assumptions to look toward as models. This is a summary of the assumptions that all people will hold in the future society of peace and brotherhood. They come from the descriptions by the luminaries who repeatedly taught us about our place in the universe. In this heaven on Earth that is humankind's destiny, all people will reply "Of course" to all of these assumptions. They will be taken for granted.

- I am an eternal being having a physical experience.
- The goal for my life, over any physical realm goals, is to grow spiritually.
- My highest calling is to serve others.
- All other people are one with me.
- My love for all others is without conditions; I love without reservation.
- I help all others grow spiritually so humankind is developing toward heaven on Earth.
- I am one with nature.
- I am one with the Higher Power.
- The intuition that guides me is the Higher Power and beings on the other side of life whose sole desire is to help me grow spiritually.

For more information and resources about what spirituality is, go to http://youreternalself.com/chapter6.htm.

7

How Do You Grow Spiritually?

Each moment, you think, act, and feel based on a set of assumptions that you've put into play. You become the person reflected in that set of assumptions for that moment. We'll call that set of assumptions a perspective.

The perspectives are what the person states when she explains why she has done something. "I went to church Sunday morning instead of the picnic because going to church is the right thing to do." The perspective just seems right and true and the way life is or should be. But behind the perspective are assumptions: "If I don't go to church the church people will think I'm not holy enough to be with them," "If I don't go to church, I'll go to hell," and other assumptions unique to the person. Most of these assumptions aren't spoken or known by the person holding them. They're hidden from awareness and cloaked by the perspective that it's the right thing to do.

Every action you perform and every thought you think has perspectives behind it. Each perspective is made up of assumptions.

These assumptions and perspectives are entirely in your mind, not in the world around you or other people. You know that's true because other people have different assumptions and different perspectives. If somehow everyone were tapping into the same set of assumptions or perspectives out in the universe somewhere, everyone would think and act the same. Of course, we don't!

Our Assumptions Comprise Our Minds

Your mind is made up of assumptions. You can identify your most deeply rooted assumptions because when someone asks you about them, you reply "Of course" or "Of course not." You feel like it's the only sensible thing.

For example, imagine that you're in a restaurant and you want to use the restroom. As you walk down the hall to the restrooms, you come to the one for the opposite sex first. Would you go into it and use it since it's closest?

"Of course not," you smirk in disbelief. "I would never go into the restroom for the opposite sex." That's based on an assumption: people don't use the restrooms designated for the opposite sex. You're amazed that I could even suggest that. We use all kinds of words to describe these things we would not do: "that's ridiculous," "what a silly thing to say." That's "crazy," "absurd," "wrong," or "stupid."

The assumptions can also be stated positively. "Walking down the hall in that restaurant, do you go into the restroom for your gender?" "Of course!" you say. And you'll call that "sensible," "right," "appropriate," or "acceptable."

We call these assumptions by other names such as "beliefs" and "common sense." In this book, I call them assumptions because most of the time, we just assume they're true—we don't even question them.

You're a collection of these assumptions and you live your life based on them. They determine the kind of fruit you'll bear. You might be an apple tree or a pear tree or an olive tree; you will bear a specific fruit as a direct, unavoidable result of your assumptions, just as a tree bears the fruit its trunk, branches, leaves, and sugar cause it to bear.

The Assumptions Are Deeply Rooted.

These assumptions are deeply rooted in our minds and we don't notice them because they are the substance that makes our minds. If we see a bat flitting through the air, we react immediately and automatically, without reviewing the assumptions. Reactions are always based on assumptions that aren't spoken, and the person most often doesn't even realize they're there. But they are behind the automatic reaction: "Bats carry rabies," "Bats are creepy," "Bats bite." "My mom was afraid of bats, so I should be." Whether they're true or not makes no difference. The person's mind thought they were true at some point and they came to form her perspective. But when you have the automatic reaction, you don't think those thoughts. You just panic and run.

In the same way, if you have the assumption that other people are your brothers and sisters, that you are one with them, and that their needs matter more than your needs, you will immediately stop and help someone in need even if you're late for a meeting. You wouldn't think of doing something else. That is the fruit in the physical realm that comes from a loving compassionate tree in the spiritual realm.

To understand why you think, feel, or act as you do, you have to go deep into yourself, perhaps even back to that time when you were a child. When you do, you may be able to describe in words what happened to create the assumptions. Somewhere back there, everything we are today was learned, and now the acting self thinks, feels, and acts immediately based on that learning, without questioning why it was learned.

We Change Our Minds from Moment to Moment.

We are very accustomed to phrases that show we've changed our mind: "I thought better of it," "I came to realize," "It dawned on me," "I figured out," "I made up my mind," "I used to think," "I decided." All of these phrases mean the person has weighed all of the assumptions that make up the perspectives in his or her mind and has come to a perspective that feels OK—a perspective the person can say "Of course" to. When an assumption changes, the person shifts the balance to a new perspective. However, all of the assumptions and the perspective that result are entirely in the person's mind, not in other people or the world. The person is really changing his reality.

This is an example. Look at the image[1] at the top of the next page. Do you see the young woman and the old woman?

To see the young woman, you have to shift your mind into "young woman" mode. Her nose is the little bump to the left; she is facing away from you and looking left. To see the old woman, you have to shift your mind into the "old woman" mode. Her mouth is the almost horizontal line above the border of the dress at the neck. Stare at the mouth line and you'll see the old woman. It will be even easier to see one or the other if you cover up the old woman's mouth and chin with your finger to see the young woman, or cover the little bump and eyelashes that are on the young woman's face and stare at the mouth to see the old woman.

You will be able to shift your perception with ease once you see the two images. You can't see both at once; you have to shift between them. You impose a whole picture on the drawing, either a young woman or an old woman; you give it meaning and organization. That's happening entirely in your mind, not in the picture. The picture doesn't change.

We all shift our balance of assumptions to a different perspective with the same ease. We "change our minds" as easily as we shift between the young woman and old woman. This is an example. A woman is in a man's office. She looks at the man, worried. He touches her breast. How do you feel about that?

You likely felt put off by the scene—it was inappropriate behavior for the man. Your perspective was "This man is doing something wrong!" The assumptions were, "Men must not fondle women in their offices," "Bosses sometimes take advantage of employees," "Women are often touched inappropriately," and so on. They all form the perspective: "This man is doing something wrong."

OK, he's a doctor and she has a lump he is examining. Now how do you feel? You probably shifted your mind to a new perspective. When I added a fact, you brought to mind another set of assumptions: "Physicians can touch women," "This man is a physician." Your perspective shifted: "It's OK for him to touch her breast." The change in your perspective was entirely in your mind. The two people standing there haven't changed.

We come to perspectives every moment of every day, in an instant, without thinking about what we're doing. We shift our perspectives just like shifting between seeing the young woman and old woman in the drawing. You don't have to work at changing from seeing the old woman or young woman—your mind just does it instantly when you want to make the change. It's the same with the instantaneous shifts in your mind you go through every moment of the day. However, all of these assumptions and the resulting perspectives are in your mind; they are not in other people and not in the world. They are what comprise you as a person. They are who you are.

The scenery around you changes: the people, location, time of day, and circumstances. They all change from moment to moment, and you shift to perspectives to fit the changes in scenery as you evaluate them. But regardless of how the scenery changes, you are in charge of the personal reality you create. You do the shifting.

We Create a Reality Where There Are Just Atoms.

The perspectives are always in you and relevant only to you, never in the world or in someone else. What you're really looking at when you see the picture of the young woman and old woman on the page is just smears of ink, with lighter and darker areas. There's no young woman there; there's no old woman. It's a piece of paper with ink unevenly deposited on it. You bring to the picture your perspectives. You then force your perspectives on the meaningless smears of ink and create meaning: either an old woman or a young woman, whichever you decide to create. If someone said, "I don't see anything on that page but ink stains, no old woman or young woman," you would think he was defiant or crazy. But it's just that that person has another perspective.

When you "make" a young woman in the picture with your mind, you're creating a reality for the moment. It becomes an experience, just like looking at a sunset, but you created the "young woman" experience entirely in your mind. When you "make" an old woman, you're creating another reality. The picture doesn't change in either event.

We do that in our lives from moment to moment of every waking day. The material realm of energy and matter we navigate through is without meaning—it's a mass of atoms. You give it meaning by shifting your mind into perspectives. You create reality, and you do it as easily as you shift between seeing an old woman or young woman in meaningless blobs of ink on paper.

It's true that our senses are registering things in the environment. If we stub our toe on a chair, we feel it. Yes, that's physical existence. But what we understand from the sense impressions is the reality of our life. Reality isn't in the chair. It's in our understanding of what a chair is and what we intend to do with the chair. We identify it as "my sitting thing." Without that conception in our minds, it is just a coagulation of atoms that has no meaning, just as it has no meaning for a newborn who hasn't yet learned about chairs.

The material universe is not our reality. We create our reality in our minds in response to the universe. The scenery is the backdrop for the play, but the scenery is not the play. Change the scenery to a different set and the play will still go on. And different plays can go on with the same scenery.

Our minds are in the realm outside of the body and the brain. The makeup of our minds is what is spiritual; nothing in the physical realm is spiritual. When we change our assumptions so we feel love, compassion, peace, and brotherhood, our spirit changes. That is how we grow spiritually. Metanoia.

The Assumptions Come from Our Culture.

Assumptions seem to be "right" because most of the people in our culture hold the same assumptions. After all, if you ask 20 people whether they would go to the restroom of the opposite sex if it were closer, they would all say, "No." That makes it seem that here's a perspective that's objective truth—out there written on a stone tablet somewhere.

That's not the case. All 20 people would agree because they have been reared in the same society. In another society or in an earlier time, you might have all 20 people saying they'd go to the nearer (or the cleaner or less crowded) one. It's just that everyone in a society learns the same assumptions, that's all. The more people in our society that share a perspective, the more we believe it's right and true and written on a stone tablet. But it still comes down to each individual person, alone, having a perspective based on a set of assumptions—it's not out there; it's in here.

Scholars today are calling the assumptions from our culture "memes" because they travel with the culture and mold our minds just as genes mold our bodies. Until we reach a point in our lives where we can examine these assumptions and develop our own selves, we remain the person society molded as we grew up.

This learning occurred because we had to follow the rules to fit in and fitting in is a primary motivation for human beings. We watched other people act as they did and from their behavior and others' reactions, we learned what was acceptable and unacceptable. We saw people get along and be rewarded for doing some things, and we heard our family talk about "those others" who didn't follow the rules in their assumptions. We were praised, "Good boy (or girl), " for some behavior and sternly warned, "Don't do that—it's bad," for other behavior. As a result, we learned which thoughts, feelings, and actions were right and good and which were bad and unacceptable, just as easily as we learned to speak our native tongue. We didn't have to go to school to learn the language; we didn't have to go to school to learn the assumptions that comprise our minds.

When people grow up in a different culture or age from someone else, they learn a different set of assumptions. Gregorio Billikopf, of the University of California, tells the following fascinating and amusing story about cultural differences. (His friend calls him "Grigorii Davidovich" in the story.)

> Toward the end of my three week trip I was invited by my young Russian host and friend Nicolai Vasilevich and his lovely wife, Yulya, out to dinner. At the end of a wonderful meal, Yulya asked if I would like a banana. I politely declined and thanked her, and explained I was most *satisfied* with the meal. But the whole time while my mind was racing: "What do I do? Do I offer her a banana even though they are as close to her as they are to me? What is the *polite* thing to do?"
>
> "Would *you* like a banana?" I asked Yulya.

"Yes," she smiled, but made no attempt to take any of the
three bananas in the fruit basket. "What now?" I thought.

"Which one would you like?" I fumbled.

"That one," she pointed at one of the bananas. So all the
while thinking about Russian politeness I picked the
banana Yulya had pointed at and peeled it half way and
handed it to her. Smiles in Yulya and Nicolai's faces told
me I had done the right thing. After this experience I
spent much time letting the world know that in Russia,
the polite thing is to peel the bananas for the ladies.
Sometime during my third trip I was politely disabused
of my notion.

"Oh no, Grigorii Davidovich," a Russian graciously
corrected me. "In Russia, when a man peels a banana for
a lady it means he has a *romantic* interest in her." How
embarrassed I felt. And here I had been proudly telling
everyone about this tidbit of cultural understanding.[2]

These assumptions that differ from culture to culture are simply held
by large numbers of people who feel they're "right" or "normal."
However, after a while, they may become rules, and people who violate
some rules may be embarrassed, or more strongly, shunned by the
society, judged by the state, punished, and even executed. Those
holding them call their assumptions "right" and everyone else's "wrong,"
but they're still assumptions that many individuals hold individually.
There's no universally written rule on a stone tablet somewhere.

The assumptions also change among whole societies over time. In
the Middle Ages in England, there were three levels of people: peasants
on one level, lords or priests on the next, and royalty at the top. The
peasants were neither fully free nor slaves. Understand that these are
like the average workers today who work in factories, restaurants, and
shopping malls. These ordinary, everyday people in the peasant class
could not leave a village, sell farm animals, or marry without the lord of
the manor's permission. Ask the average person today whether he
would like to have money and own property some day and he will say,
"Yes, of course." If you had asked a peasant in the Middle Ages whether
he would like to have money and own property some day, he would
have laughed uproariously. "Of course not. That's crazy. I'll never own
property or make money and my children won't. We're peasants."

There was no upward mobility. That was simply an assumption of life as a peasant; he was a peasant, his children would be peasants, and his grandchildren would be peasants. But these beliefs were still only assumptions. The assumptions comprised the peasant's mind and he assumed that was reality.

The peasant's physical makeup was no different from ours. The peasant had a mind that could learn theoretical physics. An individual who was a peasant in the Middle Ages could have been a nuclear scientist if she had lived in the twenty-first century. What made the difference in what the peasants believed and the way they thought? The assumptions that were in their minds. That's all! And they each created their worlds every moment based on their assumptions.

Assumptions about the Society of Peace and Brotherhood

Humankind is evolving toward a society of peace and brotherhood, but progress has been retarded over the last two millennia. Like the peasant in the Middle Ages who was sure he could never be free and own land, many today believe we're soft rocks and our goal in life is the infinite struggle to acquire infinite wealth; society reared us to believe that. But those beliefs are primitive and immature. Just as people in the Middle Ages assumed that some people were destined to be lords or priests and the rest were destined to be peasants, the belief that human beings are just accidents in time is based in ignorance and will extinguish as humankind matures.

In the first century CE, Yeshua ben Yosef referred to the society we could be living in, with spiritually wealthy and free people, when he said this society is spread out upon the face of the Earth already, but people do not see it (Gospel of Thomas, 17, 3, 51, and 113). The same saying was rendered in another text:

> The kingdom of God does not come with your careful observation, nor will people say, "Here it is, "or "There it is," because the kingdom of God is within [and among] you."
>
> *– Yeshua ben Yosef* (Luke 17:20-21)

Those who heard the words repeated them to others until they were written down toward the end of the first century, but few (or none) at the time understood them, and for two millennia, this simple, unpretentious wisdom has been buried beneath the ostentatious cathedrals of religion.

Yeshua was saying to the Galileans, "The kingdom of God is here already, inside you, but you're just choosing not to live in it through your spiritual attitudes." If those first-century Jews had listened and had chosen to start changing their assumptions about life, other people, the Higher Power, nature, and their spiritual nature, today we would have inherited the heaven on Earth they would have begun to develop.

Finding Out What Your Assumptions and Perspectives Are

You can understand how far from or how close to this society of love, peace, and brotherhood you are by drawing out and examining your assumptions about yourself, life, others, nature, and the Higher Power. And you can grow spiritually toward that society by changing the assumptions you hold to be more in keeping with the loving, peaceful, eternal self you're becoming that will create and live in that society. These are the assumptions that will be accepted as "of course" personal truths in the society imbued with love, peace, and brotherhood, the heaven on Earth:

- I am an eternal being having a physical experience.
- The goal for my life, over any physical realm goals, is to grow spiritually.
- My highest calling is to serve others.
- All other people are one with me.
- My love for all others is without conditions; I love without reservation.
- I help all others grow spiritually so humankind is developing toward heaven on Earth.
- I am one with nature.
- I am one with the Higher Power.
- The intuition that guides me is the Higher Power and beings on the other side of life whose sole desire is to help me grow spiritually.

You currently hold assumptions about each of these statements. They comprise your mind, and thus your place in your spiritual development.

For example, the first assumption is that we are eternal beings having a physical experience. If someone fears the materialists might be right and we might really be just accidents in time who will die and be gone forever, then that person holds an assumption that isn't true. She will live her life based on that and feel fear when she thinks of dying. She'll believe her loved ones who have died might be gone forever. And so she'll create a reality for herself that is full of grief and fear. But she'll be creating that reality out of ignorance.

If you go through that list of assumptions people will hold in the heaven on Earth society and write down everything you feel and think for each one, as quickly as the statements come into your mind, you'll end up with a clear picture of where you are on your eternal spiritual journey right now. You will likely have more than one statement come to your mind for each. Write them all down.

An important part of your spiritual journey now is to grow so your assumptions become increasingly like the assumptions in those statements. Ideally, you would want to be able to say "of course" to each, without doubt. That's not going to be possible for most of us in this life. We'll just mature as far as we can before we resume growing on the next plane of our eternal lives.

Who you <u>are</u> is spiritual, not what you do. Your fruit in the physical realm will result from the spiritual you in the spiritual realm, where your mind is. Change your mind by changing your assumptions. That results in spiritual growth.

How That Will Happen in Real Life

Now let's bring all of this down to an example of growing in spiritual maturity. A 10-year-old boy comes home from school crying. He explains to his father that a classmate pushed him down, so he ran away crying. When the father hears his story, his mind assembles a set of assumptions and he shifts into a perspective. Imagine the assumptions are, "Boys who don't fight back are sissies," "I want my son to grow up to be a man," and "My dad taught me that when someone hits you, you should hit him back." The father shifts his mind into this perspective: "If someone pushes you, push him back."

Having created that reality, the father says to his son, "Don't run away. Push him back."

His son responds, "It wasn't a boy. It was a girl." The father's mind shifts to a new set of assumptions: "Girls are weaker than boys and girls shouldn't beat boys," "But boys shouldn't hit girls," "The other kids will think he's a real sissy if he doesn't fight back," "The other parents are going to think my kid's a wuss."

Having changed the reality in his mind, he responds, "Don't let girls beat you. Don't hit a girl, but push her back really hard and tell her you'll kick her butt if she does that again."

This parent is forming reality and shifting it as the dialogue continues. This reality isn't in the situation; it isn't in his son; it's entirely in his mind. But now his son has learned a whole set of assumptions and perspectives about what people do to each other when there's conflict. He's learned the assumptions that boys don't hit girls, you don't try to understand what happened that resulted in the insult, and you fight back. He'll carry that set of assumptions into his business and family life, creating his realities based on them and acting accordingly. And he'll teach his sons the same assumptions.

But during the Axial Age, from around 800 BCE to 200 BCE and through Yeshua ben Yosef's teachings and into the first millennium, spiritual leaders told us repeatedly that if we are to have a brotherhood of man, we must have a different mind—a different set of assumptions and perspectives about ourselves and others.

> **Confucianism:** Do not do to others what you would not like yourself. Then there will be no resentment against you, either in the family or in the state. (Analects 12:2)

> **Taoism:** Regard your neighbor's gain as your own gain; and regard your neighbor's loss as your own loss. (Tai Shang Kan Ying P'ien)

> **Buddhism:** Hatreds never cease through hatred. Through love alone they cease. This is an eternal law. (Dhammapada 3-5)

> **Hinduism.** This is the sum of duty; do naught to others which if done to thee would cause thee pain. (From the Mahabharata 5.1517)

> **Islam:** No one of you is a believer until he desires for his brother that which he desires for himself. (Sunnah)

> **Judaism:** What is hateful to you, do not to your fellow human beings. That is the law; all the rest is commentary. (Talmud, Shabbat 3 1 a)

Yeshua said the same thing in the first century CE. As a result of his assumption that we must love our neighbor as ourselves, he said "If someone slaps you on the cheek, turn the other cheek so he can slap you on that cheek." That's based on a set of assumptions: "Peace is more important than retribution," "Forgiveness is better than striking back in anger," "Other people are our beloved—we shouldn't harm them for any reason, even if they harm us." The perspective based on these assumptions is, "Don't harm another person under any circumstances, even if that person harms you."

If the father in our story held these assumptions and shifted his mind into this perspective, he might have said to his son, "If someone pushes you, go to that person and ask her what you've done that made her feel angry with you. Tell her you want to be friends and ask her what you have to do to be a friend." That father has shifted his mind so he is shaping his reality based on the words of the spiritual teachers who taught about love and forgiveness.

You may be thinking, "Well that won't work. The poor kid'll get pushed around all day." Unfortunately, that may be true. We're still living in a spiritually primitive society where conflict and anger are accepted norms. If we're to change the world, we all need to begin by changing ourselves. Gandhi said, "We must become what we want the world to be." It will happen one person at a time. Reality is only individual, and society is simply many individuals each creating a reality moment by moment based on personal assumptions. If we shape our realities using perspectives based on the teachings of the luminaries, we will have begun progress toward the brotherhood of man.

The father in my story would have to struggle to have that perspective. He's learning and has to follow a cheat sheet to pass this test—he really has to think about it and struggle because he was reared in a violent society where many fathers tell their sons, "Be a man. Push her back." He's going to have to go against the assumptions that made up his mind from boyhood, which his father taught him. The boy's grandfather (this man's father) might be angry with the father when he hears he didn't teach his son to "be a man." But the father will accept this division, and will do it because he has a spiritual model to guide him so he can do something against his normal inclinations.

His son will see his father's example and hear his words, and he'll grow up to have that perspective in his nature. Just as he learns to speak the language and go into the right restroom without thinking twice about either, he'll learn that being nonviolent is just the better way to be. His generation will be even closer to the day when people will live in harmony. While that generation will work at being peaceful and loving in some other areas, the boy's son (the father's grandson) will grow up with a new model and will take humankind even closer to the brotherhood of man where people live in peace and love.

Reality wasn't in the coagulations of atoms around that father. His universe was in his assumptions and perspectives. He then acted out the scenes in the physical realm based on what he had already scripted in his mind. When his son responded in the physical realm, he changed the scene in his mind and acted based on the new script, but it was all still entirely in his mind; his responses in the physical world were just acting out the drama already created. His reality was in his mind.

You Grow in Spiritual Maturity by Changing Your Assumptions

The result is that if you want to grow spiritually, you have to identify the assumptions you learned from the physical realm that now are keeping you from feeling unconditional love and compassion for yourself, others, and the Higher Power. You have to change your mind.

When our descendents grow into a society that wouldn't even consider any alternative assumptions about life, one another, the Higher Power, and their inner selves, they will be living in heaven on Earth. They will be spiritual trees whose fruit in the physical realm will always be loving and compassionate, so the world will be a loving, compassionate world. We can't arrive at that destination yet; our society is too far from it. But it is humankind's destiny.

Common Practices that May Not Aid in Spiritual Growth

Two common practices are very popular in the dominant world religions, but aren't necessary for spiritual growth and may in fact hinder it.

Meditation

Some people are able to open themselves to the Higher Power and their own eternal nature through a meditation practice. As a result of consistently engaging in deep meditation, they feel a change in their understanding of their place in the universe. That experience then affects other parts of their lives and they mature spiritually. For them, it is a valuable, powerful part of their spiritual growth.

However, a meditation practice isn't necessary for spiritual growth. Even those who teach meditation admit that most people are not able to initiate or maintain a meditation practice,[3,4] and many who do are disappointed that they don't have the peak spiritual experiences that the religions advocating meditation describe.[5] That can result in the unfortunate and unjustified feeling of being a spiritual failure. Don't feel you must meditate to grow spiritually, and don't evaluate your spiritual practice or growth based on whether you've had the life-changing peak experience some people describe.

Meditation is also a solitary activity that is incomplete without the spiritual growth that comes in a community,[6] and it alone can't help a person overcome the psychological issues that must be addressed to have mental and spiritual growth.[7]

Also don't feel that only an Eastern religion or practice is spiritual. You need no religion or religious practice to mediate your relationship with the Higher Power or aid your spiritual growth. Quiet times of contemplation or prayer and listening to the Higher Power speak to you will be very rewarding for you. Enjoy them without feeling you must have a regular period of time dedicated to meditation.

You can read more about meditation and spiritual development at http://youreternalself.com/chapter7.htm.

Church Services

Church services, especially in megachurches and any other setting where people watch passively as others perform, likely will do very little to help you grow spiritually; they shut people down instead of opening them up. These passive experiences actually can interfere with spiritual growth because participants believe they're doing their spiritual duty and never bond with other people or uncover and reconsider their assumptions and perspectives. As Carl Jung, the father of Jungian psychoanalysis, wrote, "Religion is a defense against a religious experience." Churches where people sit passively in rows may bring an occasional perspective that resonates with the spiritual person you're becoming, but the growth itself will occur only as you use the insight to open yourself to reexamining your assumptions and perspectives and changing your relationships with others, face to face. Only in small, intimate groups where you talk openly will you be able to grow spiritually.

How Do You Grow to Make These Assumptions Part of Your Nature?

You grow to make these assumptions part of your nature by becoming open to guidance and reexamining the assumptions you learned during childhood. To accomplish that, you most do these things:

1. Be open and childlike.
2. Be willing to look at your assumptions and perspectives.
3. Realize the hidden assumptions.
4. Move past rationalizations.
5. Use emotions as clues to assumptions.
6. Allow time for the realizations to weave through all of your assumptions.
7. Don't judge your spiritual growth as good or bad.
8. Fill your life with spiritual experiences and people.

Be Open and Childlike.

> I tell you the truth, anyone who will not receive the
> kingdom of God like a little child will never enter it.
> - *Yeshua ben Yosef*

The first requirement for maturing spiritually is that you become humble and naively open, like a child. You must have a child's willingness to grow into spiritual adulthood without expectations and plans, just as a child grows inexorably into physical and emotional adulthood not knowing what an adult mind and life will be like.

You must be willing to clean out the closet of your mind and throw out all the old assumptions and perspectives that no longer fit you, transforming your mind with new assumptions and perspectives you likely don't even know about right now, but that fit whom you are becoming spiritually.

In other words, you must be willing to release your grip on assumptions that were called "right" and "commonsense" and "righteous" and "godly" and all the other words our parents, teachers, and clergy used to enforce the assumptions you learned from society in the physical realm. When you let go, you will find materializing in your open hands what the Higher Power has brought to you to replace what you released. But you won't know what that is until you receive it.

You are becoming a new person. You don't know what that person will be like, just as when you were 10 you didn't know the adult you would become. You couldn't know. For this person to come into your life, you have to be willing to allow yourself to be different, but you don't know what that difference will be.

If you are confident that you have arrived at the correct answers about religious practices and have the knowledge that is Truth for everyone in the universe, then you run the risk of being deluded. Just as a drunk person doesn't realize her drunkenness, when a person insists she has the Truth about existence for everyone, she likely does not realize her own ignorance. That isn't to say you shouldn't have convictions such as the need to live in brotherhood and peace, and the reality of the afterlife. It just means that with some other issues, such as religious practices, the influence of spirits on people, methods of growing spiritually, and so on, you should, at times, go through periods of reexamination and doubt. If you have no periods of self-doubt and reexamination, you may very possibly be shutting down your openness to new perspectives.

Be Willing to Look at Your Assumptions and Perspectives.

An important requirement for your spiritual growth is that you're willing to draw out the assumptions and perspectives that are deep within you, which are who you are as a person. They are creating your realities.

In your prayer or meditation, or in a group to which you belong in which you trust the members, voice your assumptions and perspectives if you're comfortable doing so. That will help you bring them out into the light where you can look at them.

You will also learn about many assumptions you hold through discomfort, pain, and suffering. The physical realm is the world of change—it provides obstacles and challenges that will bring to the surface deeply buried assumptions that you need to face but wouldn't if you weren't challenged. Your greatest understandings may come when your business fails, you are diagnosed with terminal cancer, or a loved one dies. During those times, you could collapse into a puddle of tears and never rise up again, or you could use what happens to discover more about yourself and the assumptions and perspectives behind why you feel as you do. If you go through the painful process of looking at yourself deeply, you will grow from it.

The journey is spiritual. Uncovering, understanding, and working at changing your assumptions are large parts of what you need to do. But you're given help from the Higher Power and those on the next planes of life. Whatever happens, it will work out if you're listening to that counsel. Ask and be open to the answers; they will come.

Realize the Hidden Assumptions.

When an assumption is so much a part of you that you believe it's "right" or the only way to think, then it's a foundation brick that makes up your mind. You likely won't even know about it because you just assume it's correct or the way life ought to be. It's a brick down there in the foundation somewhere and you never thought to look at it to see whether it's something you really *want* to believe.

These assumptions you don't even think about are "unrealized assumptions." You haven't made them real to yourself yet. They're simply the way life is, just as we know we have a heart but have never seen it and don't have to think about it to make it beat.

These unrealized assumptions came from your experiences in the physical realm. If someone's parents always belittled her and told her she'd amount to nothing, the unrealized assumptions she might have learned were "I'm incompetent." "No one likes me." "I'll never be a success." "What's the use of trying. I'll never get ahead." The person carries these unrealized assumptions and creates self-defeating realities from moment to moment throughout life. When given a challenge at work, she stresses out, breaks down, and fails. She fulfilled her own expectations, but they didn't exist in her work or her boss or the physical world. They were in her mind apart from the body. She lived a reality she created, but it was based on faulty, unrealized assumptions that created automatic thinking, feeling, and acting.

Squirrels and fish and puppies and people all grow up in the physical realm learning how to navigate through it. We learn from the society in which we are reared. All of this accumulated knowledge creates a bundle of unrealized assumptions about life that you use without thinking to create the reality of your life from moment to moment. You have to be willing to realize these unrealized assumptions and decide whether they fit inside the new person you're becoming.

You grow spiritually by changing the mind's assumptions and perspectives.

Move Past Rationalizations.

Sometimes, the assumptions will be cloaked by rationalizations. A rationalization is a thought that seems to be real or logical, but it's hiding what the person feels or thinks. For example, a father may not want his daughter who lives at home to be out past 10 p.m., although she's 18 years old. If he considers why, he might think, "It's dangerous for a young woman to be outside after 10 p.m." But his real assumption may be "Young women are naturally promiscuous and she'll meet men if she's out after 10" or "Young men are sex crazy and they'll influence her to do things she will regret when she's older if she's out after 10." The father's mind may not let him feel he mistrusts his daughter or is considering her sexuality, so he lets himself think only the rationalization, "It will keep her out of danger."

If you allow yourself to examine all the assumptions, the real ones likely will come out among the statements you make about why you think or feel something or why you act in a particular way. It may take a long time for it to come out, and you may need someone else helping you drag it out of its hiding place.

Your real assumptions will more likely come to your mind if you speak or write as quickly as thoughts come to you. The more you have to mull over the assumptions, the more likely they're rationalizations. Your mind will sort through the assumptions you have until it comes to a combination that creates a perspective comfortable to you. Being comfortable may mean you have found a rationalization that will make you feel OK, but which is not at the basis of your thought, feeling, or behavior. The more spontaneously you voice what you feel, the more likely it is the real assumption. The more you have to "consider" or "think through" the assumption, the more likely it's going to turn out to be a rationalization.

After you've voiced or written the assumption, let it go and relax your mind. Then look at the assumption. Does it feel like it has life in it? Does it feel true or real? Each time you return to it after leaving it for a while, you'll instantly get a feeling about it. "That sure feels like it's me; that's what I believe." Or you'll feel, "I'm not feeling like that's it. It doesn't feel like I believe that deep down." If it doesn't feel like you, relax your mind and think again of the situation, person, or whatever is the focus of the assumption. Voice or write the first things that come to you. Then look at them to see whether any of them feel like there's life in them. Eventually, you'll feel that what you're voicing is true. That's the real assumption.

And don't be dismayed if you feel something is true and real, but the next day it feels off to you. It may take some time for a real assumption to surface. Your dialogue isn't just with yourself or your group, but with people not seen, but nonetheless there and tangible. You're loved and ministered to by people in the spiritual realm and the Higher Power. Be patient. You and they will be successful. Have faith. If you ask, the answer will be given to you.

Use Emotions as Clues to Assumptions.

"She made me so angry I was red." Well, no. It's impossible for someone to make another person feel any emotion. We create our own realities—no one can impose a reality on us. All they can do is change the scenery. In this case, the angry person made *himself* angry over something she said or did. He did it to himself based on his assumptions.

Imagine this is what happened. His wife said, "I'm not cleaning the dishes." He reacted with anger immediately, but behind the anger, his mind held these assumptions: "It's women's work to do dishes," "She's trying to show me she runs the family," "Men run families and women do what they're told." He didn't consciously think those assumptions, but they resulted in his acting self's automatic response of *making himself* angry.

Imagine the same situation but a different man with a different set of assumptions: "She works hard all the time," "I don't work enough around the house." *He* made *himself* feel grateful or guilty. It's the same situation, but different assumptions resulting in different emotions.

Whether we feel angry, guilty, sad, disgusted, frustrated, joyful, grateful, or hopeful, all depend on the assumptions about the situation that comprise our minds. The emotions have nothing to do with the other people or the world around us; they come entirely from our assumptions.

The emotions tell us what the real assumptions are that a person holds. Many people in our culture fear death. They won't talk about it, won't admit they're going to die, pray for a miracle to avoid it right up to the last minute, and weep and wail at funerals as though the person were gone forever. They say, "She's in heaven and we'll meet again some day," but the emotions tell us the assumption is "She's stone cold dead and we're burying her in the ground." They go to the cemetery to "pay respects," as though the person were there, moldering away in the ground. But the person isn't there; she's blissful and happy, having the time of her eternal life!

The emotions will let you know what your assumptions are. As you look at the assumptions you hold about the statements I listed earlier that will be "of course" assumptions in the society of love, peace, and brotherhood, if you feel fearful or anxious, the feelings come from assumptions. When you feel the uncomfortable, negative emotion, uncover the assumptions that are at the basis. They're there. The negative feelings aren't built into the scenery of your life. They're not in the atoms and molecules that make up your environment. They result from the assumptions and perspectives you hold. If they're painful and you don't know how to deal with them, make an appointment with a licensed counselor. Counselors are trained to help you deal with the more difficult assumptions and fears that result from them.

Allow Time for the Realizations to Weave Through All of Your Assumptions.

When you understand something for the first time, it is a realization. In other words, you make it real. It may be something that's been there for decades, but when you finally see it, the discovery can be surprising. Your spiritual growth will be filled with these realizations because you're becoming an empty vessel, and understanding will be freely given to you. If you are in a group with others who are having realizations, theirs will inspire more of your own.

After you have a realization, you'll see that it changes your assumptions and perspectives in a broad range of areas, one at a time, over days, weeks, or years. That's called "horizontal learning" or "weaving." For example, you may learn one day that you have held the assumption that your 17-year-old son couldn't be of any help to you in day-to-day household decisions. You didn't say that and it didn't come to your mind, but you never did involve him in any of your household or important activities. That shows you that the assumption that he wouldn't be helpful was there, deep inside of you. Then one day you hear that Alexander the Great became regent of Macedonia at age 16 and Joan of Arc led the French armies to victory at Orléans at 17.

It dawns on you, out of the blue, that your 17-year-old son has all the capabilities that he needs to take a hand in family affairs. That is the realization. But you still have dozens of assumptions that don't match that realization: "He just wants to loaf all day," "He's just a kid," "He'll make mistakes if I give him a job to do." Those assumptions will still be there, even though the light bulb went on and you had the realization that he has the capabilities to participate in family decisions.

The next week, it happens that you are trying to decide whether to replace the furnace and it comes to you that you can involve him in the decision, so you talk with him about it. You're weaving your discovery into your life. You have some concerns because your old assumptions are still a part of you, but as you weave the realization that he's becoming an adult into your life, you change other assumptions to fit this new learning.

Two months later, you're settling your father's estate and it occurs to you that your son could help sort out the belongings. The old assumption was "He'll make mistakes if I give him a job to do," but you're weaving the new realization that he's capable into all of your assumptions, so your new assumption is, "He's capable of sorting, cataloguing, and making decisions." You give him the tasks with some concern because the old assumption is still active. After a year or two of weaving, you find you have a whole set of assumptions that bring you to the perspective, "My son is a capable young adult on whom I can rely at any time as I would any adult," and you can say "Of course" to that. It has become part of your mind. But it took a single realization, then the process of weaving through learning dozens of new assumptions over two years to come to that perspective.

As you're going through the weaving process, you'll find your assumptions clashing. The clash will cause you some frustration, but that is a sign that you're changing and growing. At times, you will have a new realization that creates a new set of assumptions, but the other assumption you act from is out of sync with the new ones. At that moment, you're creating a reality using the old assumption and acting based on it, but it's pretty clear that it violates what you hold to be true in the new realization. The negative term for that is "backsliding," but that's full of judgment and you really shouldn't use that term for yourself or anyone else. It's just that you're in the process of weaving, and the weaving takes time and some adjustments. Don't expect that you'll come to a realization and within a couple of days your life will be reoriented. And don't do a guilt trip on yourself or others when you or they are weaving new assumptions and there are still some old assumptions influencing your thoughts, feelings, and actions that you or they haven't finished adjusting.

For example, imagine that Ben has the assumption, "A loving family does things together in the evening," but working late keeps him from doing things with his family. As Ben thinks about it, he discovers he has the assumption, "I have to work late to earn money so my family can have the things they want." So Ben's assumptions are at odds. That is called "cognitive dissonance." It means the person has two assumptions that may not be compatible, but he holds both as "Of course" assumptions. With that realization, Ben resolves not to work so late and to spend more time with his family.

But one week, it seems he's needed at the office every night. That doesn't mean he's done anything wrong. He hasn't "backslid." It means only that he will have to work on the assumptions that he's changing as he weaves his new learning into his life. The intimate support group I describe in the next chapter can help. In the group, Ben may bring up the fact that he didn't want to be at work every night, but it just happened. If Ben gives the group permission to reflect to him what they are hearing, someone may say, "You know, it sounds like you're assuming that only you can manage the office when your company is negotiating a contract." Ben might then think for a moment, and say, "Yes, that's true, and I feel I can't hire someone to negotiate contracts with me because it would be too expensive." So part of Ben's growth is to reexamine those assumptions. He may change them by deciding, "Joan's very capable. I just have to train her. If I want to reduce my time in the office, I need to start delegating." He's growing. The fact that he had a bad week was just part of the growth because it helped him reexamine more assumptions. The dissonance between his realization and what he felt he had to do caused some pain for him, but in the end, Ben learned from it.

However, if Ben keeps working late and doesn't spend time with his family, even though he has the assumption, "A loving family spends time together in the evening," then he'll be living with great frustration and likely some guilt. The frustration and guilt come from the reality he's creating, though, not from anything in his family, his job, or the universe. He may choose to live life a frustrated person because he has the free will to do that. And no one should judge him because of where he is in his spiritual growth. But it's pretty clear that if he wants to have bliss and satisfaction, some assumptions need to be adjusted in this situation with his family.

Discovering your assumptions, weaving your learning through the dozens of other assumptions in your life, and growing spiritually so your life becomes what you want it to be will be much easier for you if you are part of a supportive group. They can listen to you explain your feelings and assumptions and share their perspectives. That will help you look at yourself from other points of view. And they'll be supportive as you struggle with new assumptions that don't feel good to you at first.

The new realizations that have caused you to weave new assumptions through your mind will change it irrevocably. Your mind will be becoming a different mind than it was when the process began, and you can never go back. Each new realization is a leap forward.

Don't Judge Your Spiritual Growth as Good or Bad.

Don't judge your spiritual growth. Don't feel that because you're doing things you wish you weren't, or you're sad and frustrated in the physical realm, it means you must be spiritually immature. You will feel sad, frustrated, and unhappy when you suffer loss and your life changes. That's normal. It's also part of your loving compassionate nature that underlies your physical nature. Your love creates sadness when you see the suffering others are enduring or when you lose someone or something you love. The love is the reason you're unhappy.

But more importantly, you are right now at the level of spiritual growth that is right for you. You're at an A+ level in the Earth school. Don't judge yourself. Don't expect more of yourself than you're experiencing right now. You're where you should be. You're at the head of your class. You'll continue to grow, but you are already a spiritually mature person, at whatever level you are, because you're open to growing and looking for answers. Spirituality is a journey, not a destination.

Also, if you spend your life trying to help the little girl or little boy who was abused as a child whom you still have in you, that is your spiritual journey in this life. Learning to understand and cope with what happened to you is spiritual; you're changing the inner you to have less trauma or stress so you can live in peace. As for the other spiritual issues, such as learning to be a servant to others, you have an eternity to learn more lessons such as those. You needn't feel you have to reach a standard in this Earthly life. Take care of yourself; that's what the Higher Power wants for you.

If you're sad or unhappy often or much of the time, talk with your physician about it. The physical realm could very possibly have given you a body that has a chemical or genetic disposition to depression that you can receive help for. The explanations in this book aren't meant to suggest that you should or could get over all your problems just by working at your assumptions. If you were given psychological or physical conditions by the physical realm that make your life difficult, they'll affect you regardless of how you change your mind. Counseling and medication are gifts from God given through scientists to help people. Accept the gifts. Then, with the limitations you still have, you can work at changing your assumptions as much as you are able to.

Emulate the Model Even If You Aren't Comfortable with the Assumptions Yet.

We're living in a law-and-order society now where laws are necessary to enforce humane behavior. Laws restrain people from doing hateful things to other people, and they provide care for the poor because no one would care for them otherwise. Some of our assumptions and perspectives are more in line with following rules and legislating behavior than with an inner sense of unconditional love and servanthood to all other people. We have our feet in both worlds. As a result, we'll be working at following the model even if internally we don't yet have the confidence in the assumptions that underlie it.

For example, we know we should rush to forgive others. Someone may know that and want to model it because it's apparent that this is an important action in the path toward spiritual maturity, but the assumptions that crowd into the person's mind come from the materialistic society in which we have been reared: "Forgive your neighbor is a fine concept, but my brother-in-law keeps spreading lies about me and if I forgive him, he'll just do it again." Or "Letting her keep doing it will just show everyone I'm a spineless wimp." Following the model may not feel comfortable; physical realm fears may crowd into the person's mind, created by the old materialistic assumptions. But eventually, following the model even against the deeply felt concerns will result in the assumptions in the model weaving through the person's mind; the assumptions will become more "Of course" beliefs and the person will grow to have the inner disposition to love unconditionally.

The actions may precede the beliefs.

Fill Your Life with Spiritual Experiences and People.

Read books and watch media that contain accounts by people who have had spiritual experiences such as ADCs, NDEs, healings, psychic realizations, and sessions with mediums. There are many wonderful DVDs and books available today in which people describe what has happened to them. You will learn from them and understand more about the greater reality and eternity.

Seek out and listen to wise souls who have had remarkable experiences or have insights into spirituality. You can learn from them. Immerse yourself in the testimonies from real people. There are many, and they will teach you about your place in the universe, your eternal nature, and the Higher Power. The material realm is bathing you in perspectives that are thoroughly physical while minimizing or hiding the spiritual. We live in a materialistic age. To understand the spiritual realm and grow from the knowledge, you must search out and experience the less-available spiritual media.

Lists of resources I recommend will be kept up to date at http://youreternalself.com/chapter7.htm.

Build happy, contented surroundings with others and look for opportunities to join in on loving, compassionate activities. Seek out loving people and spend time with them. Avoid all negative emotions. If you choose to meditate, focus on love, peace, and brotherhood during your contemplative periods. Rush to forgive and overcome separation and barriers. As you feel love, you will learn to love more deeply. Conversely, if you feel anger, mistrust, hatred, and separation, you will paint your life with the dark colors in those brushes.

Your world will be whatever you are. And as you love, your world will become more loving.

8

Become Part of an Intimate Spiritual Group

To grow spiritually, you should be part of an intimate group that grows together. You learn to love by loving. During the group meetings, you'll be learning about spirituality, the realities of life and the universe, how to understand your own assumptions and perspectives, how to grow spiritually, and how to accept others' assumptions that may be very different from yours.

You'll be learning about others, about yourself, about your eternal nature and the afterlife, and about God.

Learning about Others

The intimate group will help you learn about listening, understanding, accepting, and loving unconditionally. You'll learn how to

- Focus on another person and listen genuinely and wholly, losing yourself in loving unity with that person
- Listen without judging

- Empathize without feeling the need to solve the problem
- Avoid giving advice
- Just reflect back what you're hearing without insinuations
- Understand perspectives that are different from yours as being only different, not right or wrong

Nothing a group member can say would separate you from that person or make you feel less loving and accepting. When you feel a negative emotion, try to understand the assumptions behind the negative feeling. In your quiet times of prayer or contemplation, or in the group, bring out the hidden assumptions behind the feelings and decide whether they fit with the spiritual person you're becoming.

Learning about Yourself

You'll also be learning about yourself:

- How to love unconditionally
- What it's like to be loved unconditionally
- How to trust others without reservation
- How to serve without expectation for return or compensation
- What your assumptions and perspectives are that create your realities
- How to stand back from yourself as a watcher and understand your assumptions and perspectives with less involvement and less letting them control you
- What you cling to that makes you feel frustrated, worried, or fearful
- How to change your assumptions and perspectives to grow spiritually
- How to trust that you are learning lessons and to see that challenges in life are opportunities to grow

Learning about Your Eternal Nature and the Afterlife

You'll be learning about your eternal nature and the afterlife:

- You are a spiritual being having a physical realm period of your eternal life.
- The afterlife is as real as, or more real than, this life.

- Your loved ones are just a step away, blissfully involved in their new spiritual lives.

- Death is simply a graduation into the next wonderful stage of your eternal life.

- Your spiritual nature affects you, others, and the environment in which you live.

- You can communicate with those who have transitioned into the next stage of their eternal lives.

Learning about God

You'll learn about the Higher Power that is the basis of all life in the universe and from whom the universe comes into being. You'll learn

- The nature of the Higher Power

- That the Higher Power is one with you and provides guidance and counseling to help you grow spiritually

- How to trust that the Higher Power will provide what is in your best interest

Characteristics of Your Intimate Group

Establish the intimate group with care. Include a small number of people. Choose participants carefully and follow the protocol below until the group is established. Have all group members read these guidelines and agree to them before the group meets.

The guidelines are going to sound a little constraining and unusual. The reason is that in our normal conversations, we've all developed some bad habits from childhood. When someone speaks, we often don't listen; we're getting ready to say what we have in mind. Conversations are sometimes like two radios facing each other, each blaring out its message with no hearing and no understanding.

We also tend to give advice as though we had the right answer. When someone describes a problem, we feel the need to solve it for the speaker. It's unusual for us to listen only to understand, not to voice our beliefs or give advice. This intimate group must be grounded in listening, focusing on others to the exclusion of the self, nonjudgment, tolerance, and understanding. Most of us haven't learned how to have those kinds of conversations. They must be learned.

Content

Foremost, the purpose of the group is to come together in love and openness, without expectations. Whatever happens will benefit everyone if the group has these qualities. Coming together in love will catalyze experiences and result in knowledge far beyond what we can anticipate. Feeling this love and freely giving love will fill you with a sense of peace and fulfillment.

Have a time when group members can share their spiritual growth, describe realizations, and discuss assumptions and perspectives. Anyone may ask for help in understanding something, but the purpose of the time is to share only, not solve problems.

Have group members read books and watch media that contain accounts by people who have had spiritual experiences; then discuss them in the group. There are many wonderful DVDs and books available today in which people describe what has happened to them. You may ask people who have had remarkable experiences or have insights into spirituality to speak to your group. Have group members describe testimonies from real people and encourage members to share their own experiences. Resources I recommend will be kept up to date at http://youreternalself.com/chapter8.htm.

Go through the list of assumptions I presented earlier in this book that will underlie a loving, peaceful society. Share your assumptions about each and talk about them. As long as the assumptions and perspectives are hidden, you'll be living from within them. When you uncover and discuss them, you can look at them from outside of them. Then you can decide whether they fit the spiritual person you're becoming.

Protocol

The protocol will evolve as the group develops. These guidelines are important to begin the group, but once it is established, the group will evolve its own guidelines. If the group seems to be becoming too loose or uncomfortable for even one person, that person may ask that the group return to this protocol. There is no discussion of that request. The group does it in appreciation and love for the person who requested it.

1. Confidentiality is critical. Nothing said in the group leaves the group meeting. Spouses not present should not hear about something someone says in confidence. Don't talk about the group or a person in the group outside of the group meeting.

2. Assume there is no "truth" outside of each person and no one in the group has the truth for anyone else. You are attempting to understand others' assumptions and perspectives, and you are opening to others as they help you understand your own assumptions and perspectives. If you are from the same church or faith, don't enforce belief in the assumptions of the religion or insist on obedience during the meetings.

3. Be open and transparent, without pretences and without putting on a face because you want to appear knowledgeable or righteous or mature, or because you're afraid your weaknesses will be judged and you won't be regarded as highly. You'll learn that others can accept you as you are, with all the things you might normally hide from people. You'll, in turn, learn to accept others without judgment.

4. However, don't feel you have to reveal more than you're comfortable talking about. It isn't a sign of strength or spirituality to say something you're uncomfortable saying. Wait until you feel comfortable to speak about it. If you're troubled by something you'd rather not reveal or you feel overwhelmed by some feelings, talk with a counselor about it, not the group. This is not a therapy group.

   The group may meet for months or years before everyone begins to share more intimate feelings. You have to learn to trust everyone and feel comfortable. Don't expect to have completely open dialogues for the first months. That will evolve naturally.

5. Focus on understanding the other people. Avoid giving advice, although anyone may feel free to ask for reflections on what they've just said. The group is not intended to solve problems. As you share perspectives, the person may arrive at a solution, but that is entirely within the person's reality.

6. Don't psychologize. As you hear someone talk about a thought, feeling, or behavior and the assumptions behind it, you may think of psychological reasons for it, or may feel you want to probe to get to the psychological implications. Don't do that. You're not psychologists and you're not trying to make everyone feel better or be psychologically healthy. Just listen and don't interpret what you hear.

7. Anyone may speak. No one is required to speak. Don't go around the room and have everyone speak. Let the person speak without interruption. When the person is finished, someone else may speak. If the group has some overenthusiastic speakers, use a "talking

stick." The person holding the talking stick is the only one permitted to speak until he or she relinquishes it by giving it to someone else.

8.   Listen with empathy and concern. As you listen, focus on the other person; become the other person. Shut down the flow of your own assumptions as much as possible. Imagine yourself with this person's assumptions and sense what that would be like. You'll learn to be more empathetic and stand in someone else's shoes. Share your assumptions that might be different, but don't insinuate that they're right or more rational or more spiritual.

9.   Never judge. Never believe someone is wrong or weird, and never speak negative words. Listen to the statements and assumptions openly, without judging.

10. When someone shares something personal and you want to ask a question, ask whether the person is open to questions. If not, don't ask questions. The person is not obligated to answer any question. If your question is met with silence, don't pursue it. Then share your assumptions and perspectives about the same subject. The purpose is not to show them what is right, but for them to understand your assumptions and perspectives. The group's purpose is to share and understand, not arrive at the truth or solve problems.

11. Don't ask questions that make statements, such as "Don't you think you could go and talk to your sister." That's not a question; it's a statement: "You should go and talk to your sister." Notice that the question has no question mark ending it.

12. Early on especially, as you sense some judgment or insinuation of "right" or advice in a statement, stop and talk about it. But don't argue about it and don't defend a position. You're putting something on the table only. Speak your feelings about it and go on. No one is required to respond to any statement, but everyone may ask for a response. The insights about what is said will come naturally.

13. Learn to love openly and unconditionally. There are no wrongs and nothing is unlovable. If someone wants to hear other perspectives about what he has just said, that person may ask for them.

14. If someone is not present, don't discuss him or her.

You can learn more about forming and participating in the intimate group to grow spiritually at http://youreternalself.com/chapter8.htm.

9

What Are the Facts About the Afterlife?

Life is eternal; and love is immortal; and death is only a horizon; and a horizon is nothing save the limit of our sight. - *R. W. Raymond*

We're now all sharing what we know about life and the universe as humankind could never do prior to the present age. In the process, experiences people have and knowledge we gain from the experiences are openly shared. The result is that we've learned that people are having regular, normal communications with those who have gone on to the next plane of life. What was previously hidden because people could talk about their experiences only among a small group of relatives and friends is now known by masses of people. Our accumulated knowledge is demonstrating continually, indisputably, the reality of the afterlife. We're learning as a society what people as individuals and small groups knew about all along.

Just as the seventeenth through the nineteenth centuries saw the discovery of the Newtonian universe, and the twentieth century saw the discovery of the quantum universe, the twenty-first century is seeing the discovery of the spiritual universe.

The Sources of Our Knowledge about the Afterlife

Here are some of the communications we're having commonly now that are teaching us about the afterlife:

Near-death experiences: A Gallup poll in the United States indicated 8-12 million people (approximately the population of New York City) claimed experience of life beyond the grave; in Britain, a Mori poll showed seven people out of 10 believed NDEs happen and constitute evidence of an afterlife.[1] We know about the afterlife from NDE experiences.

After-death communications: A broad range of studies of after-death communication have shown that around 40 percent of people say they have had an after-death communication experience, with the percentage as high as 70 or 80 percent for widows.[2] We have learned about the afterlife from what those there have told people. Loved ones in the afterlife are describing what their lives are like there.

Induced after-death communications (IADC™): From 70 to 98 percent (depending on the environment) of people who undergo IADCs™ report that they experience an after-death communication, with virtually all insisting that they actually communicated with the deceased person for whom they are grieving. Thousands of people have now had the experience.[3] The reports experiencers give to their psychotherapists after these sessions have added to our understanding of the afterlife.

Mental medium communications: Thousands of mediums have had communication with people who have crossed over to the next plane of life, with the results of the medium readings being verified by the family members. The shelves of bookstores are now crowded with books containing mediums' accounts of the readings and what the sessions have taught them about the afterlife. Perhaps the best compilation of reports is in *The Supreme Adventure, Analyses of Psychic Communications*, by Robert Crookall.[4] These reports have provided insights into the afterlife that are consistent across time, geography, and cultures.

Direct voice and physical medium communications: A number of direct-voice and physical mediums have made it possible for people in the afterlife to speak. Direct-voice mediums have held carefully controlled séances in which unmistakable voices of those in the afterlife are heard. Their voices have been recorded and now exist in thousands of recordings (see David Thompson[5] and Leslie flint[6]). They have provided the clearest descriptions of the afterlife. If you want to listen to some recordings, link to http://youreternalself.com/chapter9.htm.

In all, we have a vast amount of information from the citizens of the afterlife. What we now know is not based simply on religious texts, musings by mystics, or ancient traditions. It is based on first-hand accounts from sources whose reliability has been verified in tests by skeptics, scientists, and scholars from a variety of disciplines. This storehouse of knowledge has given us an understanding of what happens to someone when they leave the body, what life is like on the next planes of life, and what those in the afterlife advise for us who are still on the Earth plane. The remainder of this chapter summarizes what we know.

I don't cite the individual speakers from the afterlife or medium sources because the endless citations from hundreds of recordings and other sources would be cumbersome and the knowledge is repeated often by many on the next planes of life. Be assured that every fact was spoken by someone who is a resident of the next plane of life.

How Our Loved Ones Are

The most important issue for most people, of course, is whether their loved ones who have passed away are all right. I can tell you with great assurance that they're fine—in fact, they're joyous. Everyone who speaks from the afterlife describes their happiness at being without worries, healthy, feeling light as a feather, with a young body that has no aches and pains. They're delighted.

As to why they don't communicate with you often or at all, one reason is that it is difficult for them to communicate with us. It isn't something they can do easily, and just as few people on our side of life can communicate with those on the other side of life, most people on the next planes of life aren't adept at getting through to us. They do register our thoughts, but may not be able to communicate back easily or at all.

They're also not worried about you, unless you're grieving and unhappy. They now know the truth that you and they are eternal beings. You'll live your life and transition into the next plane of life where you'll reunite; in the meantime, they know you need to continue to learn lessons and they know they can't really do anything to help you with your struggles. You have to work them out yourself. They're happy and they know you're fine as well. They'll be happiest when you're happy.

And they're busy learning about life and eternity. They have occupations and preoccupations, often what they wished they could have done on the Earth plane but couldn't. They haven't forgotten you, but just as you have to go to work or have activities each day and leave your family members to whatever they're doing, those who are on the next plane of life aren't preoccupied with staying around you. They're busy, and they know you have your life to live.

However, you may receive assistance from them in taking care of yourself and learning your life lessons. You may have a sudden insight or a feeling of calm and peace in the midst of worrying. Someone on the Earth plane may contact you unexpectedly with a message you need to hear, or you may chance upon some information in a book or on television that helps you through a crisis. Any of these insights may have been brought to you by that person you wish you could hear from. They do offer assistance, although it may not be in the way you might expect or wish.

They will often return to be with you when you think of them. They don't observe birthdays and anniversaries because there is no time as we know it in the afterlife. However, when you think of them and they know the family is coming together, they often will stand among you. They're with you, but you can't see them. Your thoughts come to them in the afterlife and they respond by going to be with you on special occasions.

Just know that they are happier than they've ever been; they are always within thought range of you; and they know you're just separated from them for a short time. They're fine.

If your loved one was an infant or a child, that little one will be with your loved ones who have gone before. They will continue to rear your child in love, and you will be reunited when you transition to the other side.

Pets also are kept by family members until the owners transition over, at which time, the pet returns to the owner without question.

Preparation for Death

When a person has been ill and can prepare for death, the spirit "calls" deceased loved ones to let them know that the passing will occur soon. The person may then have dreams about deceased loved ones or visions of them in waking moments. These are intentional efforts to prepare the person for the coming transition. Then, when the death occurs, the loved ones are there to greet the person who crosses over.

Those who are more self-centered and have no belief in the life to come may not send out such a call to those on the other side. However, they are still cared for by guides who help them until they grow out of the self-centeredness and disbelief.

That is not the case when a person dies suddenly in war or an accident. The loved ones come as soon as they can, but the person may be assisted in the transition by a guide or a "rescuer," a person now in the afterlife who has dedicated his or her life to helping people make the transition into the next life.

At the Moment of Death

When a person dies, the person leaves the Earthly body with very little ceremony. The separation is quite natural and happens without the person's being fully aware that it has happened.

While people who have nearly drowned and been revived describe drowning as a terrible experience, people who actually die as a result of drowning describe themselves as "skipping" the terrible part. It is common for people who have crossed over not to remember anything about the circumstances at the moment of death.

People often describe floating above their bodies while the body is still alive. They see the efforts to revive them and the results. If they are revived, they recall the events in a near-death experience. If they do not survive, they easily, gently move into the next plane of life. Crookall explains that about an hour before the person's body dies, the person's ethereal self often stands nearby with complete consciousness. Natural death is not accompanied by pain or fear.[7]

Awakening on the Other Side of Life

After the physical body dies, a variety of events have been described by those who have crossed over. Those who have died a violent, sudden death, as in war or an accident, may not realize they have died. They remain in an Earthly "vibration" as they call it, where they can walk on the Earth, sit on chairs, climb stairs, and take busses, but they are spirit, so no one can see them. One WWI soldier described himself running toward the enemy on the battlefield, but noticing that the enemy was running past him as though they couldn't see him. It wasn't until some time later that he realized he had been killed on the battlefield, but was still running on the Earth plane as the spirit person. His physical body was lying on the battlefield somewhere but all the rest—his mind, personality, and memories—were exactly the same.

Another man said that before his death, he was walking down the street with his wife and remembered seeing something coming at him. He then saw a crowd of people standing around staring at something. He "had a look" and saw someone lying on the street who looked just like him. "Could've been my twin brother," he said. His wife was crying hysterically, but for some reason, she couldn't see him. The reason was that he had been hit by a runaway truck and died. He got into the ambulance with the body and sat next to his grief-stricken wife, who still couldn't see him. Then he went to his own funeral. He remarked, "It was all very nice, but it was so damned silly because there I was!"

For some reason, some people find themselves next to the body or in the same room after the body dies. One man described trying to wake his body up before his sister came in and found him.

Others who pass away describe awakening in an open field, where at times a guide comes to help them. Some awaken on a couch in a home where their loved ones are. Others awaken in a hospital-like setting called a "reception area" where people help them make the adjustment to being dead and their loved ones come to visit. It seems that this common period of sleep is around two or three Earth days.

The transition is quite smooth and without incident. The person may not realize he or she has died, however, and needs help understanding the change. Some are bewildered for a period of time until they make the adjustment. A number of those who spoke during séances described how, in the moments after their bodies died, they felt that they must be dreaming and would wake up.

Several of those who spoke in the Leslie Flint séances described being "earthbound." They stayed on the Earth plane for weeks or years, walking about unnoticed by people, trying to communicate. A few described acting as poltergeists, banging things and moving things about to get attention. But it was just in trying to communicate, not to harm anyone.

After a while, however, most people do leave the Earth plane and go on to higher levels. Some explain that the excessive grief of the survivors depressed them and retarded them from progressing into happier conditions. Their most fervent wish was to reassure their loved ones that they were fine. Some describe the fact that they couldn't reassure their loved ones as the greatest difficulty in making the transition.

Guides, Rescuers, and Loved Ones

Guides, "rescuers," and loved ones on the other side help each person make the transition into the new life. The rescuers focus on people who have died suddenly in accidents or war, who are not prepared for death and are surprised or shocked to see their new surroundings. These rescuers are often people whom themselves have died in accidents or war and have dedicated themselves to helping others make the transition. The rescuers also help people who are earthbound because of their attachment to the Earth to grow in their assumptions and perspectives to leave the Earth plane.

Guides are like teachers, who help the person understand the new life. The guides continue to work with people for a long period to help them mature away from the Earth plane to higher levels.

The deceased's loved ones are often the ones who help the deceased understand that they are dead and what the new surroundings are.

Condition after Death

After death, all who cross over describe having a tangible body just as they had when in a physical body. They have no aches and pains, however, and they feel healthy and light. When they see themselves in a reflection, they look as they did in their twenties or thirties if they died at an older age. If they died as children, they grow up on the other side of life.

Those in the afterlife remark often about how completely natural their bodies are, just as they had on the Earth plane. When the body stops functioning, the person is still completely as he or she was just before dying. Their personalities, memories, concerns, and intentions are exactly the same. They are the mind without the physical body. However, they do have an ethereal body that has all the same tangible qualities as the physical body.

People do not lose their individuality in the afterlife and don't suddenly become omniscient or clairvoyant. They don't change. They also don't transform into being good or angelic. They carry their fears, conflicts, and problems into the afterlife. However, the perspective they have, if they allow it to influence them, changes them more quickly.

They learn what all on Earth would benefit from learning—that they are in fact eternal beings who just finished an Earthly period. That helps them to alleviate the problems, fears, and negative thoughts they had while on Earth, but they don't suddenly change.

We absolutely know that people don't enter millennia of sleep waiting for a resurrection after death. When the body is no longer attached to the eternal self, the person goes on just as before, with an ethereal body and all the memories, personality, knowledge, inclinations, and interests they had while still using the body. Many people are surprised to see that they're dead when everything is so natural. They experience exactly the same things we do on the Earth plane: their bodies, trees, buildings, homes, walking, daylight, warmth, joking with people, playing games, listening to talks, going to the theater, listening to concerts—it's all just as though they were on the Earth plane, but with none of the negatives.

As it turns out, the Earth is the nursery where the mind grows and becomes what it will be as it continues to evolve through eternity. When people leave the Earth plane, they enter an environment that suits their mental condition, attitudes, and spiritual level of growth. Those who have been selfish and cruel on the Earth plane will be on a sphere or plane with others who are also selfish and cruel. That isn't a punishment and it certainly isn't a hell. It's a condition they create by their own expectations for the way life is and ought to be. They expect life to be dog-eat-dog, full of greed and selfishness, so that is the way it is for them. And they are with others who have the same inclinations.

They remain on that lower plane until they grow out of it. They are given help and are taught by higher-level people who work with them to help them understand their self-centeredness and hostile, cruel, or violent minds. However, they will remain on that level as long as they choose to continue to hold the assumptions that comprise their spiritually backward minds. No one put them there; no one demands they change; no one punishes them. They remain there until they choose to grow into a higher spiritual level. Then, they simply evolve into another level naturally.

Some materialist scientists are still materialists in the afterlife. They are on the next plane of life certain that there's some physical explanation for what has happened to them. They are endeavoring to understand it, working in teams as they did on the Earth plane to study what has taken place. They still won't allow themselves to believe in the afterlife and spiritual existence.

People find themselves in a comfortable environment that is familiar to them so the transition is easier. They carry their expectations into the afterlife and those shape what they encounter. They actually create their realities. The realities are "collective," however. Groups of people with similar attitudes and expectations are on the same plane or sphere and the reality fits all of them, just as the reality of the Earth plane applies to all who are here.

When people are earthbound after death and unable to accept their own deaths, they may grow to understand what has happened by learning that others cannot see or hear them. They may see their own funerals, meet loved ones who have died years before them, and have new abilities, such as being able to pass through walls, float, or be transported by simply thinking of a destination.

Some describe a life review as one of the ways they grow spiritually. It helps them understand their assumptions and perspectives, but is not a punishment.

The Hell Myth

No one in any of the séances by physical mediums ever describes a hell or place of torment. The concept of hell is a myth invented by the church in the first and second centuries CE. For more about why hell is a myth, link to http://youreternalself.com/chapter9.htm.

Environment

The environment depends on the person's state of being. If someone is still tied to the Earth and its environment, they will experience a very Earthlike existence, for as long as they remain at that level of thought. Eating and drinking aren't necessary in the afterlife, but when a person first enters, eating and drinking are available as the person wishes, to help acclimate them to living their new life. The person will no longer eat and drink when they grow out of the need to do so.

Each person lives in a home with loved ones. The homes are very often duplicates of the homes they loved on the Earth plane. Sometimes, people who were wealthy on the Earth plane are in smaller houses to help them learn that wealth isn't important. The homes have no heating or air conditioning because the temperature is always pleasant. Unless the person wants to experience Earthlike conditions, there is no sun, no moon, and no stars. There is a continual pleasant light that comes from no source. There is no night, although some describe a "twilight." People do "rest," but don't sleep.

The buildings are described as being made of a solid material, but it has a pearl-like luminescence. There are large buildings housing schools, art galleries, and libraries in vast, beautiful, clean cities.

Houses have gardens around them, with natural soil, just as on Earth. People who enjoyed gardening tend the gardens, and beautiful flowers grow continually and profusely. No one picks the flowers, however. They are left to grow naturally. There are no seasons; the flowers don't die.

The afterlife has all the attributes of the Earth plane. There are mountains, rivers, lakes, forests, and vast fields of flowers. There are birds and all the animal species, but they don't prey on one another and they are not afraid of each other. The animals are described as living in separate areas, but people can walk up to them and hold them. The animals are at a higher state of being than on the Earth plane, able to communicate through a telepathy that doesn't require speech. They know they are one with humankind and are completely understood by those with whom they come into contact. No animals are killed. No animal products are used in making things.

Music and art are integral, vital components of the afterlife planes. There is continual music, although a person doesn't have to listen to it. The choice is entirely up to each individual. There are vast orchestras made up of thousands of people playing instruments, some of which are like those on the Earth plane while others are unique. As an orchestra plays, beautiful colors appear around the orchestra in keeping with the music.

There are no cars, busses, or other machinery. People walk to destinations, although they do have the ability to simply focus on where they would like to be and they are transported there. Most, however, explain that they prefer to walk.

Occupations and Preoccupations

A person may continue his occupation from the Earth plane. Artists still paint; builders still build houses; teachers still teach. Shakespeare and Oscar Wilde are still writing plays. However, people are not required to be anything they don't wish to be. If a person always desired to play the piano while on the Earth plane, but never had the chance, she may learn to play the piano on the next plane of life and give recitals or be part of the vast orchestras. Someone who loved to grow flowers on Earth but ended up being an auto mechanic can become a gardener in the afterlife.

Since there are no manufacturing plants, people who engaged in manufacturing occupations on Earth find other occupations and preoccupations. Many teach children who have left the Earth plane and grow up in the afterlife. Some people do "rescue" work, helping people who have died to understand where they are and guiding them along as they adjust to their new lives.

There is no money. People act out of love for one another. They give of themselves in ways that make both them and the receiver joyful.

The Vastness of the Afterlife

The afterlife, they explain, is vaster than we can imagine. There are millions of planes of existence, occupied by vast numbers of people at various levels of spiritual maturity and interest. It is incorrect to view the afterlife as a few discrete planes. Instead, there is level after level of continuously different planes where people are together based on their interests and attitudes.

There are some levels that are actually below the Earth plane in spiritual advancement. There, the people are in a kind of darkness of thought. They are at that level because of their own mindset, however, and are given guidance to grow out of it. Eventually, everyone advances beyond the darker levels. These lower planes are not a hell, however. There is no such place of torment.

Some in the afterlife refer to a transition plane between the Earth and the next levels of existence where a person may remain until acclimated to being in the next life.

Spiritual Development

People in the afterlife find themselves in conditions of their own making based on their mental condition, attitude, and spiritual growth. They then may stay on that level if they wish, or advance into higher levels of spiritual growth. Some people prefer to stay where they are for long periods of time. Higher level teachers and guides try to help them learn so they can advance, but there is no pressure, and no one requires anyone to leave a level and progress to another level.

The conditions in the life close to the Earth plane that most people enter are so pleasant that many choose not to evolve into higher levels of being for a long time. They remark that they are content to stay where they are, although they know there are higher levels.

Time

Because the afterlife has no sun, there are no days or years to count. There are changes that occur, and people have the same types of experiences they had on Earth that occur over time, so there is a time of sorts. However, they don't count time, and since they realize their eternal nature, there is no hurry to accomplish things. Their sense of time, in other words, is quite different.

Suicides

People who commit suicide are met with compassion and understanding on the next plane of life. There is no judgment or condemnation. However, there is great sadness among all living on the next plane of life when the suicide victim arrives, and he or she feels deep remorse. That person sees the grief family and friends still on Earth suffer, because their thoughts and emotions are known by the person who has committed suicide. Many attend the funeral unseen, and because they then understand that life really is eternal, they realize that they could have worked out the problems and lived full lives with those who loved them on Earth. Now the opportunity is gone. What could have been a wonderful, rewarding life has been cut off. And in the afterlife, the person still has to face and work out the problems he or she was experiencing, but with all the remorse and sadness that accompanies the suicide.

Suicide is not an alternative if the body is free of unbearable pain. Most difficulties will pass with time and the person will live a rewarding life, growing, learning, loving, and experiencing. The problems still must be faced in the afterlife, with the added burdens of remorse and the knowledge that nothing can now be done to go back to life to make things better and have a joyful, fruitful lifetime.

Imminence of the Afterlife with the Earth Plane

Those on the next planes of life explain that the Earth plane is saturated with other planes of existence that we simply can't see. There are earthbound people who wander about until they are able to release themselves by their change of thought, from the Earth. They crave the pleasures and experiences of the Earth plane but, of course, can't experience them. As a result, they may stay around living people who have the same inclinations, influencing them through their thoughts. Destructive people in the afterlife, for instance, will be attracted to people with destructive tendencies still alive and focus their thoughts on influencing them to consider destructive behavior.

They also describe the fact that beings on other vibration planes coexist with us. Changes in our atmosphere on the Earth plane affect them, so pollution is affecting the other planes as well as our own.

Ghosts, Poltergeists, and Earthbound Spirits

Ghosts are described by those in the afterlife as being impressions on the memory of the "ether," the unseen spiritual atmosphere surrounding Earth. When emotional events occur, the ether may retain a memory of the event. Later, sensitive people may be able to see the memory act out. The memories are described as ghosts, and generally appear in relationship to traumatic events. These ethereal memories have no spirit attached to them, can move only in the ways the living person moved when the memory was created, cannot communicate, and are completely harmless. That is why hauntings often involve the same spirit seeming to perform the same actions repeatedly, with no communication between the apparitions and the witnesses. When the conditions between the Earth's atmosphere and the ether are just right, the memories may play out like a movie so more than one living person witnesses them. That is what happens when people witness a battle scene being played out by what people call "ghosts." In any event, there is no living spirit there when the memory comes from the ether.

Poltergeists, on the other hand, can be earthbound people who are not able or willing to change their mental condition to allow themselves to leave the Earth plane. They are almost always simply trying to attract attention and are frustrated that no one can see them or respond to their communication. As a result, they may bang on things, move things about if they can, and otherwise disrupt the Earth plane.

Some are immature spiritually, and may have been mischievous on Earth. They continue their mischievous activities by staying on the Earth plane and influencing people on this side of life who are susceptible because of their natural inclinations toward the same sort of mischief. Drugs or alcohol make a person on the Earth plane even more susceptible. In addition, some people still alive on Earth open themselves to influence because they have latent medium abilities, but they are not spiritually mature enough to keep the lower-level people in the afterlife from intruding.

Many children have mediumistic ability because they are more open and naïve, but they lose it as they grow older and become more jaded. Poltergeists are often associated with children and adolescents because of this latent medium ability the poltergeists can draw from to act in the physical realm.

If children use a device such as a Ouija board, they can hear from earthbound people who intentionally deceive them. In those cases, the lower level spirits can provide misleading and disruptive messages. In no circumstances, however, can a lower level spirit possess someone.

Some on the next planes of life have also said clearly that these earthbound spirits are the cause of many cases of psychosis, paranoia, depression, addiction, manic depression, criminal behavior, and phobias. They cannot "possess" a person, but people who are sensitive to the other realms of life and easily influenced can become the focus of earthbound spirits who wish to use them to have vicarious experiences. Dr. Carl A. Wickland, a member of the Chicago Medical Society and American Association for the Advancement of Science, and director of the National Psychological Institute of Los Angeles, describes his experience with people afflicted by these influences:

> Spirit obsession is a fact – a perversion of a natural law – and is amply demonstrable. This has been proven hundreds of times by causing the supposed insanity or aberration to be temporarily transferred from the victim to a psychic sensitive who is trained for the purpose, and by this method ascertain the cause of the psychosis to be an ignorant or mischievous spirit, whose identity may frequently be verified.[8]

Some mediums have warned that those who are conduits for automatic writing can hear from earthbound spirits:

Both Smith and Rosher [mediums using automatic writing] were warned by their communicators about intruders. "Mother said the misinformation had been written by spirit intruders who were sometimes able to exert more power than she and so could push her aside and take control of the pencil," Smith wrote, further stating that "everyone who dies rebellious is a potential source of mischief." Burdick warned Rosher that there are spirits on his side "who would try to use you in a wrong way."[9]

Evil, Demons, and Satan

Those on the next planes of life do not talk about a devil or demons. Those mythical creatures developed in religions out of a need to give an identity to the evil and suffering humankind endures, but there never were such creatures. You can read more about the devil and demons at http://youreternalself.com/chapter9.htm.

However, they do speak often about "thought regions" where people who were degenerate on Earth are together because of their common attitudes. And they do indicate that these people are still bent upon impeding humankind's growth to spiritual maturity. As such, they sometimes use the word "hell" to describe the thought region, but never suggest that it is a place of torture. That hell with fire and brimstone is a myth. This account by Mike Tymn on his always-fascinating and informative blog contains a deceased soldier's description of the thought region where some degenerate people remain out of their own choosing:

> . . . Private Thomas Dowding, a 37-year-old British soldier, was killed on the battlefield in WWI. On March 12, 1917, he began communicating through the mediumship of Wellesley Tudor Pole. After floundering in the ethers, not even realizing he was dead for a time, as time goes on that side, he was met by his brother, William, who had died three years earlier, and began his orientation.
>
> "Hell is a thought region," Thomas Dowding communicated on March 17, 1917. "Evil dwells there and works out its purposes. The forces used to hold mankind down in the darkness of ignorance are

generated in hell! It is not a place; it is a condition. The
human race has created the condition."[10]

This thought region, he explains, "depends for its existence on
human thoughts and feelings." People are there because they choose to
be there, but "Release will come from within some day." When any
person chooses to mature out of the condition, they rise from it
immediately.

Materializations on the Earth Plane

People on a higher spiritual plane can materialize on the Earth plane
(see Chapter 2 for examples). Dr. Elisabeth Kübler-Ross tells of her
experience with Mrs. Schwartz, a patient who had died and appeared to
her two years later in fully materialized form. Kübler-Ross had a
conversation with her and touched her. In all respects, Mrs. Schwartz
was fully human in form and substance.[11] A friend of mine named Mike
Thomson had the surprise of having his ex-wife's uncle suddenly appear
in the seat next to him as he was driving. The uncle spoke to him, then
disappeared. Mike learned several hours later that his ex-wife's uncle
had died at the moment he appeared to Mike. Such stories are common.

Physical mediums can also enable people from the next plane of life
to materialize using a substance called ectoplasm drawn from the
medium's body. The medium doesn't make it happen; instead, it occurs
naturally during a séance. The ectoplasm is attracted to the form of the
deceased's etheric body and envelopes it, with all the feel of the body,
including the feel of bones and soft flesh that are not actually present.

The Afterlife is a World of Thought

Our eternal selves are the assumptions, perspectives, thoughts,
feelings, memories, intentions, insights, creativity, revelations, and all
other inner processes that make up our minds. None of these are in
matter or energy, the physical realm. When the person leaves the
physical body behind, what is left is the eternal self, the real person. As
a result, the afterlife is a world of thoughts. There, everything is very
real and tangible, but it is a result of a person's attitude, thoughts, and
intentions that create the world.

In this world of thought, people can communicate through speaking, but most communicate through thoughts. Animals also communicate by thoughts with people.

Books read themselves to people. When someone wants to read a book, she just needs to focus on the book and the author's thoughts at the time of the book's creation will communicate the book to the person, exactly as the author intended it. Reading word by word isn't necessary.

People create using a combination of intention, creativity, and effort, but the effort isn't like pounding nails. It takes work, but it is a mental form of work. When someone wants a new suit or dress, they just have to imagine the type of fabric and someone else will create the fabric using mental images and an effort like work. They say we won't be able to fully understand the process they describe as well as they can.

Buildings are constructed through thought and effort. At higher levels of spiritual development, things can come into being by just thinking them into existing, but that is not the preferred way and that is not available at the lower levels of development. Most people prefer to exert the effort involved in bringing the imagined thing into being.

Communication from the Afterlife

Several on the other side have described working to influence people to experience after-death communication. One person in the afterlife named Alfred Higgins described both giving a message to his wife directly and to a medium to give to his wife. You can hear the recording of his séance at http://youreternalself.com/chapter9.htm. Soon after his death, he went to his home and found his wife standing in the kitchen peeling potatoes. She couldn't see him, of course. He stood close to her and concentrated his thoughts on her, calling her name. She suddenly dropped the knife she was holding and looked up. She then burst into tears because she had heard him, but couldn't see that he was standing next to her.

Some time later, he influenced his wife, by thinking, to go to a Spiritualist church. There, he gave the medium the thought message that he had died as a result of a fall from a ladder to let his wife know the message was for her. The medium got the ladder image, and told those assembled about it. When the man's wife responded, the medium misinterpreted the message and suggested it meant she would be ascending upward into new endeavors. Higgins was frustrated, but kept focusing on the medium.

He concentrated his thoughts on the medium to have her tell his
wife he knew about "the ring," and that it wasn't the right ring. While he
was still alive, his wife had lost the wedding band he had given to her
and she bought a new one identical to it, not telling him she had lost the
original. In the afterlife, he learned what had happened. He influenced
the medium with the message and the medium did get the message
correctly. His wife understood, but was very surprised that he knew
about the ring.

Frederic W. H. Myers, a pioneer in psychical research,
communicated through medium Geraldine Cummins using automatic
writing. He provided this description of how those on the other side
influence the living in automatic writing:

> The entity identifying himself as Myers explained the
> difficulty in communicating by means of automatic writing.
> "The inner mind is very difficult to deal with from this side,"
> Cummins recorded. "We impress it with our message. We
> never impress the brain of the medium directly. That is out of
> the question. But the inner mind receives our message and
> sends it on to the brain. The brain is the mere mechanism.
> The inner mind is like soft wax, it receives our thoughts, their
> whole content, but it must produce the words to clothe it."

> Myers went on to explain that success in sending the thought
> through depends on the inner mind of the automatist
> [medium doing automatic writing], which must contribute to
> the body of the message. "In other words, we send the
> thoughts and the words usually in which they must be
> framed, but the actual letters or spelling of the words is
> drawn from the medium's memory. Sometimes we only send
> the thoughts and the medium's unconscious mind clothes
> them in words."

> Myers also offered that when discarnate beings want to
> communicate through a sensitive, they must enter a dream or
> subjective state which detaches them from the memory of
> concrete facts in their past lives. "Further, if we communicate
> directly through the medium, though we often retain our
> personality, our manner of speech, we are frequently unable
> to communicate through the medium's hand."[12]

Inspiring People on the Earth Plane

People in the afterlife who were scientists and artists on Earth explain that they discovered after death that they had been inspired often when they made discoveries or created great works of art while on Earth. Those on the next planes of existence are greatly interested in inspiring people on the Earth plane and helping them to make discoveries and create beautiful art works. Some explain that they are looking for promising people to inspire. It is, in a sense, continuing their work on the Earth plane, although they also are doing their own work in the afterlife.

Religious Beliefs and the Afterlife

Those in the afterlife all agree there are no churches or religions, although some people still cling to dogma and beliefs from the Earth plane for a while until they grow out of them. God is at the base of all existence, the power behind all consciousness. God is pure love that permeates matter, energy, consciousness, and the seen and unseen realms.

There are no "holy scriptures," no rituals, and no dogma among those who have released themselves from the Earth plane's belief systems. Some people temporarily cling to the old beliefs, staying in groups with others who have the same worldviews. Everyone enters the next plane of life with all the same assumptions and perspectives they had on Earth. As a result, there are some Christian groups living together there who are sure they're in a holding pattern waiting for the rapture and their return to a physical existence on the Earth plane. Some who believed that the spirit sleeps until the resurrection, are "sleeping," although they're given guidance and inspiration to begin understanding that they're already in the next stage of their eternal life.

All of these people with narrow, restricting views eventually grow out of them into freedom and spiritual maturity. No one stays in these conditions forever.

The fact that people's attitudes and expectations create the reality they're in is one of the reasons people from different faiths see different personages when they have near-death experiences. Some Christians expect to see Jesus, so that is who the guide coming to meet them is. I don't suggest that the figure who greets them isn't really the Jesus they expected to meet, just that a person may be greeted by Jesus because they expect it. If they were Hindu, they might see Yamraj, Hindu king of the dead, when the guides come to help them. Compassionate, loving people greet everyone. People carry their beliefs and expectations into the afterlife and those shape the environment in which they find themselves.

Many are very disillusioned with the Christian church, and warn that religious dogma is the greatest obstacle to spiritual growth and the spiritual evolution of humankind.

They also are unhappy with the Spiritualist movement, which they describe as being shallow. People in the movement, they say, focus on the display of mediumship, rarely going beyond the weekly readings in services to helping people grow spiritually based on the underpinning knowledge that they are spiritual beings having a physical experience.

They emphasize that humankind has no understanding of the power of the Holy Spirit, and if it simply allowed the power of God to manifest itself, humankind would be dramatically changed.

Those in the next planes of eternal life consistently describe reincarnation, not just onto the Earth plane, but into other "spheres" or locations in the universe and other planes of reality. However, they don't describe a process of reincarnating into animal forms and finally merging with a greater consciousness when they have been liberated from reincarnation. They do say that while people may continue to reincarnate onto the Earth plane, they will do so only until they have learned all of the lessons the Earth plane can teach. They then go on into other realms to learn higher-level spiritual lessons without reincarnating on the Earth plane again.

Individuals choose to reincarnate in the physical realm for three reasons: to help someone in their Earth life, to serve humanity in general, or to learn life lessons that will help them mature spiritually. However, they emphasize consistently that most individuals make the choice. Few are reincarnated without choosing to do so. We are in charge of our eternal spiritual growth. The exception is for people who have not progressed at all on the Earth plane and must return to learn the lessons. They may reincarnate soon after death.

When loved ones make the transition into the afterlife, those who preceded them are still there to greet them—they're not "absent" because they're engaged in another incarnation. That could mean the part of the eternal self that was involved in that incarnation remains to greet loved ones or that the person simply waits to reincarnate until all those she loved have crossed over. The record isn't clear.

10

Recent Indications the Mind Forms the Brain

Recent research into brain functioning provides further indications that the mind, outside of the body and the brain, brings consciousness and memories to the brain and forms the brain resulting in what we experience as thinking, memories, and sensory experiences. The effect is the same as a signal coming to a television and forming the components so you can see the picture and hear the sounds coming from a source outside of the television. Larry King isn't in the television set. The sets, cameras, broadcasting equipment, and all the vast resources of people and technology required to produce and broadcast the signal are outside of the television; the television just lights up and gives you the experience when the signal comes to it. But Larry King's interviews have already finished before the television even gets the signal.

In the same way, it appears that the brain takes on the configuration in its neurons that fits with your experiences of sight, hearing, tasting, touching, smelling, sense of motion, body sense, and emotion when a signal from outside the body and brain forms the brain to have the experience. Recent research in this chapter seems to support that view.

The Mind in the Brain Would Have to Create Electricity, but Has No Mechanism to Do So.

Pim van Lommel, a cardiologist in the Division of Cardiology, Hospital Rijnstate, Arnheim, Neetherlands, explains that the mind, which is non-physical, couldn't create physical electricity to make the brain recreate an image. For the image to be recalled, the brain would have to generate electricity causing millions of neurons to fire in exactly the same way they were active in the brain when photons coming to the brain through the eye created the image in the first place. But the brain has no ability to create the electricity. This fact has been discussed repeatedly in the literature, including in the *Journal of Physiology,*[1] *Journal of Neurophysiology,*[2] and *Truth Journal, International Interdisciplinary Journal of Christian Thought.*[3] Pim van Lommel summarizes the comments:

> For decades, extensive research has been done to localize consciousness and memories inside the brain, so far without success. In connection with the unproven assumption that consciousness and memories are produced and stored inside the brain, we should ask ourselves how a non-material activity such as concentrated attention or thinking can correspond to an observable (material) reaction in the form of measurable electrical, magnetic, and chemical activity at a certain place in the brain, even an increase in cerebral blood flow is observed during such a non-material activity as thinking.[4]

In other words, a thought doesn't exist in matter, and yet, when you intend to recall a face, the image appears in your mind and the brain lights up with electrical activity. But the brain doesn't have a mechanism to cause the electricity that science has assumed is necessary to recreate the image in the brain. Pim van Lommel is suggesting that the mind outside of the brain causes the brain to light up.

Biophysicists Detect No Electricity in Sensory Neurons.

Attempts to measure electricity along the sensory neurons when a person is sensing something have failed to find traces of it. The laws of thermodynamics dictate that electrical impulses must produce heat. Thomas Heimburg, associate professor of biophysics at the Niels Bohr Institute at Copenhagen University, and Andrew D. Jackson, professor of theoretical physics at Copenhagen University, have been attempting to detect the heat from the electricity when impulses are traveling along nerves to produce sensory experiences. They can find none.

All medical and biological textbooks state that nerves function by sending electrical impulses along their length. Heimburg says that their research shows the textbooks are wrong:

> But for us as physicists, this cannot be the explanation. The physical laws of thermodynamics tell us that electrical impulses must produce heat as they travel along the nerve, but experiments find that no such heat is produced . . .[5]

In other words, there appears to be no electrical activity coming from the sensory organs, although the brain does register electrical activity that shows the person is having a sensory experience.

The most likely explanation is that sensory experience is already in the mind and the brain is simply being formed by consciousness to reflect the sight, hearing, smelling, tasting, touching, or emotion. That fits with the research showing that the mind can know the type of picture to be shown several seconds before a computer even selects a picture and shows it on a monitor where the body can sense it.

The Brain Just Reflects What the Mind Has Already Seen.

When a person "sees" something, the neuroscience explanation is that signals from the eye travel along the optic nerve to the parts of the

brain where the image is received and processed. In an optical illusion, a person looks at an image, but the mind thinks the image is different from what it actually is. The illusion to the right is an example.

In the illusion, the ball at the bottom (front) of the picture looks smaller than the ball at the top. However, both are actually the same size. The mind has interpreted the two balls as being different even though, in reality, they're the same.

We experience the same illusion as the moon looks larger when closer to the horizon. Our mind registers it in relationship to things on the horizon, but it seems smaller as it rises into the expanse of the night sky.

Scott Murray, University of Washington psychology professor, and two colleagues wanted to know how people's brains registered the difference between the apparent size (one appearing to be larger than the other) and the actual size, since the two are identical. To find out, they used fMRI, that measures neuron activity in the brain or spinal cord. They measured the parts of the brain that register sight (the optical cortex) as people looked at the image of the two balls in the picture.

Remarkably, even though the two balls are identical in size, looking at the ball in the back that seems larger activated 20 percent more brain area than looking at the ball in the front that looks smaller. The 20 percent difference was identical to the estimate the subjects made when asked about the difference in size between the two balls.

If the mind were in a brain that is a machine, it wouldn't register a difference between the two balls; it would simply see two circles of the same size and the mind would register the information in the same area within the brain. That's not what happens. Murray reported,

> Researchers have long believed that the visual system is
> organized hierarchically, with early visual areas such as
> the primary visual cortex simply registering the physical
> input from the eyes and "higher" visual areas attempting
> to put all the information together. This work challenges
> these theories of the organization of the visual system.[6]

If the brain is a machine receiving the image through the retinas, we would expect that the photons striking the retinas would cover the same area of retina for both balls and the brain would register the two balls as being identical in size, just as a camera would recreate the actual balls at their actual sizes on the exposed film. Instead, the brain becomes active with an image that has registered the illusion in the mind.

A reasonable interpretation of these results is that the mind outside of the brain observes the image and decides about the illusion before the brain is even involved. The mind then sends the message to the brain and the brain registers the mind's message just as the mind outside of the body sent it, with the errors in estimating size.

This is more evidence supporting the suggestion that the mind has the experience, then tells the brain about it and the brain becomes active, reflecting what the mind has already processed and experienced.

Conclusion

You are an eternal self having a physical experience. The Earth world is the realm of joy and sadness, success and failure, excitement and frustration, elation and tragedy, comfort and disease, and finding and losing loved ones. How well you recover and learn from the dark periods depends on your spiritual understanding.

When you know without a doubt that you are eternal, you'll have no fear of death. You'll feel deep sadness when a loved one graduates from Earth school and leaves you behind, but not lasting grief, and you'll learn to accept your new relationship with them more easily. You'll know that for just a few brief moments in eternity, you'll be separated because they're going on to higher education for a while. They'll stay in contact, though, and you'll receive their messages if you've grown spiritually to realize they're still with you.

When you learn without a doubt that you're eternal, you'll have a new perspective on the mundane things in your life that have seemed so important that they have kept you from being with your family, lavishing love on those around you, and enjoying every moment of your physical life. With your new spiritual understanding, you'll realize how remarkably trivial and inconsequential those mundane things are. On the day you come to know your eternal self, you'll stride into the room where your loved ones are and give each the grandest, most heartfelt hug you've ever given, and you'll vow to fill the rest of your life with such loving moments.

On the day it finally becomes real to you that your life will never end and you'll never be separated from those you love, you'll be reborn into a new life with a peace that surpasses all Earthly understanding. Your joy will inspire love and happiness in those around you, and you'll live with them in harmony and love. The tragedies will still happen, but you'll face them in love together, knowing they're just moments in eternity.

That day is in your future, but for it to dawn, you must open yourself to spiritual understanding like a little child, without clinging to religious beliefs or materialist skepticism that inhibit you from accepting what those on the other side of life and God are opening up to you. If you seek, you will find; if you knock, the door will open for you.

You will learn the truth. And the truth will set you free.

Endnotes

Chapter 1 Endnotes

[1] Patt, n.d.

[2] Schroeder, 2001, p. 158.

[3] Hameroff, n.d.

[4] Presti, 2006.

[5] Chalmers, 1997.

[6] Sheldrake, "Nature As Alive . . ." n.d.

[7] Sheldrake, "Nature As Alive . . ." n.d.

[8] Carter, 2007.

[9] Hamani, McAndrews, Cohn, et al. 2008.

[10] Tippit, n.d.

[11] Berkovich, n.d.

[12] Grof, 1998.

[13] Carter, 2007.

[14] Burt, 1975.

[15] Carter, 2007.

[16] Touber, 2007.

[17] Hamani, McAndrews, Cohn, et al. 2008.

[18] Carter, 2007.

[19] Radin, 1997, p. 259.

[20] Mars, n.d.

[21] Restak, 2006, p. 596.

[22] Weiss, 1969.

[23] Choi, 2007.

[24] Choi, 2007.

[25] "Tiny-brained man's lifestyle . . ." 2007.

[26] Images from H. E. Puthoff, "CIA-Initiated Remote Viewing At Stanford Research Institute." Institute for Advanced Studies.

[27] Radin, 1997, p. 101.

[28] Utts, 1995.

[29] Schnabel, 1997.

[30] Radin, 1997, p. 104.

[31] Radin, 1997, p. 105.

[32] Targ & Puthoff, 1974; Targ & Harary 1984; Puthoff & Targ 1976.

[33] Penman, 2008.

[34] Targ & Katra, 1998.

[35] Radin, 1997, pp. 96-97.

[36] Radin, 1997, pp. 96-97.

[37] Ring & Cooper, 1999.

[38] Dossey, 1989, p. 18.

[39] "Study suggests brain . . ." 2005.

[40] Begley, 2007.

[41] Weiskrantz, 2007.

[42] "Amazing Blind Teen . . ." 2006.

[43] "Humans with Amazing Senses . . ." 2006.

[44] Moody, 2001.

[45] Linzmeier, 2006.

[46] Fenwick, 2007.

[47] Sabom, 1982.

[48] "Study Suggests Life After Death . . ." 2007.

[49] "Study Suggests Life After Death . . ." 2007.

[50] Van Lommel, 2001.

[51] Van Lommel, 2001.

[52] Sharp, 2003.

[53] Ring & Lawrence 1993.

[54] Cook, Greyson, & Stevenson 1998.

[55] Van Lommel, 2001.

[56] Van Lommel, Wees, Myers, & Elfferic, 2001.

[57] Sabom, 1998.

[58] Kelly, Kelly, Crabtree, & Gauld, 2006.

[59] Sabom, 1998.

[60] Twemlow et al., 1980.

[61] Myers, 2007.

[62] Twemlow et al., 1980.

[63] Rogo, "Researching . . ." Cited in Schmicker, *Best Evidence*, p. 203.

[64] Morse with Perry, 1994.

[65] Tart, 1968.

[66] Zammit, 2006, p. 69.

[67] Zammit, "Australian Psychics . . ." n.d.

[68] Ramsland, 2007.

[69] "Psychic Detectives," 2005.

[70] "Psychic Detectives," 2005.

[71] Radin, 1997, pp. 118-124).

[72] Bierman & Radin, 1997.

[73] Honorton & Ferrari, 1989.

[74] Penman, 2007.

[75] Sheldrake, "Experiments on Telephone Telepathy" n.d

[76] Libet, 1984.

[77] Libet, 1979.

[78] Penman, 2007.

[79] Penman, 2007.

[80] Radin, 1997, p. 101.

[81] "Prodigy, 12, Compared to Mozart," 2007.

[82] "Prodigy, 12, Compared to Mozart," 2007.

[83] "Prodigy, 12, Compared to Mozart," 2007.

[84] "Prodigy, 12, Compared to Mozart," 2007.

[85] Akiane's Web site.

[86] Akiane's Web site.

[87] Olivia Bennett's Web site.

[88] Cited in Jacques Hadamard, 1949, pp. 142-143.

[89] "Graham Wallas' model," 2007.

[90] Dossey, 1989, pp. 32-33.

[91] Quoted in Chesterman, 1974, p. 186.

[92] Kendall, 1955, p. 138.

[93] Knoll, 1957, p. 270.

[94] Treffert, 2007.

[95] Treffert, n.d.

[96] Orlando Serrell Web site. http://www.orlandoserrell.com.

[97] Martin, 2006.

[98] Kelly, 2000.

[99] Basar, 2005.

Chapter 2 Endnotes

[1] "Yeshua" is the Aramaic name mistranslated "Iesous" in Greek, "Iesus" in Latin, and finally "Jesus" in English. His followers and family never uttered the name "Jesus." The letter "J" wasn't even in the English language until after the sixteenth century, so before that no one ever pronounced the name "Jesus."

[2] Russell, 2004.

[3] "Skeptics who declared . . ." 2007.

[4] "Max Planck quotes," 2007.

[5] Morin, 2000.

[6] Vargas et al., 1989.

[7] Hay, n.d.

[8] Morse, 1994.

[9] Rees, 1971.

[10] Holden, 2005.

[11] Haraldsson, 1988-1989.

[12] Kalish & Reynolds, 1973.

[13] Matchett, 1972.

[14] Stevenson, 1983.

[15] Guggenheim & Guggenheim, 1995.

[16] Mayer, 2007.

[17] Botkin with Hogan, 2005.
[18] Botkin with Hogan, 2005, p. 158.
[19] Holzer, 1963.
[20] Moore, 2006.
[21] Wagner, 2007.
[22] Morse with Perry, 1990.
[23] Komp, 1992.
[24] Kübler-Ross, 1983.
[25] Osis, 2007.
[26] Osis, 2007, page 192.
[27] Wills-Brandon, 2007.
[28] Wills-Brandon, 2007.
[29] Wills-Brandon, 2007.
[30] Fenwick, 2007.
[31] Osis, 1998.
[32] Osis, 2007.
[33] Hallenbeck, 2003.
[34] Moore, 2006.
[35] Wills-Brandon, 2007.
[36] "Types of Experiences We Study," 2007.
[37] Barrett, 1926.
[38] Barrett, 1926.
[39] Tymn, "A Veridical Death-Bed Vision," n.d.
[40] Zammit, 2006, p. 148.
[41] *Journal of the Society for Psychical Research,* 1904.
[42] *Proceedings of the Society for Psychical Research*, Volume 6, p. 20.
[43] Gurney, Myers, & Podmore, 1886.
[44] Gurney et al., 1886.
[45] Gurney et al., 1886.
[46] Zammit, 2006.
[47] McKenzie, 1971, pp. 116-117.
[48] Rogo, 1993, pp. 16-17.
[49] Spraggett, 1974, pp. 45-46.
[50] Johnson, 1982, pp. 198-199.
[51] Bennett, 1939, pp. 131-132.
[52] Tymn, "A Veridical Death-Bed Vision," n.d.
[53] Easton, 2005.
[54] Larson & Witham, 1998.
[55] Amatuzio, 2007.
[56] Kübler-Ross, 2006.
[57] Hamilton, 1942.
[58] Hamilton, 2007.
[59] Rommer, 2000.
[60] Rowse, 1993.

[61] Morse, 1994, p. 190.

[62] Zammit, 2006.

[63] Tymn, "Distinguished Researchers . . ." 2007.

[64] Zammit, 2006.

[65] Pearson, 1991.

[66] Pearson, 1993.

[67] Pearson, 1997.

[68] Pearson, 1990.

[69] "Conversation with Victor Zammit . . ." 2007.

[70] Snyder, 2007.

[71] Tymn, "Distinguished researchers . . ." 2007.

[72] Tymn, "Distinguished researchers . . ." 2007.

[73] Tymn, "Distinguished researchers . . ." 2007.

[74] Tymn, "Distinguished researchers . . ." 2007.

[75] Tymn, "Distinguished researchers . . ." 2007.

[76] Tymn, "Distinguished researchers . . ." 2007.

[77] Tymn, "Distinguished researchers . . ." 2007.

[78] Tymn, "Distinguished researchers . . ." 2007.

[79] Tymn, "Distinguished researchers . . ." 2007.

[80] Tymn, "Distinguished researchers . . ." 2007.

[81] Tymn, "Distinguished researchers . . ." 2007.

[82] Tymn, "Distinguished researchers . . ." 2007.

[83] Baird, 1988.

[84] Meek, 1998.

[85] Archie Roy, in a letter to Michael Roll, May 19, 1983.

[86] Bander, 1973, p. 132.

[87] Bander, 1973, p. 132.

[88] Tymn, "Distinguished researchers . . ." 2007.

[89] Botkin with Hogan, 1995, p. 168.

[90] Lombroso, 2006.

[91] Tymn, "Distinguished researchers . . ." 2007.

[92] Greyson, 2000.

[93] Tymn, "Distinguished researchers . . ." 2007.

[94] Tymn, "Distinguished researchers . . ." 2007.

[95] Geley, 1927.

[96] Tymn, "Distinguished researchers . . ." 2007.

[97] Tymn, "Distinguished researchers . . ." 2007.

[98] Schwartz & Simon, 2003.

[99] Tymn, "Distinguished researchers . . ." 2007.

[100] Tymn, "Distinguished researchers . . ." 2007.

[101] Fontana 2005.

[102] Tymn, "Distinguished researchers . . ." 2007.

[103] Bander, "Voices from the Tapes . . ." p. 132.

[104] Jung, 1973.

[105] Tymn, "Distinguished researchers . . ." 2007.
[106] Tymn, "Distinguished researchers . . ." 2007.
[107] Tymn, "Distinguished researchers . . ." 2007.
[108] Tymn, "Distinguished researchers . . ." 2007.
[109] Tymn, "Distinguished researchers . . ." 2007.
[110] Tymn, "Distinguished researchers . . ." 2007.
[111] Tymn, "Distinguished researchers . . ." 2007.
[112] "Hornell Hart (1888-1967)," 2007.
[113] Murphet, 1990, p. 64.
[114] Balfour, 1879.
[115] Tymn, "Distinguished researchers . . ." 2007.
[116] Zammit, 2007.
[117] Doyle, 1926, p. 129.
[118] Randall, 2004.
[119] Zammit, 2006.
[120] Zammit, 2006.
[121] Tymn, "Physician Travels Out of Body," 2007.
[122] Tymn, "Distinguished researchers . . ." 2007.
[123] Tymn, "Distinguished researchers . . ." 2007.
[124] Brune, "The Rediscovered Beyond," n.d.
[125] Bander, 1973.
[126] Bander, 1973.
[127] "The Church of England and Spiritualism," 1979.
[128] Tymn, "Distinguished researchers . . ." 2007.
[129] Tymn, "Distinguished researchers . . ." 2007.
[130] Crookall, 1961.
[131] Schwartz & Simon, 2003.
[132] Schwartz et al., 2001.
[133] Schwartz & Simon, 2003.
[134] Beischel & Schwartz, 2007.
[135] Zammit, 2006.
[136] "Helen Duncan: The Official Pardon Site."
[137] Tymn, "Ghost loses chess match" n.d.
[138] Zammit, 2006, pp. 123.
[139] Smith, 2004.
[140] Rogge, n.d.
[141] Spraggett, 1973.
[142] Tymn, "Proof Positive of Spirit Communication" n.d.
[143] Blum, 2006.
[144] Hodgson, 1897-1898, p. 297.
[145] Schmicker, 2002, pp. 249-250.
[146] Schmicker, 2002, pp. 250-251.
[147] Schmicker, 2002, p. 251.
[148] Zammit, 2006, pp. 116-117.

[149] Hyslop, 1918.

[150] "James Hyslop 1854-1920" n.d.

[151] Carrington, 1973, p. 54.

[152] Carrington, 1973, p. 54.

[153] Schmicker, 2002, pp. 252-253.

[154] Bray, 1990, p. 15.

[155] Hapgood, 1975, pp. 224-227.

[156] "Daniel Dunglas Home (1833-1886)," n.d.

[157] Oppenheim, 1985, p.11.

[158] Flint, 1971, page 94.

[159] "Paranormal Voices Assert: Death No End," n.d.

[160] Zammit, "The Direct-Voice Mediumship of Leslie Flint," n.d.

[161] Flint, 1971, p. 220.

[162] Keen, 2003.

[163] Keen & Ellison, 1999.

[164] Zammit, 2006, p. 75.

[165] Butler & Butler, 1947, p. 78.

[166] Meek, 1987.

[167] Zammit, 2006.

[168] Inglis, 1984, p. 226. Cited in Zammit, "10. Materialization Mediumship."

[169] Cassirer, 1996, p. 103. (as cited in Zammit, 2006, p. 95).

[170] Cassirer, 1996, p. 103. (as cited in Zammit, 2006, pp. 95-96).

[171] Cassirer, 1996, p. 115. (as cited in Zammit, 2006, p. 96).

[172] Kubler-Ross, 1997.

[173] Kübler-Ross, 1991.

[174] Kübler-Ross, 1991.

[175] Fodor, 1934.

[176] Fisher, 1986.

[177] Stevenson, 1974.

[178] Lazarus, 1993, p. 85.

[179] Lazarus, 1993, p. 119.

[180] Zammit, 2006, p. 12.

[181] Zammit, 2006, p. 127.

[182] Zammit, 2006, p. 128.

[183] "Cross-Correspondence," n.d.

[184] Zammit, 2006, p. 131.

[185] Dodds, 1962.

[186] Currie, 1995.

[187] Schoonmaker, 1996.

[188] Sabom, 1982.

[189] Schroeter-Kunhardt, 1993.

[190] Penman, n.d.

[191] Sabom, 1982, p. 183.

[192] Greyson, 2000.

[193] Van Lommel et al., 2001.
[194] Sabom, 1982.
[195] Morse & Perry, 1991.
[196] "An Introductory Analysis of the NDE . . ." n.d.
[197] Stevenson, Owens, & Cook, 1990.
[198] Stevenson, Owens, & Cook, 1990.
[199] Marshall, Lazar, & Spellman, 2001.
[200] Fenwick, "Dying: a spiritual experience . . ." n.d.
[201] Sabom, 1982.
[202] Sudduth, n.d.
[203] Gabbard & Twemlow, 1984.
[204] Schroeter-Kunhardt, 1993.
[205] Blackmore, 1986.
[206] Greyson, 1983.
[207] Bates, 1985.
[208] Lisansky, Strassman, Janowsky et al., 1984.
[209] Latz, Agle, DePalma et al., 1972.
[210] Schroter-Kunhardt, 1990.
[211] Morse, 1994.
[212] Greyson, "Near Death Experiences as . . ." n.d.
[213] Sabom, 1982.
[214] Zaleski, 1987.
[215] Grey, 1985.
[216] Giovetti, 1982.
[217] Counts, 1983.
[218] Pasricha, 1986.
[219] Zammit, 2006.
[220] Sabom, 1982.
[221] Sabom, 1982.
[222] Hertzog & Herrin, 1985.
[223] Gabbard & Twemlow, 1984.
[224] Morse, 1994.
[225] Becker, 1993.
[226] Fenwick & Fenwick, 1996.
[227] Fenwick & Fenwick, 1995, p. 47.
[228] Botkin with Hogan, 2005.
[229] Botkin with Hogan, 2005, pp. 82-84.
[230] Botkin with Hogan, 2005, pp. 84-85.
[231] Botkin with Hogan, 2005, pp. 86-87.
[232] Botkin with Hogan, 2005, pp. 87-88.
[233] Botkin with Hogan, 2005, pp. 88-89.
[234] "Fate of the Universe>Anthropic Principle," n.d.
[235] "Fate of the Universe>Anthropic Principle," n.d.

[236] Gonzalez & Richards, 2004.

[237] Bryner, 2007.

[238] Schroeder, 2001, p. 58.

[239] Gonzalez & Richards, 2004.

[240] Gonzalez & Richards, 2004.

[241] Richards & Gonzalez, 2004.

[242] Corey, 2007.

[243] Heffern, 2003.

[244] Happold, 1991.

Chapter 3 Endnotes

[1] Hamilton, n.d.

[2] Radin, 1997, p. 79.

[3] Radin, 1997, page 86.

[4] Varvoglis, 1999.

[5] Radin, 1997, pp 87-88.

[6] Schlitz & Honorton, 1992.

[7] Schlitz, 2003.

[8] Schlitz, 2003.

[9] Smith, Burke, Rhine, Stuart, & Greewood, 1966.

[10] Lazlo, 1996.

[11] Grinberg-Zylverbaum, Delaflor, Sanchez-Arellano, Guevara, & Perez, 1993.

[12] Grinberg-Zylverbaum, Delaflor, Sanchez-Arellano, Guevara, & Perez, 1993.

[13] Thaheld, 2003.

[14] Radin, Rae, & Hyman, 2000.

[15] Braud & Schlitz, 1983.

[16] Braud & Schlitz, 1989.

[17] Schlitz & Braud, 1985.

[18] Schlitz & LaBerge, 1997.

[19] Braud, n.d.

[20] Radin et al., 2000.

[21] Achterberg & Cooke, 2005.

[22] Montecucco, 1992.

[23] Montecucco, 2007.

[24] Ullman & Krippner, 1970; Persinger & Krippner 1989.

[25] Botkin with Hogan, 2005, pp. 92-98.

[26] Tart, 1969.

[27] Moody, 1993.

[28] Moody, 1993.

[29] Braud, Shafer, & Andrews, 1993.

[30] Sheldrake, "The 'Sense of Being Stared At," 1998.

[31] Laberge & Schlitz, 1997.

[32] Radin, Rae, & Hyman, 2000.
[33] Braud et al., 1990.
[34] McKenna & O'Bryen, 1997.
[35] Playfair, 2003.
[36] Radin et al., 2000.
[37] Playfair, 2003.
[38] Emerson, 1883.
[39] Parish, n.d.
[40] Grinberg-Zylverbaum, 1993.
[41] Dunne, 1991.
[42] Interview with B. Dunne, 1998.
[43] Montecucco, 1992.
[44] Murphy & White, 1978.
[45] Novak, 1976.
[46] Kenny, n.d.
[47] Kenny, n.d.
[48] McCraty, 2003, p. 9.
[49] Schwartz & Russek, 1999.
[50] McCraty, 2003, pp. 12-13.
[51] Hagelin, Orme-Johnson, Rainforth, Cavanaugh, & Alexander, 1993.
[52] Dillbeck et al., 1981.
[53] Orme-Johnson et al., n.d.

Chapter 4 Endnotes

[1] Hamani, McAndrews, & Cohn, et al., 2008.
[2] Carter, 2007.
[3] Dossey, 1997.
[4] Harris et al., 1999.
[5] Sicher, Targ, Moore, & Smith, 1998.
[6] Krieger, 1975.
[7] Grad, 1965.
[8] Wilkinson, Knox, Chatman, Johnson, Barbour, Myles, & Reel, 2002.
[9] Woods & Dimond, 2002.
[10] Astin, Harkness, & Ernst, 2000.
[11] Jonas & Crawford, 2003.
[12] Miller, 1982.
[13] LeShan, 1974.
[14] Goodrich, 1974.
[15] Goodrich, 1976.
[16] Winston, 1975.
[17] Byrd, 1988.
[18] Abbot, 2000.

[19] Ring, "Dr. Larry Dossey Champions . . ." n.d.
[20] Ring, "Dr. Larry Dossey Champions . . ." n.d.
[21] Rein, 1986, pp. 76-80.
[22] Braud & Schlitz, 1988, pp. 5-9.
[23] Grad, Cadoret, & Paul, 1961.
[24] Solfvin, 1982.
[25] Watkins & Watkins, 1971.
[26] Watkins & Watkins, 1973.
[27] Wells & Klein, 1972.
[28] Wells & Watkins, 1975.
[29] Bengston & Krinsley, 2000.
[30] Onetto & Elguin, 1966.
[31] Barry, 1968.
[32] Tedder & Monty, 1981.
[33] Nash, 1984.
[34] Borysenko, 1993.
[35] Haraldsson & Thorsteinsson, 1973.
[36] Tiller, Dibble, & Kohane, 2001.
[37] Tiller, 1999.
[38] Radin, Taft, & Yount, 2004.
[39] Dunne & Jahn, 1992.
[40] Radin, 1997, p. 167.
[41] Von Buengner, n.d.
[42] Von Buengner, n.d.
[43] Emoto, 2005.
[44] Radin, Hayssen, Emoto, & Kizu, 2006.

Chapter 6 Endnote

[1] Chopra, D. 1999.

Chapter 7 Endnotes

[1] Adapted from an anonymous German postcard . . . 1915.
[2] Encina, n.d.
[3] "Reasons for failure in meditation," n.d.
[4] Kornfield (as cited in Kearney), n.d.
[5] "A Conversation with John Giorno," n.d.
[6] Heath, n.d.
[7] Kearney, n.d.

Chapter 9 Endnotes

[1] Lougrhan, 2001.
[2] Holden, 2005.
[3] Botkin with Hogan, 2005.
[4] Crookall, 1961.
[5] Circle of the Silver Cord.
[6] http://adcguides.com.
[7] Crookall, 1961, pp. 14-16.
[8] Tymn, "Distinguished researchers . . ." 2007.
[9] Tymn, "Automatic Writing . . ." 2007.
[10] Tymn, 2008.
[11] Kübler-Ross, 1991.
[12] Tymn, "Automatic Writing: Like Holding a Live Bird," 2007.

Chapter 10 Endnotes

[1] Desmedt and Robertson, 1977.
[2] Roland and Friberg, 1985.
[3] Eccles, 1988.
[4] Van Lommel, "6. Neurophysiology in . . ." (n.d.).
[5] "Physicists challenge notion . . ." 2007.
[6] "There's more than meets the eye . . ." 2007.

Bibliography

4 in 10 Americans are under stress: Gallup poll. (n.d.). Health and Fitness, Netscape. Retrieved July 24, 2007, from http://health.netscape.com/ story/2007/01/31/4-in-10-americans-are-under-stress-gallup-poll/.

A conversation with John Giorno. (n.d.). Artful Dodge, Department of English, College of Wooster. Retrieved October 14, 2007, from http://wooster.edu/ ArtfulDodge/interviews/giorno.htm.

Abbot, N. C. (2000). Healing as a therapy for human disease: a systematic review, *Journal of Alternative and Complementary Medicine.* 6(2), 159-169.

Achterberg, J., & Cooke, K. (2005). Evidence for correlations between distant intentionality and brain function in recipients: A functional magnetic resonance imaging analysis. *Journal of Alternative and Complementary Medicine,* 11(6), 965-971.

Akiane's Web site. http://www.artakiane.com/.

Amatuzio, J. Web site. http://www.foreverours.com/.

Amazing blind teen uses echolocation to "SEE." (2006, October 26). Familes.com. Retrieved August 25, 2007, from http://special-needs.families.com/blog/ amazing-blind-boy-uses-echolocation-to-see-watch-the-video-clip.

An introductory analysis of the NDE (near-death experience). (n.d.). Retrieved September 23, 2007, from http://www.fortunecity.com/roswell/séance /78/nde.htm.

Astin, J. A., Harkness, E., & Ernst, E. (2000). The efficacy of "distant healing": a systematic review of randomized trials. *Annals of Internal Medicine,* 132, 903-910.

Baird, J. L. (1988). *Sermons, Soap and Television — Autobiographical Notes.* London: Royal Television Society.

Balfour, A. J. (1879). *A Defence of Philosophic Doubt.* University of Michigan.

Bander, P. (1973). *Voices from the Tapes.* New York: Drake Publishers.

Barrett, W. (1926). *Death-Bed Visions — The Psychical Experiences of the Dying.* Rider & Co.

Barry, J. (1968). General and comparative study of the psychokinetic effect on a fungus culture. *Journal of Parapsychology.* 32, 237-43.

Basar, E. (2005). Memory as the "whole brain work" A large-scale model based on "oscillations in super-synergy." *International Journal of Psychophysiology,* 58(2-3), 199-226.

Bates B. C., & Stanley, A. (1985). The epidemiology and differential diagnosis of near death experience. *American Journal of Orthopsychiatry,* 55, 542-9.

Becker, Carl B. (1993). *Paranormal Experience and Survival of Death*. Suny Series in Western Esoteric Traditions. New York: State University of New York Press.

Begley, S. (2007, April 9). In our messy, reptilian brains. *Newsweek* online. Retrieved April 9, 2007, from http://www.msnbc.msn.com/id/17888475/site/newsweek/.

Beischel, J., & Schwartz, G. E. (2007, January/February). Anomalous information reception by research mediums demonstrated using a novel triple-blind protocol. *Explore*, 3(1).

Bengston, W. F., & Krinsley, D. (2000). The effect of the "laying on of hands" on transplanted breast cancer in mice. *Journal of Scientific Exploration*, 14(3), 353-364.

Bennett, E. (1939). *Apparitions and Haunted Houses: A Survey of Evidence*. London: Faber and Faber.

Berkovich, S. (n.d.). A scientific model why memory aka consciousness cannot reside solely in the brain. Retrieved October 25, 2007, from http://www.nderf.org/Berkovich.htm.

Berman, M. (1981). *Reenchantment of the World*. Cornell University Press.

Bierman, D. J., & Radin, D. (1997). Anomalous anticipatory response on randomized future conditions. *Perceptual and Motor Skills*, 84, 689-690.

Blackmore, S. (1986). Out of body experiences in schizophrenia. *Journal of Nervous and Mental Disease*, 174, 615-9.

Blum, D. (2006). *Ghost Hunters: William James and the Search for Scientific proof of Life After Death*. Penguin Press.

Borysenko, J. (1993). *Fire in the Soul: A New Psychology of Spiritual Optimism*. Warner Books, Inc.

Botkin, A., with Hogan, R. C. (2005). *Induced After-Death Communication: A New Therapy for Grief and Trauma*. Charlottesville, VA: Hampton Roads.

Braud, W., & Schlitz, M. (1983). A methodology for the objective study of transpersonal imagery. *Journal of Scientific Exploration*, 3, 43-63.

Braud, W., & Schlitz, M. (1988). Possible role of intuitive data sorting in electrodermal biological psychokinesis (bio-PK). In *Research in Parapsychology* (pp. 5-9). Metuchen, New Jersey: The Scarecrow Press.

Braud, W., & Schlitz, M. (1989). Remote mental influence of animate and inanimate target systems: A method of comparison and preliminary findings. *Proceedings of Presented Papers*, 32nd Annual Parapsychological Association Convention. San Diego, California, 12-25.

Braud, W. A. (n.d.). Empirical explorations of prayer, distant healing, and remote mental influence. Institute of transpersonal psychology. *Journal of Religion and Psychical Research*, 17:2, 62-73. Retrieved July 15, 2007, from http://www.integral-inquiry.com/docs/649/empirical.pdf.

Braud, W., Shafer, D., & Andrews, S. (1990). Electrodermal correlates of remote attention: Autonomic reactions to an unseen gaze. *Proceedings of Presented Papers*, Parapsychology Association 33rd Annual Convention, 14-28.

Braud, W., Shafer, D., & Andrews, S. (1993). Reactions to an unseen gaze (remote attention): A review, with new data on autonomic staring detection. *Journal of Parapsychology*, 57, 373-390.

Bray, S. (1990). *A Guide for the Spiritual Traveler*. Queensland Australia: Scroll Publishers.

Brune, P. C. (n.d.). The rediscovered beyond. Retrieved March 31, 2007, from http://www.worlditc.org/.

Bryner, J. (2007, October 1). Huge stores of oxygen found deep inside Earth. MSNBC. Retrieved October 4, 2007, from http://www.msnbc.msn.com/id/21082196/.

Buengner, P. (n.d.). Morphic Fields can now be measured scientifically! The Global Oneness Commitment. Retrieved October 13, 2007, from http://www.experiencefestival.com/a/Morphic_fields/id/10320.

Burt, C. (1975). *The Gifted Child*. New York: Wiley.

Butler, T., & Butler, L. (1947). *There is No Death and There are No Dead*. AA-EVP Publishing.

Byrd, R. C. (1988). Positive therapeutic effects of intercessory prayer in a coronary care unit population. *Southern Medical Journal*, 81(7), 826-829.

Carrington, H. (1973). *The World of Psychic Research*. New Jersey: A.S Barns & Co., Inc.

Carter, C. (n.d.). Rebuttal to Keith Augustine's attack of "Does consciousness depend on the Brain?" Retrieved May 30, 2007, from http://www.survivalafterdeath.org/articles/carter/augustine.htm.

Cassirer, M. (1996). *Medium on Trial—the Story of Helen Duncan and the Witchcraft Act*. Stanstead. Essex: PN Publishing.

Chalmers, D. J. (1997). The puzzle of conscious experience. *Scientific American*, special issue "Mysteries of the mind." Retrieved October 5, 2007, from http://www.healthstones.com/mineraldata/beliefs/parapsychology/parapsychology.html.

Choi, C. (2007, May 24). Strange but true: When half a brain is better than a whole one," ScientificAmerican.com. Retrieved May 30, 2007, from http://www.sciam.com/article.cfm?articleId=BE96F947-E7F2-99DF-3EA94A4C4EE87581&chanId=sa013&modsrc =most_popular.

Chopra, D. (1999). *Everyday Immortality*. Audio book. Random House, Inc.

Circle of the Silver Cord. Web site at http://silvercordcircle.com.

Cook, E. W., Greyson, B., & Stevenson, I. (1998). Do any near-death experiences provide evidence for the survival of human personality after death? Relevant features and illustrative case reports. *Journal of Scientific Exploration*, 12, 377-406. Retrieved July 17, 2007, from http://www.near-death.com/evidence.html#a2.

Corey, M. (2007). *The God Hypothesis: Discovering Design in Our "Just Right" Goldilocks Universe.* Rowman & Littlefield Publishers, Inc.

Counts, D. A. (1983). Near-death and out of body experiences in a Melanesian society. *Anabiosis*, 3(2), 115-135.

Crookall, R. (1961). *The Supreme Adventure, Analyses of Psychic Communications.* James Clarke & Co., Ltd.

Cross-correspondence. (n.d.). Answers.com. Retrieved August 25, 2007, from http://www.answers.com/topic/cross-correspondence.

Current results, empirical normalization. (n.d.). Global Consciousness Project. Princeton University. Retrieved October 22, 2007, from http://noosphere.princeton.edu/.

Currie, I. (1995). *You Cannot Die.* Book Club Associates.

Daniel Dunglas Home (1833-1886). (n.d.). SurvivalAfterDeath.org. Retrieved July 16, 2007, from http://www.survivalafterdeath.org/mediums/home.htm.

DePanfilis, Children's Bureau. (n.d.). *Child Neglect: A Guide for Prevention, Assessment and Intervention.* Child Welfare Information Gateway. Retrieved October 25, 2007, from http://www.childwelfare.gov/pubs/usermanuals/neglect/chaptertwo.cfm.

Desmedt, J. E., & Robertson, D. (1977). Differential enhancement of early and late components of the cerebral somatosensory evoked potentials during forced-paced cognitive tasks in man. *Journal of Physiology*, 271, 761-782.

Dillbeck, M. C., et al. (1981). The Transcendental Meditation program and crime rate change in a sample of 48 cities. *Journal of Crime and Justice*, 4, 25-45.

Dodds, E. R. (1962). Presidential Address. *Proceedings of the Society for Psychical Research.* London.

Dolgoff, S. (2007, November 28). Life is good. So why can't you stop worrying? MSNBC. Retrieved November 28, 2007, from http://www.msnbc.msn.com/id/21993569/.

Dossey, L., & Schwartz, S. (n.d.). *Therapeutic Intent/Healing Bibliography of Research.* Retrieved December 15, 2007 from http://www.stephanaschwartz.com/distant_healing_biblio.htm/.

Dossey, L. (1989). *Recovering the Soul: A scientific and Spiritual Search.* Bantam Books.

Dossey, L. (1997). *Healing Words.* HarperOne.

Doyle, A. C. (1926). *The History of Spiritualism, Vols. I and II.* New York: Arno Press.

Dunne, B. J. (1998). Cited in McTaggart, L. *The Field* (p. 119). Harper Paperbacks.

Dunne, B. J. (1993). Co-operator experiments with an REG device. PEAR Technical Note 91005. In Rao, K.R. (Ed.), *Cultivating consciousness for enhancing human potential, wellness and healing* (pp. 149-163). Westport, CT: Praeger.

Dunne, B., & Jahn, R. G. (1992). Experiments in remote human/machine interaction. *Journal of Scientific Exploration*, 6(4), 311-332.

Easton, J. C. (2005, July 14). Survey on physician's religious beliefs shows majority faithful. *The University of Chicago Chronicle*. Retrieved March 31, 2007, from http://chronicle.uchicago.edu/050714/doctorsfaith.shtml.

Eccles, J. C. (1988). The effect of silent thinking on the cerebral cortex. *Truth Journal*. Retrieved December 15, 2007 from http://www.leaderu.com/truth/2truth06.html,.

Emerson, R. W. (1883). Essays: first series. In the *Riverside Edition, Vol. II, of Emerson's Complete Works*. Boston: Houghton Mifflin and Co.

Emoto, M. (2005). *The Secret Life of Water*. Atria.

Encina, G. B. (n.d.). Cultural differences? Or, are we really that different? University of California. Retrieved October 31, 2007, from http://www.cnr.berkeley.edu/ucce50/ag-labor/7article/article01.htm.

Farby, J. (2007, October 25). Study finds stress levels for Americans on the rise. All Headline News. Retrieved October 25, 2007 from http://www.allheadlinenews.com/articles/7008947268.

Fate of the universe>Anthropic principle. (n.d.). Oracle Thinkquest.org Educational Foundation. Retrieved May 24, 2007, from http://library.thinkquest.org/C0126626/fate/fate%20of%20universe.anthropic%20principle.main.htm.

Fenwick, P., & Fenwick, E. (1995, March 2). All the questions are essentially simple but the answers remain elusive. *The Daily Mail*. London.

Fenwick, P., & Fenwick, E. (1996). *The Truth in the Light—An Investigation of Over 300 Near-Death Experiences*. Headline Book Publishing.

Fenwick, P. (n.d.). Approaching-death experiences and the NDE: A model for the dying process. International Association for Near-Death Studies. Retrieved June 21, 2007, from http://www.iands.org/research/important_studies/dr._peter_fenwick_m.d._science_and_spirituality_6.html.

Fenwick, P. (n.d.). Dying: a spiritual experience as shown by near death experiences and deathbed visions. Royal College of Psychiatrists. Retrieved June 21, 2007, from http://www.rcpsych.ac.uk/PDF/PFenwickNearDeath.pdf.

Fenwick, P. (n.d.). People have NDEs while brain dead. *Near-Death Experiences and the Afterlife*. Retrieved April 1, 2007, from http://www.near-death.com/experiences/evidence01.html.

Fisher, J. (1986). *The Case for Reincarnation*. London: Grafton Books.

Flint, L. (1971). *Voices in the Dark*. Macmillan.

Fodor, N. (1934). Chapter 3: The voice of Confucius: Story of George Valiantine. In *These Mysterious People* (p. 238). Rider & Co. Retrieved June 21, 2007, from http://www.survivalafterdeath.org/books/fodor/chapter2.htm.

Fontana, D. (2005). *Is There an Afterlife?: A Comprehensive Overview of the Evidence*. O Books.

Frontier Perspectives. (1997, Spring/Summer). 6(2), 70-78.

Gabbard, G. O., & Twemlow, S. W. (1984). *With the Eyes of the Mind: An Empirical Analysis of Out-of-Body States.* New York: Praeger.

Geley, G. (1927). *Clairvoyance and Materialization: A Record of Experiments.* London: T. Fisher Unwin Limited.

Giovetti, P. (1982). Near-death and deathbed-experiences: An Italian survey. *Theta,* 10(1), 10-13.

Gonzalez, G., & Richards, J. (2004). *The Privileged Planet: How Our Place in the Cosmos is Designed for Discovery.* Regnery Publishing, Inc.

Goodrich, J. (1974). Psychic healing: A pilot study. Unpublished doctoral dissertation, Union Graduate School, 1974.

Goodrich, J. (1976). Studies of paranormal healing. *New Horizons,* 2(2), 21-24.

Grad, B., Cadoret, R., & Paul, G. I. (1961). The influence of an unorthodox, method of treatment on wound healing in mice. *International Journal of Parapsychology,* 3, 5-24.

Grad, B. R. (1965). Some biological effects of laying-on of hands: a review of experiments with animals and plants. *Journal of the American Society for Psychical Research,* 59, 95-127.

Graham Wallas' model. (n.d.). Retrieved September 11, 2007, from http://members.optusnet.com.au/charles57/Creative/Brain/wallis_intro.htm.

Grey, M. (1985). *Return from Death.* London: Arkana.

Greyson, B. (1983). The near death experience scale: construction, reliability and validity. *Journal of Nervous and Mental Disease,* 171, 369-75.

Greyson, B. (2000). Near death experiences as evidence for survival of bodily death. Survival of Bodily Death: An Esalen Invitational Conference, February 11-16, 2000. Retrieved June 3, 2007, from http://www.esalenctr.org/display/confpage.cfm?confid=9&pageid=95&pgtype=1.

Grinberg-Zylverbaum, J., Delaflor, M., Sanchez- Arellano, M.E., Guevara, M. A., & Perez, M. (1993). Human communication and the electrophysiological activity of the brain. *Subtle Energies,* 3, 3.

Grof, S. (1998, January 1). Life after death: The testimony of science. A documentary by Tom Harpur. Wellspring Media.

Guggenheim, B., & Guggenheim, J. (1995). *Hello from Heaven.* Bantam Books.

Gurney, E., Myers, F. W. H., & Podmore, F. (1886). *Phantasms of the Living.* London: Trubner.

Hadamard, J. (1949). *The Psychology of Invention in the Mathematical Field.* Princeton: Princeton University Press.

Hagelin, J. S., Orme-Johnson, D.W., Rainforth, M., Cavanaugh, K., & Alexander, C. N. (1999). Effects of group practice of the Transcendental Meditation Program on preventing violent crime in Washington, D.C.: Results of the National Demonstration Project to Reduce Crime and Improve Governmental Effectiveness in Washington, D.C., June-July, 1993. *Social Indicators Research,* 47, 153-201.

Hallenbeck, J. L. (2003, June 26). Altered states of consciousness at the end of life. *Palliative Care Perspectives,* Oxford University Press. Retrieved June 20, 2007, from http://www.mywhatever.com/cifwriter/library/70/4961.html.

Hamani, C., McAndrews, M.P., Cohn, M., et al. Memory enhancement induced by hypothalamic/fornix deep brain stimulation. *Annals of Neurology, 63,* 119-123.

Hameroff, S. (n.d.). Overview: Could life and consciousness be related to the fundamental quantum nature of the universe? *Quantum Consciousness.* Retrieved December 15, 2007, from http://www.quantumconsciousness.org/overview.html.

Hamilton, C. (n.d.). Is God all in your head? *What is Enlightenment?* magazine. Retrieved October 4, 2007, from http://www.wie.org/j29/consciousness.asp?page=9.

Hamilton, T. G. (1942). *Intention and Survival.* Regency Press.

Hapgood, C. H. (1975). *Voices of Spirit.* New York: Nordon Publications.

Happold, F. C. (1991). *Mysticism: A Study and an Anthology.* Penguin. (as cited in Miller, G. (n.d.), Reading revolutions: intellectual history. Retrieved November 21, 2007, from http://hua.umf.maine.edu/Reading_Revolutions/Emerson.html.

Haraldsson E., & Thorsteinsson T. (1973). Psychokinetic effects on yeast. An exploratory experiment. In *Research in Parapsychology* (pages 20-21). Metuchen, NJ: Scarecrow Press.

Haraldsson, E. (1989). Survey of claimed encounters with the dead. *Omega, 19,* 103-13.

Harris, W. S. et al. (1999). A randomized, controlled trial of the effects of remote, intercessory prayer on outcomes in patients admitted to the coronary care unit. *Archives of Internal Medicine,* 159(19), 2273-2278.

Hay, D. (n.d.). The spirituality of the unchurched. British and Irish Association for Mission Studies. Retrieved March 12, 2007, from http://www.martynmission.cam.ac.uk/BIAMSHay.htm, March 12, 2007.

Heath, I. (n.d.). Self-awareness and meditation. *Discover Your Mind.* Retrieved October 14, 2007, from http://www.discover-your-mind.co.uk/faqs/r5-self-awareness.htm.

Heffern, R. (2003, December 12). Spirituality and the fine-tuned cosmos. *National Catholic Reporter.* Retrieved May 24, 2007, from http://ncronline.org/NCR_Online/archives2/2003d/121203/121203a.php.

Helen Duncan: The Official Pardon Site. Retrieved July 29, 2007, from http://www.users.zetnet.co.uk/helenduncan/.

Hertzog, D. B., & Herrin, J. T. (1985). Near death experiences in the very young. *Critical Care Medicine,* 13, 1074-5.

Hill, W.E. (1915). Image adapted from an anonymous 1888 German postcard by W.E. Hill for *Puck* magazine.

Hodgson, R. (1897-1898). A further record of observations of certain phenomena of a trance. *Proceedings of the Society for Psychical Research,* 13, 297.

Holden, J. (2005, November 5). Holden describes the frequency of after-death communication. University of North Texas News Service. Retrieved November 11, 2007, from http://web2.unt.edu/news/ story.cfm?story=9441.

Holladay, A. (2007, December 7). Expanding space. WonderQuest. Retrieved December 10, 2007, from http://www.wonderquest.com/ ExpandingUniverse.htm.

Holmes and Rahe Stress scale says divorced men seeking contact are at most risk. (n.d.). BBC Action Network. Retrieved October 25, 2007, from http://www.bbc.co.uk/dna/actionnetwork/A3539522.

Holzer, H. (1963). *Ghost Hunter*. New York: Bobbs Merril Co.

Honorton, C., & Ferrari, D. C. (1989). Future telling: A meta-analysis of forced-choice precognition experiments, 1935-1987. *Journal of Parapsychology*, 53, 281-308. Retrieved October 23, 2007, from http://www.boundaryinstitute.org/articles/timereversed.pdf.

Hornell Hart (1888-1967). (n.d.). SurvivalAfterDeath.org. Retrieved April 16, 2007, from http://www.survivalafterdeath.org/researchers/hart.htm.

Humans with amazing senses. (2006, August 9). ABC Primetime. Retrieved August 25, 2007, from http://abcnews.go.com/Primetime/story? id=2283048&page=1.

Hyslop, J. H. (1918). *Life After Death: Problems of the Future Life and Its Nature*. Kessinger Publishing.

Indicators of School Crime and Safety: 2006. (2007). Institute of Education Sciences, U.S. Department of Education. Retrieved September 24, 2007, from http://nces.ed.gov/programs/crimeindicators/.

Inglis, B. (1984). *Science and Parascience—A History of the Paranormal 1914-1939*. London: Hodder and Stroughton.

James Hyslop 1854-1920. (n.d.). Retrieved December 22, 2007, from http://www.survivalafterdeath.org/researchers/hyslop.htm.

Johnson, R. C. (1982). *The Imprisoned Splendour*. Quest Books.

Jonas, W. B, & Crawford, C. C. (2003). Science and spiritual healing: a critical review of spiritual healing, "energy" medicine, and intentionality. *Alternative Therapies*, 9(3), A56-71.

Journal of the Society for Psychical Research, February 1904.

Jung, C. G. (1973). *Letters, Volume 1*. Translated from the German by R. F. C. Hull. Princeton: Princeton University Press.

Kalish, R. A., & Reynolds, D. K. (1973). Phenomenological reality and post death contact. *Journal for the Scientific Study of Religion*, 209-21.

Kearney, P. (n.d.). Still crazy after all these years: Why meditation isn't psychotherapy. Retrieved October 15, 2007, from http://www.buddhanet.net/crazy.htm.

Keen, M., & Ellison, A. (1999). Scole: A response to the critics? The Scole Report. *Proceedings of the Society for Psychical Research*, 58(220).

Keen, M. (2003). Physical phenomena at the David Thompson séance of October 25th 2003. Retrieved July 16, 2007, from http://silvercordcircle.com/ newsletters/montague_keens_report.pdf.

Kelly, E. (2000). Inadequacies of contemporary mind/brain theories. Paper presented at the Esalen Invitational Conference on Survival of Bodily Death, February 11-16, 2000. Retrieved September 11, 2007, from http://www.esalenctr.org/display/ confpage.cfm?confid=9&pageid=87&pgtype=1.

Kelly, E. F., Kelly, E. W., Crabtree, A., & Gauld, A. (2006). *Irreducible Mind: Toward a Psychology for the 21st Century.* Rowman & Littlefield Publishers.

Kendall, J. (1955). *Michael Faraday.* London: Faber.

Kenny, R. (2004, May-July). The science of collective consciousness. *What is Enlightenment.* Retrieved October 13, 2007, from WIE Unbound at http://www.wie.org/j25/kenny.asp.

Kenny, R. (n.d.). What can science tell us about collective consciousness? Leaderful Teams Consulting. Collective Wisdom Initiative. Retrieved October 13, 2007, from http://www.collectivewisdominitiative.org/ papers/kenny_science.htm#end63.

Knoll, M. (1957). Transformations of science in our age. In *Man and Time,* Joseph Campbell (Ed.), Bollingen Series. Princeton: Princeton University Press.

Komp, D. M. (1992). *A Window to Heaven: When Children See Life in Death.* Grand Rapids, Michigan: Zondervan Publishing.

Kornfield, J. *A path with heart: A guide through the perils and promises of spiritual life.* New York: Bantam, 1993 (as cited in Kearney, n.d.).

Krieger, D. (1975). Therapeutic touch: the imprimatur of nursing. *American Journal of Nursing, 7,* 784-787.

Kübler-Ross, E. (2006). *Is There Life After Death?* Sounds True audio.

Kübler-Ross, E. (1983). *On Children and Death.* New York: MacMillan Publishing.

Kübler-Ross, E. (1997). *On Death and Dying.* Scribner.

Kübler-Ross, E. (1991). *On Life After Death.* Celestial Arts.

Laberge, S., & Schlitz, M. (1997). Covert observation increases skin conductance in subjects unaware of when they are being observed: A replication. *The Journal of Parapsychology, 61.*

Larson, E. J., & Witham, L. (1998). Leading scientists still reject God. *Nature, 394,* 313.

Latz, N. M., Agle, A. P., & DePalma, R. G., et al. (1972). Delirium in surgical patients under intensive care. *Archives of Surgery, 104,* 310-3.

Lazarus, R. (1993). *The Case Against Death.* London: Warner Books: London.

LeShan, L. (1974). *The Medium, the Mystic, and the Physicist.* New York: Viking Press.

Libet B., et al. (1979). Subjective referral of the timing for a conscious sensory experience. *Brain, 102,* 193-224.

Libet, B. (1984). Subjective antedating of a sensory experience and mind-brain theories: Reply to Honderich. *Journal of Theoretical Biology*, 144, 563-570.

Linzmeier, B. M. (n.d.). Attitudes toward near-death experiences. Retrieved December 6, 2006, from http://www.nderf.org/nde_attitudes.htm.

Lisansky J., Strassman R. J., Janowsky D., et al. (1984). Drug induced psychoses. In Tupin, J. P., Halbreich, U., Pena, J. J., (Eds.), *Transient psychosis: diagnosis, management and evaluation* (pp. 80-111). New York: Bruner/Mazel.

Lombroso, Cesare Lombroso. (2006). *Criminal Man*. Duke University Press.

Lougrhan, G. (2001). Can there be life after life? Ask the atheist! Near-Death Experiences and the Afterlife. Retrieved May 8, 2007, from http://www.near-death.com/experiences/atheists01.html.

Machado, C., & Shewmon, D. A. (Eds.). (2004). *Brain Death and Disorders of Consciousness. Springer*. Retrieved October 20, 2007, from http://www.opuslux.com/continuityofconsciousness.htm.

Mars, B. (n.d.). Improve your brain power – with a healthy diet. BNET Research Center. Retrieved October 10, 2007, from http://findarticles.com/p/articles/mi_m0HKL/is_5_7/ai_66918296.

Marshall, R. S., Lazar, R. M., & Spellman, J. P. (2001). Recovery of brain function during induced cerebral hypoperfusion. *Brain*, 124, 1208–1217.

Martin, D. (2006, September 18). Savants: Charting 'islands of genius.' CNN.com. Retrieved December 7, 2007, from http://www.cnn.com/2006/HEALTH/09/06/savant.genius/index.html.

Matchett, W. F. (1972). Repeated hallucinatory experiences as part of the mourning process among Hopi Indian women. *Psychiatry*, 35, 185-194.

Max Planck quotes. (n.d.). Retrieved November 30, 2007, from http://thinkexist.com/quotation/a_new_scientific_truth_does_not_triumph_by_/158371.html.

Mayell, H. (2002, February 12). Thousands of women killed for family "honor," *National Geographic News*. Retrieved on October 15, 2007, from http://news.nationalgeographic.com/news/2002/02/0212_020212_honorkilling.html.

Mayer, E. L. (2007). *Science, Skepticism, and the Inexplicable Powers of the Human Mind*. New York: Bantam Books.

McCraty, R. (2003). *The energetic heart: Bioelectromagnetic interactions within and between people*. Boulder Creek, CA: Institute of HeartMath.

McKenna, P., & O'Bryen, G. (1997). *The Paranormal World of Paul McKenna*. Faber & Faber.

McKenzie, A. (1971). *Apparitions and Ghosts: A Modern Study*. London: Arthur Baker Ltd.

McTaggart, L. (2002). *The Field*. Harper Paperbacks.

Meek, G. (1987). *After We Die What Then*. Columbus, Ohio: Ariel Press.

Miller, L. H., & Smith, A. D. (n.d.). The stress solution: An action plan to manage the stress in your life. Retrieved October 25, 2007, from http://www.apahelpcenter.org/articles/article.php?id=103.

Miller, R.N. (1982). Study of the effectiveness of remote mental healing. *Medical Hypotheses*. 8, 481-490.

Montecucco, N. (1992, November). Report by Cyber: Ricerche Olistiche. Retrieved December 17, 2007, from http://www.goertzel.org/dynapsyc/1996/subtle.html.

Montecucco, N. (2007). Experimental evidence of nonlocal correlation between the brain/consciousness of subjects in different locations during the Global Peace Meditation/Prayer Day of 20th May, 2007. Retrieved December 15, 2007, from http://www.globalpeacemeditationprayerday.org/PDF/italy_experiment.pdf.

Moody, R. (1993). *Reunions: Visionary Encounters with Departed Loved Ones*. Ivy Press.

Moody, R. (2001). *Life after Life: The Investigation of a Phenomenon — Survival of Bodily Death*. HarperOne.

Moore, C. A. (2006, February 18). The unseen realm: Science is making room for near-death experiences beyond this world. *Desert Morning News*.

Morin, R. (2000, April 24). Do Americans believe in God? Retrieved April 23, 2007, from http://www.washingtonpost.com/wp-srv/politics/polls/wat/archive/wat042400.htm.

Morse, M. L., & Perry, P. (1991). *Closer to the Light*. London: Souvenir Press.

Morse, M. L. (1994). Near death experiences and death-related visions in children: implications for the clinician. *Current Problems in Pediatrics*, 24, 55-83.

Morse, M. L. with Perry, P. (1994). *Parting Visions*. New York: Villard Books.

Mozart, A. M. (1974). Quoted in John Chesterman, *An Index of Possibilities: Energy and Power* (p. 186). New York: Pantheon Books.

Murphet, H. (1990). *Beyond death — The Undiscovered Country*. London: Quest.

Murphy, M., & White, R.A. (1978). *The psychic side of sports*. Reading, MA: Addison-Wesley.

Myers, F. W. H. *Human Personality and Its Survival of Bodily Death*. Kessinger Publishing, LLC.

Nash, C. B. (1984). Test of psychokinetic control of bacterial mutation. *Journal of the American Society for Psychical Research*. 78(2), 145-52.

Novak, M. (1976). *The joy of sports*. New York: Basic Books.

Olivia Bennett's Web site. Retrieved July 29, 2007, from http://www.oliviabennett.com/.

Onetto B., & Elguin G. H. (1966). Psychokinesis in experimental tumorgenesis. (Abstract of dissertation in psychology, University of Chile 1964.) *Journal of Parapsychology*, 30, 220.

Oppenheim, J. (1985). *The Other World*. Cambridge: CUP.

Orlando Serrell Web site. (n.d.). http://www.orlandoserrell.com.

Orme-Johnson, D. W., Cavanaugh, K. L., Alexander, C.N., Gelderloos, P., Dillbeck, M. C., Lanford, A.G., & Abou Nader, T.M. (In press, pp. 2532-2548). The influence of the Maharishi Technology of the Unified Field on world events and global social indicators: The effects of the Taste of Utopia Assembly. Cited in Robert Kenny, "What can science tell us about collective consciousness?" Leaderful Teams Consulting. Retrieved November 10, 2007, from http://www.collectivewisdominitiative.org/papers/kenny_science.htm#end63.

Osis, K. (1998, July). Core visions of psychical research: Is there life after death? A cross-Cultural Search for the Evidence. *Journal of the American Society for Psychical Research, 92*, 252.

Osis, K. (2007). *At the Hour of Death: A New Look at Evidence for Life After Death.* Hastings House.

Paranormal voices assert: Death no end. (n.d.). Man and the Unknown. Retrieved October 3, 2007, from http://www.xs4all.nl/~wichm/deathnoe.html.

Parish, C. (2007). The ultimate adventure. An interview by *What is Enlightenment?* WIE Unbound audiotape.

Pasricha, S. (1986). Near-Death experiences in South India: A systematic survey." *Journal of Scientific Exploration.* Society for Scientific Exploration. 9(1), 4.

Patt, S. (n.d.). Brain localization of consciousness? Neurological considerations. Retrieved October 21, 2007, from http://fondazionerui.eterbit.net/servlets/resources? contentId=16741&resourceName=Inserisci%20allegato.

Pearson, R. (1990). *Intelligence Behind the Universe!* Headquarters Publishing Company.

Pearson, R. (1991, September). Alternative to relativity including quantum gravitation. Second International Conference on Problems in Space and Time, St. Petersburg, Petrovskaja. Academy of Sciences & Arts, 278-292.

Penman, D. (2008, January). Could there be proof to the theory that we're ALL psychic? *Daily Mail.* Retrieved January 31, 2008, from http://www.dailymail.co.uk/pages/live/articles/news/news.html?in_article_id=510762&in_page_id=1770.

Penman, D. (n.d.). Have scientists really proved that man can see into the future? NewsMonster, (May 9,2007). Retrieved May 11, 2007, from http://www.newsmonster.co.uk/content/view/186/72/on May 11, 2007.

Penman, D. (n.d.). Near-death experiences are real and we have the proof, say scientists. Newsmonster. Retrieved August 6, 2007, from http://www.newsmonster.co.uk/near-death-experiences-are-real-and-we-have-the-proof-say-scien.html.

Persinger, M. A., & Krippner, S. (1989). Dream ESP experiments and geomagnetic activity. *The Journal of the American Society for Psychical Research, 83*.

Physicists challenge notion of electric nerve impulses; say sound more likely. Science Blog. (n.d.). University of Copenhagen. Retrieved October 3, 2007, from http://www.scienceblog.com/cms/physicists-challenge-notion-of-electric-nerve-impulses-say-sound-more-likely-12738.html.

Playfair, G. L. (2003). *Twin Telepathy: The Psychic Connection.* Vega.

Presti, D. (2007). Review of Edward F. Kelly, et al., *Irreducible Mind: Toward a Psychology for the 21st Century.* Retrieved October 5, 2007, from http://www.rowmanlittlefield.com/Catalog/SingleBook.shtml?command=Search&db=%5EDB/CATALOG.db&eqSKUdata=0742547922.

Proceedings of the Society for Psychical Research, 6, 20.

Prodigy, 12, compared to Mozart. (July 29, 2007). CBS News. Retrieved July 29, 2007, from http://www.cbsnews.com/stories/2004/11/24/60minutes/main657713.shtml.

Psychic Detectives. (December 30, 2005). *Nancy Grace.* Retrieved May 13, 2007, from http://transcripts.cnn.com/TRANSCRIPTS/0512/30/ng.01.html.

Puthoff, H. E., & Targ, R. (1976). A perceptual channel for information transfer over kilometer distances: historical perspective and recent research. *Proceedings of the IEEE,* 64.

Puthoff, H. E. (n.d.). CIA-initiated remote viewing at Stanford Research Institute. Institute for Advanced Studies. Retrieved December 10, 2007, from http://www.biomindsuperpowers.com/Pages/CIA-InitiatedRV.html.

Radin, D. (1997). *The Conscious Universe: The Scientific Truth of Psychic Phenomena.* New York: HarperCollins Publishers.

Radin, D., Hayssen, G., Emoto, M., & Kizu, T. (2006). Double-blind test of the effects of distant intention on water crystal formation. *Explore,* September/October 2006, 2(5).

Radin, D., Rae, C., & Hyman, R. (2000). Is there a sixth sense? *Psychology Today.* July/August 2006. Retrieved October 6, 2007 from http://www.psychologytoday.com/articles/index.php?term=pto-20000701-000034&page=3.

Radin, D., Taft, R.,, & Yount, G. (2004). Possible effects of healing intention on cell cultures and truly random events. *The Journal of Alternative and Complementary Medicine,* 10(1), 103-112.

Ramsland, K. (May 13, 2007). Psychic detectives. CourtTV Crime Library. Retrieved May 13, 2007, from http://www.crimelibrary.com/criminal_mind/forensics/psychics/index.html.

Randall, E. C. (2004). *The Dead Have Never Died.* Kessinger Publishing, LLC.

Reasons for failure in meditation. (n.d.). *Meditation Is Easy.* Retrieved October 14, 2007, from http://www.meditationiseasy.com/mCorner/failure_in_meditation.htm

Rees, W. D. (1971). The hallucinations of widowhood. *British Medical Journal,* 4, 37-41.

Rein, G. (1986). A psychokinetic effect on neurotransmitter metabolism: Alterations in the degradative enzyme monoamine oxidase. In Weiner, D. H., & Radin, D. (Eds.), *Research in Parapsychology 1985* (pp. 77-80). Metuchen, NJ: Scarecrow Press.

Restak, R. (2006). Cited in Cy Wenberg, *Gadflies*. Trafford Publishing.

Richards, J., & Gonzalez, G. (2004, May 1). Are we alone? *The American Spectator*. Retrieved April 16, 2007, from http://www.discovery.org/scripts/viewDB/index.php?command=view&id=2143.

Ring, K., & Cooper, S. (1999). *Mindsight: Near-Death and Out-of-Body Experiences in the Blind*. Institute of Transpersonal Psychology.

Ring, K., & Lawrence, M. (1993). Further evidence for veridical perception during near-death experiences," *Journal of Near-Death Studies*, 11(4), 223-229.

Ring, P. (n.d.). Dr. Larry Dossey champions the healing power of prayer. *Mysteries Magazine, 16*. Retrieved October 21, 2007, from http://www.mysteriesmagazine.com/articles/issue16.html.

Rogge, M. (n.d.). Direct Voice: Conversation between mother and her deceased son. Death No End. Retrieved October 5, 2007, from http://www.xs4all.nl/~wichm/fearon.html.

Rogo, D. S. (1993). *Leaving the Body: A Complete Guide to Astral Projection*. Fireside/Simon & Schuster.

Rogo, D. S. (n.d.). Researching the out-of-body experiences. Retrieved from www.paradigm-sys.com/cttart/sci-docs/ctt97-ssooo.html by Michael Schmicker. Cited in Schmicker, *Best Evidence*, p. 203.

Roland, P. E., & Friberg, L. (1985). Localization in cortical areas activated by thinking. *Journal of Neurophysiology*, 53, 1219-1243.

Rommer, B. (2000). *Blessings in Disguise: Another Side of the Near Death Experience*. Llewellyn Publications.

Rowse, A.L. (1993). Justice for Robert Bridges—20th century British poet. LookSmart. Retrieved September 21, 2007, from http://findarticles.com/p/articles/mi_m2242/is_n1531_v263/ ai_14482537/pg_4.

Roy, A. (1983, May 19). Letter to Michael Roll. Retrieved from http://www.cfpf.org.uk/letters/1983/1983-05-19_ar2mr/1983-05-19_ar2mr.html, September 22, 2007.

Russell, P. (2004). *From Science to God: A Physicist's Journey into the Mystery of Consciousness*. New World Library.

Sabom, M. (1982). *Recollections of Death: A Medical Investigation*. New York: Harper & Row.

Sabom, M. (1998). *Light and Death*. Zondervan.

Schlitz M., & Braud, W. G. (1985). Reiki-Plus natural healing: An ethnographic/experimental study. *Psi Research*, 4, 100-123.

Schlitz, M. (2003, December 13). Embracing the mystery. *What Is Enlightenment?* WIE Unbound interview by Craig Hamilton.

Schlitz, M. J., & LaBerge, S. (1997, September). Covert observation increases skin conductance in subjects unaware of when they are being observed: a replication. *The Journal of Parapsychology.* Retrieved October 6, 2007, from http://findarticles.com/p/articles/mi_m2320/is_n3_v61/ai_20749204.

Schlitz, S., & Honorton, C. (1992). Ganzfeld psi performance within an artistically gifted population. *Journal of the American Society for Psychical Research,* 86, 83-98.

Schnabel, J. (1997). *Remote Viewers—The Secret History of America's Psychic Spies.* Dell.

Schoonmaker, F. (1996). An introductory analysis of the NDE (near-death experience). Originally published in *Two Worlds.* Retrieved July 17, 2007, from http://www.fortunecity.com/roswell/seance/78/nde.htm.

Schmicker, M. (2002). *Best Evidence.* Lincoln, NE: Writers Club Press.

Schroeder, G. L. (2001). *The Hidden Face of God.* New York: Simon and Schuster.

Schroeter-Kunhardt, M. (1993, Fall). A review of near death experiences. *Journal of Scientific Exploration.* Society for Scientific Exploration, 7(3) 219-39, 1. Retrieved July 17, 2007, from http://www.scientificexploration.org/se/abstracts/v7n3a1.php.

Schroter-Kunhardt, M. (1990). Erfahrungen sterbender während des klinischen Todes. Z *Allg Med,* 66, 1014-21.

Schwartz, G., & Russek, L. (1999). *The living-energy universe: A fundamental discovery that transforms science and medicine.* Charlottesville, VA: Hampton Roads.

Schwartz, G. E., & Simon, W. L. (2003). *The Afterlife Experiments, Breakthrough Scientific Evidence of Life After Death.* Atria.

Schwartz, G., et al. (2001). Accuracy and replicability of anomalous after-death communication across highly skilled mediums. *Journal of the Society for Psychical Research,* 65(1).

Schweitzer, T. (n.d.). U.S. workers hate their jobs more than ever. Tamara Schweitzer, Inc.com. Retrieved October 15, 2007, from http://www.inc.com/criticalnews/articles/200703/work.html.

Sharp, K. C. (2003). *After the Light.* Authors Choice Press.

Sheldrake, R. (1998). The "sense of being stared at" experiments in schools. *Journal of the Society for Psychical Research,* 62, 311-323.

Sheldrake, R. (n.d.). Experiments on telephone telepathy. Retrieved February 28, 2007, from http://www.sheldrake.org/experiments/telephone_experiment.html.

Sheldrake, R. (n.d.). Nature as alive: morphic resonance and collective memory. Primal Spirit. Retrieved October 2, 2007, from http://www.primalspirit.com/pr1_1sheldrake_nature_as_alive.htm.

Sicher, F., Targ, E., Moore, D., & Smith, H. S. (1998). A randomized, double-blind study of the effects of distant healing in a population with advanced AIDS. *Western Journal of Medicine,* 169(6), 356-363.

Sir Isaac Newton Conference. St. Petersburg, March 1993, pp 39-55.

Skeptics who declared discoveries and inventions impossible. (n.d.). Alternative Science. Retrieved July 14, 2007, from http://www.alternativescience.com/skeptics.htm.

Smith, G. (2004). *The Unbelievable Truth*. Hay House. Retrieved October 15, 2007, from http://www.thepsychicbarber.co.uk/bookextract.html.

Smith, J. G., Burke, M., Rhine, J.B., Stuart, C. E., & Greewood, J. P. (1966). *Extra-Sensory Perception after Sixty years; A Critical Appraisal of the Research in E.S.P.* Bruce Humphries.

Snyder, J. J. (n.d.). Science confirms survival. The Campaign for Philosophical Freedom. Retrieved September 20, 2007, from http://www.cfpf.org.uk/articles/background/snyder.html.

Solfvin, G. F. (1982). Psi expectancy effects in psychic healing studies with malarial mice. *European Journal of Parapsychology*, 4(2), 160-197.

Spraggett, A. (1973). *Probing The Unexplained*. New American Library.

Spraggett, A. (1974). *The Case for Immortality*. Scarborough, Canada: New American Library of Canada.

Stammar, G. (2007, September 20). Drill preps personnel for violence at school. *The Daily Pantagraph*.

Stevenson, I. (1974). *Xenoglossy*. University Press of Virginia.

Stevenson, I. (1983). Do we need a new word to supplement "hallucination?" *American Journal of Psychiatry*, 140, 1609-11.

Stevenson, I., Owens, J. E., & Cook, E. W. (1990). Features of "near-death experience" in relation to whether or not patients were near death. *The Lancet* 336, 1175-1177.

Stevenson, M. (2007, April 18). Ancient child sacrifices found in Mexico. Associated Press. Retrieved April 18, 2007, from http://www.msnbc.msn.com/id/18164233/.

Study suggests brain may have "blindsight." (October 31, 2005). Associated Press. Retrieved June 4, 2007, from http://www.msnbc.msn.com/id/9879390/.

Sudduth, M. (n.d.). Near death experiences: An outline. Retrieved September 23, 2007, from http://www.homestead.com/mscourses/files/NearDeathExperiences.htm.

Targ, R., & Harary, K. (1984). *The Mind Race*. New York: Villard Books.

Targ, R., & Katra, J. (1998). *Miracles of Mind*. Hampton Roads Publishing Co.

Targ, R., & Puthoff, H. (1974). Information transmission under conditions of sensory shielding. *Nature*, 251.

Tart, C. T. (1968). Psychophysiological study of out-of-the-body experiences in a selected subject. *Journal of the American Society for Psychical Research*, 62, 1, 3-27.

Tart, C. (1969). Psychedelic experiences associated with a novel hypnotic procedure, Mutual Hypnosis. In *Altered States of Consciousness* (pp 291-308). New York: John Wiley & Sons.

Tedder, W. H., & Monty, M. L. (1980). Exploration of long-distance PK: A conceptual replication of the influence on a biological system. In W. G. Roll, et al. (Eds.) *Research in Parapsychology* (pp. 90-93). Metuchen, NJ: Scarecrow Press.

Teen suicide. (n.d.). National Youth Violence Prevention Resource Center. Retrieved August 23, 2007, from http://www.safeyouth.org/scripts/teens/suicide.asp.

Thaheld, F. (2003). Biological non-locality and the mind-brain interaction problem: comments on a new empirical approach." *Biosystems*, 2209, 1-7.

The Church of England and Spiritualism—the full text of the Church of England Committee appointed by Archbishop Lang and Archbishop Temple to investigate Spiritualism. (1979). London: Psychic Press Ltd.

The State of Depression in America. (February 2006). Depression and Bipolar Support Alliance. Retrieved November 23, 2007, from http://www.dbsalliance.org/site/PageServer?pagename=about_iniatives_stateofdepression1.

There's more than meets the eye in judging the size of an object. (n.d.). The All I Need Web Site. Retrieved August 25, 2007, from http://www.theallineed.com/medicine/06032012.htm.

Tiller, W. A. (1999, May/June). Subtle energies. *Science and Medicine*. May/June 1999. Vol. 6, No. 3.

Tiller, W., Dibble, W., & Kohane, M. (2001). *Conscious Acts of Creation: The Emergence of a New Physics*. Pavior Publishing.

Tiny-brained man's lifestyle wows doctors; He lived a normal life despite the fluid buildup in his skull. (July 19, 2007). Reuters. Retrieved July 24, 2007, from http://www.msnbc.msn.com/id/19859089/.

Tippit, S. (n.d.). Study suggests life after death: brains of dead heart attack patients still function. Retrieved December 1, 2007, from http://neardeath.home.comcast.net/news/020629.html.

Touber, T. (2007, January). Life goes on. *Ode* 29.

Trained to kill: Virus of violence. (n.d.). Killology Research Group. Retrieved October 25, 2007, from http://www.killology.com/art_trained_virus.htm.

Treffert, D. (n.d.). Is there a little rain man in each of us? Talent Development Resources. Retrieved December 8, 2007, from http://talentdevelop.com/articles/ITALRMIEOU.html.

Treffert, D. (n.d.). Kim Peek—The real rain man. Wisconsin Medical Society. Retrieved September 11, 2007, from http://www.wisconsinmedicalsociety.org/savant_syndrome/savant_profiles/kim_peek.

Twemlow et al. (1980). The out-of-body experience: 1. Phenomenology. Paper presented at the annual meeting of the American Psychiatric Association, San Francisco.

Tymn, M. (2007, August 15). Ghost loses chess match. Lightlink. Retrieved September 23, 2007, from http://www.lightlink.com/arpr/tymn/ghost_loses_chess_match.htm.

Tymn, M. (2008, January). A glimpse of hell. Metgat's Blog. Retrieved January 7, 2007, from http://metgat.zaadz.com/blog.

Tymn, M. (n.d.). A veridical death-bed vision. Lightlink.com. Retrieved September 23, 2007, from http://www.lightlink.com/arpr/tymn/a_veridical_deathbed_vision.htm.

Tymn, M. (2007, August 4). Automatic writing: like holding a live bird. Posted to zaadz.com. Retrieved August 10, 2007, from http://metgat.zaadz.com/blog.

Tymn, M. (n.d.). Distinguished researchers found evidence for survival. Lightlink.com. Retrieved March 31, 2007, from http://www.lightlink.com/arpr/tymn/testimonials.htm.

Tymn, M. (2007). Physician travels out of body. Mysterial Forums. Retrieved December 15, 2007, from http://www.e-hq.co.uk/mysterial.co.uk/web/cgi-bin/index.cgi?action=forum&board=spirit&op=printpage&num=9004. Cited from Funk, I. (1907). *The Psychic Riddle.* (Funk and Wagnalls).

Tymn, M. (n.d.). Proof positive of spirit communication. Retrieved August 27, 2007, from http://metgat.zaadz.com/blog/2007/5/proof_positive_of_spirit_communication.

Types of experiences we study. (n.d.). University of Virginia Health System Division of Perceptual Studies. Retrieved June 20, 2007 from http://www.healthsystem.virginia.edu/internet/personalitystudies/case_types.cfm#Deathbed.

Ullman, M., & Krippner, S. (1970). *Dream Studies and Telepathy: An Experimental_Approach.* New York: Parapsychology Foundation.

Utts, J. (1995). An assessment of the evidence for psychic functioning. Division of Statistics, University of California, Davis.

Van Lommel, P. (n.d.) 6. Neurophysiology in a normal functioning brain. *About the continuity of our consciousness.* Retrieved November 15, 2007, from http://www.iands.org/research/important_studies/dr._pim_van_lommel_m.d._continuity_of_consciousness_6.html.

Van Lommel, P. (December 15, 2001). Near-death experience in survivors of cardiac arrest; a prospective study in the Netherlands. *Lancet*, 358, 2039-45.

Vargas, L., et al. (1989). Exploring the multidimensional aspects of grief reactions. *American Journal of Psychiatry*, 146(11), 1484-9.

Varvoglis, M. (2001, August). Telepathy. *Psi Explorer*, 1. Retrieved December 20, 2007, from http://www.psiexplorer.com.

Von Buengner, P. (n.d.). Morphic Fields can now be measured scientifically! The Global Oneness Commitment. Retrieved October 13, 2007, from http://www.experiencefestival.com/a/Morphic_fields/id/10320.

Wagner, S. (n.d.). Deathbed visions. About.com. Retrieved June 20, 2007, from http://paranormal.about.com/library/weekly/aa021901a.htm.

Watkins, G. K., & Watkins, A. M. (1971). Possible PK influence on the resuscitation of anesthetized mice. *Journal of Parapsychology,* 35(4), 257-72.

Watkins, G. K., Watkins, A. M., & Wells, R. A. (1973). Further studies on the resuscitation of anesthetized mice. *Research in Parapsychology* (pp. 157-59). Metuchen, NJ: Scarecrow Press.

Weiskrantz, L. (1996). Blindsight revisited. *Cognitive Neuroscience,* 6, 215-220. Retrieved July 10, 2007, from http://www.le.ac.uk/pc/nk70/ Weiskrantz_COIN96.pdf.

Weiss, P. A. (1969). The living system: Determinism stratified. In Koestler, A., & Smythies, J. R. (Eds.) *Beyond reductionism: New perspectives in the life sciences.* London: Hutchinson.

Wells, R., & Klein, J. (1972). A replication of a "psychic healing" paradigm. *Journal of Parapsychology.* 36: 144-47.

Wells, R., & Watkins, G. K. (1974). Linger effects in several PK experiments. *Research in Parapsychology* (pp. 143-47). Metuchen, NJ: Scarecrow Press.

Wilkinson, D., Knox, P., Chatman, J., Johnson, T., Barbour, N., Myles, Y., & Reel, A. (2002). The clinical effectiveness of Healing Touch. *Journal of Alternative and Complementary Medicine,* 8(1), 33-47.

Williams, G. (1989). *A Life Beyond Death.* London: Robert Hale.

Wills-Brandon, C. (2007). *One Last Hug Before I Go: The Mystery And Meaning Of Deathbed Visions.* Hastings House.

Wills-Brandon, C. (n.d.). Understanding departing visions or deathbed visitations. empowering caregivers. Retrieved June 21, 2007, from http://www.care-givers.com/DBArticles/pages/viewarticle.php?id=137.

Winston, S. (1975). Research in psychic healing: A multivariate experiment. Unpublished doctoral dissertation, Union Graduate School.

Woods, D.L., & Dimond, M. (2002). The effect of therapeutic touch on agitated behavior and cortisol in persons with Alzheimer's disease. *Biological Research for Nursing,* 4(2), 104-114.

Zaleski, C. (1987). *Otherworld Journeys.* New York: OUP.

Zammit, V. (2006.). *A Lawyer Presents the Case for the Afterlife.* Sydney, Australia: Ganmell Pty. Ltd.

Zammit, V. (n.d.). 10. Materialization mediumship. Retrieved December 12, 2007, from http://www.victorzammit.com/book/chapter10.html.

Zammit, V. (n.d.). Australian psychics beat "orthodox" science. Retrieved May 13, 2007, from http://victorzammit.com/articles/sensingmurder.html.

Zammit, V. (n.d.). Conversation with Victor Zammit. Victor Zammit's Web site at http://victorzammit.com. Retrieved September 21, 2007.

Zammit, V. (n.d.). The direct-voice mediumship of Leslie Flint. Retrieved October 25, 2007, from http://www.survivalafterdeath.org/experiments/direct-voice/flint.htm.